MUSEUMS AND MONEY

IU Center on Philanthropy Series in Governance

James R. Wood and Dwight F. Burlingame, editors

MUSEUMS AND MONEY

The Impact of Funding on Exhibitions, Scholarship, and Management

VICTORIA D. ALEXANDER

INDIANA UNIVERSITY PRESS

Bloomington and Indianapolis

Publication of this book was supported
by a grant from the KD Endowment Fund.

The paper used in this publication meets the minimum requirements of American National Standard for Information Sciences—Permanence of Paper for Printed Library Materials, ANSI Z39.48-1984.

Manufactured in the United States of America

Library of Congress Cataloging-in-Publication Data

Alexander, Victoria D.
Museums and money : the impact of funding on exhibitions.
p. cm. — (IU Center on Philanthropy series in governance)
Includes index.
ISBN 0-253-33205-2 (cloth : alk. paper).
1. Art museums—United States—Management. 2. Art museums—United States—Finance. 3. Art patronage—United States. I. Title.
II. Series
N510.A43 1996
708.13'068'1—dc20 95-49863

1 2 3 4 5 01 00 99 98 97 96

In its deepest sense, the art museum speaks in the language of Greek mythology. The nine Muses were, after all, the daughters of Mnemosyne, the goddess of memory, by Zeus, the god of power. Art museums can be seen as temples of remembered power: creative, dynastic, financial, political.

—Karl E. Meyer,
The Art Museum: Power, Money, Ethics.

CONTENTS

ACKNOWLEDGMENTS

Many people have helped me along the path of this project. My warmest and most heartfelt thanks to Ann Swidler, John Meyer, Dick Scott, Jim Benson, and the members of SWCP at Stanford University (Kathy Lyman, Conníe McNeely, Amy Roussel, JoEllen Shively, Yasemin Soysal and, especially, Sarah Corse), and FSC at MIT/Harvard (Elaine Backman, Robin Ely, Hermie Ibarra, and Maureen Scully).

In addition, I have appreciated (and gratefully appropriated) comments on various drafts and papers relating to this project. Paul DiMaggio and Vera Zolberg have been particularly helpful. I would also like to thank Judith Blau, Neil Fligstein, Richard Hackman, Volker Kirchberg, Peter Marsden, Roseanne Martorella, Woody Powell, and Jim Wood.

Funding for this project was provided by the Program on Governance of Nonprofit Organizations at the Indiana University Center on Philanthropy, the American Association of University Women, the Program on Nonprofit Organizations at Yale University, and the Clark Fund at Harvard University. The research would have suffered without the cooperation of the anonymous directors, curators and educators I interviewed, and I would like to express my appreciation to them and to Patrick Coman of the Thomas J. Watson Library at the Metropolitan Museum and Susan Perry of the Ryerson and Burnham Libraries of the Art Institute of Chicago and their staffs who made annual reports available to me.

This book has been improved by the skills of the folks at Indiana University Press and the Center on Philanthropy. My thanks to Dwight Burlingame, Brad Johns and, especially, Lois Sherman.

PREFACE

Sometime around 1965, a rumble was heard in the museum world. It was the sound of an old funding system cracking as a new one emerged to displace it. Before 1960, museums were supported by a relatively stable set of individual philanthropists. By the mid-1970s, museums had transformed into organizations largely supported by a mosaic of institutional funders, that is, by a variety of corporations, foundations, and government agencies. When the dust settled, around 1980, museums were fundamentally changed, reflecting this dramatic shift in their resource base. I chronicle the impact of funding on large art museums from 1960 to 1986, concentrating on exhibitions, museum missions, and management styles. I also discuss how museums manage and try to avoid pressures that bear upon them from their external sources of support. In effect, I explore how museums dealt with their funding environment as it became increasingly multifaceted and turbulent. The lessons from this study continue to be relevant today as museums face, once again, a complex, changing, and increasingly uncertain funding base.

Museums, like all nonprofit organizations, must raise funds while they pursue their primary missions. Without money, museums cannot operate. But while it provides resources, the Trojan Horse called funding also carries the goals and demands of donors. Funders always have reasons for giving and always seek something in return for their gifts. Desires for prestige, visibility, access to the museum, free advice on the funder's collection, or a sense of importance may seem innocuous. Yet these demands are problematic when they are inconvenient for museums or, worse, when the means of their fulfillment conflicts with museum missions. Moreover, funders often wish to support programs or activities that vary from the ideal activities a museum might choose if money were no object. As all nonprofit managers know, this disjuncture between funder goals and recipient goals poses serious difficulties. Museum managers face a daily quandary—how to raise enough funds without acceding too much to funder pressures.

When I started this project in the late 1980s, museum personnel talked less about government funding than they do today (although President Reagan had already thrown the fear of recisions into the hearts of museum managers). An important concern then was corporations. The debate in the museum world concerned the impact of corporate funding: Do corporations somehow distort exhibitions by, for example, pressuring museums to drop controversial pieces from shows? Are corporations like tobacco or oil companies trying to clean up a sullied reputation by aligning themselves with culture organizations? If so, should they be allowed to do this? Might such alliances tarnish the museum's halo while they burnish the corporation's image? Should museums, or for that matter any culture organization, ever accept corporate donations? It was this debate that sparked my interest in the interaction of funder and museum.

After the mid-1980s, when my detailed study ends, the funding of museums became even more turbulent and complex. The museum-world debate about corporate funding was joined by national debates over federal support of the controversial art produced by Serrano, Mapplethorpe, and a continuing cast of artists who, in their work, challenge mainstream values and traditional definitions of art. Corporations, facing an extended recession in the late 1980s, cut back their philanthropic donations. They did not step up culture funding when the recession ended, as they attended to trends in the corporate world that pressure them to become lean and mean and to fashions in corporate philanthropy that, on days when corporations still feel fat and generous, favor health and education over culture.

Currently, the state of cultural funding in America is in flux. The elections of 1994 ushered in a new era and a new Congress. With Newt Gingrich leading the ax-wielding House, our country could lose the National Endowment for the Arts, the National Endowment for the Humanities, and the Corporation for Public Broadcasting. This would be a shame. These agencies have been extraordinarily helpful to the culture organizations of our nation. Theaters, symphonies, dance companies and, as I show in this book, art museums have benefited enormously from the availability of federal funds—and the public has benefited as well.

The relentless pressure of fundraising and funder demands is made more difficult when resources are scarce. Indeed, many museums these days are severely strapped for funds. Though the specifics will change, understanding the general dynamics of museums and funding in the past may provide a rough guide to the future as the funding environment of museums grows even more complex and unstable. Moreover, in the current era of government cutbacks and corporate downsizing, the types of pressures museums have experienced are shared not only by other culture organizations, but also by all nonprofit organizations that rely on philanthropy and government support. Thus, understanding the effects of funding pressures and museums' efforts to manage them can shed light on how other types of nonprofit organizations both shape and are shaped by their turbulent funding environments.

The main lesson from this study is that funding matters, but in complex ways. The people who run museums and who work there, not surprisingly, have opinions about what their organizations should do. It is not clear that funders want to dictate museum policy, but it is clear that they could not do so even if they tried. Still, funders pressure museums in a variety of ways, both direct and indirect, and museum personnel do their best to avoid pressures or to forge new arrangements that conform to the museum's desires. But in forging such arrangements, museums become crucibles of conflicting factions where tempers flare and ideals clash. Over time, the relentless pounding of funders' preferences can reshape museum missions and exhibitions, though the reshaping is always wrought against an anvil of the museum's own making. The details of this process are the subject of this book.

V.D.A.
CAMBRIDGE, MASS.
SEPTEMBER 28, 1995

MUSEUMS AND MONEY

INTRODUCTION

This book is about American art museums since 1960, focusing on changes in exhibitions and museum organization spurred by funders new to cultural philanthropy. American museums have experienced a tremendous shift in sponsorship. Traditionally, wealthy individuals supported museums. Starting in the mid-1960s, however, grants from corporations, foundations, and government agencies rapidly increased. I wondered how this shift in contributions affected museums.

Organizations such as art museums, galleries, symphonies, record companies, radio stations, and theaters all have an effect on the art they produce. How these organizations garner resources, attract audiences, and choose repertoires, productions, or exhibits bears on their cultural output. As I started this research, I wanted to find out how museums' actions shape exhibitions and whether exhibitions changed during the era of corporate and government funding. As an organizational sociologist, I have learned that organizations are profoundly shaped by their environments. Therefore, I suspected the shift in museum sponsorship might have very important ramifications for museum exhibits, as well as for the internal management of museums themselves. I also wondered what extra-aesthetic criteria influence museums' decisions about mounting exhibitions. How might funding affect art museum exhibitions? How might the organization of museums change as funding streams change?

Historically, individual philanthropists and local city governments supported museums. Traditional contributors to the arts were individual patrons, wealthy men and women who collected paintings and sculptures and who often ran museums. Municipal governments offered buildings, land, or a small appropriation. During the past three decades, however, federal and corporate contributions have come to rival individual patronage, while the role of municipal government has faded. Currently, arts funding is drawn from a wide variety of sources (DiMaggio, 1986a). The U.S. Congress established the National Endowment for the Arts (NEA) and the National Endowment for the Humanities (NEH) in 1965, and the Institute of Museum Services (IMS) in 1978. All fifty states had formed public arts councils by 1974 (NEA, cited in DiMaggio, 1983, p. 151). In addition, corporate support of the arts has dramatically increased since 1960 (Porter, 1981). Finally, increasing numbers of foundations have been established and are funding cultural institutions (Odendahl, 1990). Crane sums up the situation, "patronage of the arts [has] shifted from wealthy collectors to *organizations*" (1985, emphasis added). These new organizationally based funders are called "institutional funders" to distinguish them from individual philanthropists (DiMaggio, 1986a; Crane, 1987, 5–9).

Funders are extraordinarily important to all nonprofit organizations, providing a very important resource—money. Clearly, recipients accomplish something with the money given to them in grants. So there is an enabling effect of funding. But there are also constraints. Do recipients change their activities in accordance with donors' explicit requests? Do recipients change what they say they are going to do, in the hopes of getting funding for a changed mission? And since time is limited, does doing one activity connected with funding squeeze out other activities that are less able to attract resources? I wondered what these enablements and constraints might do to museum missions and activities. Have museum missions changed as museum support has shifted from individual philanthropy to institutional funding? Is there disagreement in museums about what museums should be doing? Does funding in any way create or heighten such disagreement?

Donors to nonprofit organizations, including museums, have goals that focus their giving. How do funders' goals affect what the recipient organizations do? Funders present museums with a wealth of conflicting goals. Both government agencies and corporations are interested in the audience appeal of exhibitions they sponsor. The government stresses wide public enjoyment or education, and corporations are interested in public relations. Corporations believe that cultural philanthropy is a good way to improve corporate reputations—a highbrow form of advertising. Government agencies know that reaching constituents is key to receiving continued appropriations. Further, both government and corporations want to sponsor art that is exciting, yet corporations shun art that is particularly controversial or difficult to understand. When awarding exhibition grants, government panels, made up of museum curators, are caught between their professional, curatorial tastes (often for challenging, esoteric art) and their public mission, which requires that they attend to projected attendance figures and consider the likelihood that the museum will be able to raise matching funds for a show. Currently, government agencies also must walk a fine line by not supporting "pornographic" or "anti-American" art while at the same time avoiding charges of "censoring" or "sugar coating" the art they do sponsor. In contrast, traditional patrons, individual donors, are object-oriented connoisseurs. They are more interested in the art itself (especially if that art is part of their own collections) than in publicity value or attracting broad audiences. Indeed, because individual wealthy philanthropists look for recognition from their peers, they prefer smaller, narrower exhibitions.

These goals—for broad public access, on the one hand, and for small, esoteric exhibitions on the other—conflict. Consequently, pressures from funders pose problems for museum managers. Further, museum curators prefer to mount scholarly, prestigious shows that may not mesh with funder goals. How do museum managers solve the dilemmas of pleasing both funders and curators, let alone critics and the public? What do museums exhibit? And does funding affect exhibition contents?

These issues are important because museum exhibitions have a direct bearing on larger aesthetic questions. Art is not produced in a vacuum. Along with aesthetic issues, social and production factors affect the content of art. Artists in their studios are influenced by social factors, in mundane and profound ways. As Howard Becker demonstrates so convincingly in *Art Worlds* (1982), artists' works are shaped by artistic conventions, social conventions, available technology, prevailing fashionable styles, and the work of support personnel, along with political concerns, which manifest themselves in the statement the art is making.

But it is even more important to recognize that art created is not equal to art remembered. Museums are essential to the remembrance process. Museum exhibitions legitimate the work of new artists and reinforce the legitimation of the already-established work of living artists or old masters. Museum exhibitions can even legitimate the lost or forgotten work of long-dead artists.

Indeed, museums *frame* art works, and not just in the literal sense. Objects displayed in museums carry the label of "art," while similar objects not exhibited are often considered "craft," "decoration," or "non-art" (Becker, 1982). As many scholars have noted (Danto, 1987; Williams, 1981; Meyer, 1979), objects must be labeled "art" for observers to recognize and interpret them as art. Along with galleries and collectors, museums validate art. The artistic canon, by definition, includes only validated art. Thus, the canon is shaped by the actions of a system of artistic production, in which museums play a crucial role. If exhibitions are shaped by the tastes and concerns of funders, then changes in museum funding may have ramifications far beyond what is mounted on the museum wall today.

If the maxim that art is not produced in a vacuum is true for the art that individuals make, it is doubly true for the art that the public sees. A museum is subject to social and production effects as it chooses the art that will be displayed in exhibitions. Relatively few Americans visit artists' studios, and of those who do, fewer still visit artists who are not represented by a gallery that sells their work. Thus, most "average people" see art and learn about artists in art museums. In addition, professional artists, art historians, art collectors, and curators—who have much deeper access to the visual art world—also study and experience art alongside the general public, inside museums. So, not only are exhibitions very important in legitimating artists and creating canons, exhibitions are pivotal in educating the public about artwork.

As I write, understanding the impact of funding on museums has taken on a new urgency as the Republican majority in Congress contemplates eliminating the three central federal agencies that fund culture: the National Endowment for the Arts, the National Endowment for the Humanities, and the Corporation for Public Broadcasting. I believe that this would be a mistake, because the NEA, an extraordinarily important institutional funder for museums, has influenced museums and museum exhibitions in ways that I will argue are largely beneficial.

This book reports findings from a study of 30 large art museums from 1960 to 1986. I draw upon theories from organizational and cultural sociology to understand what goes on in museums. The research relies on two sources of data. First, open-ended interviews with museum directors, curators, and educators provide insight into museum funding and exhibition procedures. Second, an analysis of annual reports of the museums provides information on museum exhibitions themselves, specifically funding and its correlation with the number, format, and content of exhibitions.

The study also addresses how changes in funding are related to consensus and conflict inside museums, especially between the curatorial and administrative sides. Closely related to the issue of conflict, and a point of debate, is how funding influences conceptions of museum missions. For example, museums can be oriented to education, scholarship, conservation, or entertainment, but they cannot easily manage all four tasks. External funding influences the orientation of a museum to its community, and this orientation affects exhibition design. Trustees, along with directors, play a crucial role in managing the image and role of the museum in the community.

Organizationally, I am concerned with museums' methods of choosing the number, content, and format of exhibitions and how these decisions are affected by the mixture of museums' funding sources. Moreover, my research highlights shifts in goals and personnel within museums engendered by funding changes. It shows, for instance, the increasing prominence of exhibitions in the museum industry, the greater role of non-art professionals within the museum, and the implications of these shifts for museum governance. How museum managers endeavor to place themselves within this new and complex funding environment is a central question in the research. All of these factors have broad implications for the very definition of art.

In this research, I chose to code exhibitions from large museums. Large museums form a conceptually distinct population since they play a gatekeeping role in the visual arts sector that small museums do not (Crane, 1987, Chapter 7). I concentrate on the interaction between the museum and one aspect of its environment—its exhibition funders. Though there are other external constituencies, such as audiences and contributing members, I have focused on the funding environment to develop a more detailed understanding of this key aspect of nonprofit organizations.

Clearly, I hope this book will be of interest to scholars from my own discipline, sociology.[1] In addition, I believe that the lessons from the research will be useful to museum professionals, art historians, scholars of philanthropy, and nonprofit organization theorists and managers. Thus, I've written the book with as little jargon as possible to make my findings accessible to scholars from a variety of backgrounds.

Chapter 1 develops the theoretical underpinnings of the book by introducing the relevant work from the sociology of culture and the sociology of organizations. Here, I develop a model of how museums work as organizations. Chapter 2 discusses the change from philanthropic to institutional support and discusses the goals of funders as they decide their charitable portfolios. In it, I demonstrate the increasing importance of institutional funding to museums. The research explores funding effects at two different levels, the exhibition (output) level and the museum (organization) level. At the exhibition level (Chapter 3), I attempt to link measures of funding to various types of exhibitions to determine whether funding affects artistic style chosen for display or the format of such displays. I attempt to answer such questions as: Are pieces of artwork or formats for exhibitions chosen for shows differently than they were in the past? For instance, are museums doing more Impressionist shows or more large, "blockbuster" shows? Are shows of certain types of artwork more likely to get funded than others? Does funding change individual exhibitions? Does funding change the mix of exhibitions shown in museums? Chapter 3 uses archival and quantitative data to answer questions concerning effects of external funding on the number, format, and content of exhibitions and to examine changes in the exhibition pool. At the museum level (Chapter 4), I examine changes in museum missions and internal conflict. I attempt to answer such questions as: Have museums become more oriented toward the public and their audiences? Do museums pay more attention to funders? Do museums pay more attention to other museums? How might external changes relate to profound conflicts within museums? Have museum programs changed, either in content or in the audience they focus on? Chapter 4 addresses the ramifications of the shifting funding environment for museum management, relying on findings from annual reports and interviews. Chapter 5 discusses the broader implications of the study and addresses the important issues of censorship, self-censorship, and debates over the "democratization" of museums.

NOTE

1. I have written two papers using data from this project that specifically address questions in the sociology of culture (Alexander, 1996a) and the sociology of organizations (Alexander, 1996b).

I

MUSEUMS AND MONEY

UNDERSTANDING THE EFFECTS OF EXTERNAL FORCES ON CULTURAL ORGANIZATIONS

Museums are supported by a variety of external funders. In sociology, there are two general theoretical approaches to understanding systems like funding arrangements, the sociology of culture, especially production of culture theories, and organizational sociology, especially theories that focus on the interaction of organization and environment. In this chapter, I review these two approaches to learn more about how museums might operate with regard to their funding systems and how funding might affect art exhibits.

The Production of Culture

How do organizational arrangements affect culture? This is the broad question raised in this study, and the general question addressed by the production of culture approach to the sociology of culture (Becker, 1982; Crane, 1992; Peterson, 1976, 1979). The production of culture approach recognizes that societal arrangements affect cultural products. For instance, White and White (1965) show how the change in art markets—from an academic system to a dealer-critic system around 1880—encouraged Impressionism. Their argument works like this: The French Academy was a viable system for handling the work of artists for several centuries. The Academy institutionalized a particular approach to painting with a rigid hierarchy of subject matter (history painting had the most prestige, still life and landscape, the least). Painters spent years working on a masterpiece, because the rewards of winning a prize in the Academy's juried shows, *Salons*, were extensive. Prestige, fellowships for study abroad, appointments as academicians, and commissions all flowed from winning *Salon* medals.

In the nineteenth century, the Academy became a victim of its own success. As more painters flowed into Paris seeking the prestige of Academy training and medals, the Academy was unable to handle them all. Although the population of artists was growing, the Academy at that time was restricting its numbers and raising its standards for judging art. Painters unable to enter the system or frustrated by their inability to win awards turned to other avenues to make livings as painters. This situation contributed to the creation of the dealer-critic system, a market system where dealers showed paintings in galleries and sold them to a growing middle class. Independent critics also played an important role in the system. They helped create an audience by writing about the virtues of painters and paintings.

This system was more conducive to some styles than others. It favored smaller paintings because art needed to fit into middle class houses. The fact that paintings hung in living rooms encouraged genre and landscape paintings that were more decorative than the allegorical and historical paintings that hung in Academy *Salons*. Furthermore, to maintain their livelihood, dealers needed to sell many paintings; therefore, they fostered an interest among their customers in the growth of the artist's individual style. As a rule, art connoisseurs interested in stylistic development buy more than one example of a particular artist's work. These requirements led to paintings that were completed relatively quickly, so dealers would have a flow of new works to sell. Paintings also needed to be differentiated from the work of other artists, so dealers could demonstrate the painter's unique style and development. This dealer-critic system contrasts with the academic system, where artists spent several years on one work, and where they painted in the approved style, as close to the style of the established masters as they could manage. The new practices led to the modern focus on the *career* (stylistic development) of a painter, instead of the Academy's focus on *canvases* (single masterpieces considered without regard to the master's other work).

White and White show how societal arrangements shape art. Production systems favor certain art forms over others, thus encouraging the favored forms. However, White and White do not argue that the dealer-critic system, by itself, caused Impressionism, nor that Impressionism is the only style amenable to such a system. Rather, they argue that the system influenced the very way artists painted in that it functioned well for some types of paintings and not for others. The growth of Impressionism involved many complex and interrelated developments. Yet the dealer-critic system was crucial to the development and dispersion of Impressionist work and to the creation of the concept of a stylistic career, just as the *Salons* of the Academy encouraged large-scale historical and allegorical masterpieces.

More contemporary effects of production systems on art have been documented. DiMaggio and Stenberg (1985) show that changes in the innovation and diversity of performances in resident theaters depend on the theater's size, location, and funding environment. The funding environment is a key point, as they demonstrate. Market support of theaters leads to a more popular, conformist repertoire, while performances in patronage-supported theaters are more likely to be innovative or experimental. Another example of effects of production systems on art can be found in the music industry. Peterson and Berger (1975) show that changes in recorded music are influenced by the market concentration of record companies. As the record industry moved through cycles of relative concentration (measured by the percentage of top ten hits owned by the largest firms in the industry in a given year), the diversity of records, performers and lyrical content of hits available also moved cyclically. Less diversity occurred after the industry consolidated and more diversity followed the breakup of consolidation.[1]

Wendy Griswold studied the effects of literary distribution systems and found that laws can favor one type of art enough to make it the only type published. Griswold (1981) points out that American copyright law protected American authors but not British authors. This situation encouraged the publishing of peculiarly American novels in the following manner: American publishers pirated British novels and declined to publish novels with similar themes written by Americans. Publishers accepted American work and paid royalties only when no similar novels were available free from Britain. Whereas British novels focused more on love and marriage, American novels espoused themes of the great outdoors and "man against nature" that generations of literary critics linked to the vagaries of American character rather than to the vagaries of American law. Interestingly, after American copyright law changed in 1891, the themes of British and American novels converged. In a recent article, Griswold (1992) demonstrates that British publishers are more likely to publish Nigerian novels with a "traditional" village theme than those with an urban theme, even though Nigerian authors write more books focusing on contemporary social problems. Because publishers selected books for publication in this particular manner, the impression of Nigeria that British and American readers get from Nigerian novels is of rural communities struggling with problems of tradition and modernity brought about by colonialism. Such village themes better fit the British publishers' preconceptions of Nigeria. Thus Griswold demonstrates that the ideas of individuals in production and distribution systems, along with the arrangement of the systems themselves, make a difference in what art reaches the public.

A key concept from production of culture research involves the institutions (and people) that select the cultural objects that reach the public.

Hirsch (1981) identifies such institutions as "gatekeepers"—entities that filter cultural objects as they are taken into the system.[2] In museums, there are many gatekeepers. Curators are gatekeepers because they choose which objects to include in a show. So too are museum directors when they decide what gifts of painting or sculpture should be accepted, or when they determine what part of the permanent collection, if any, should be sold. Directors and museum trustees are also gatekeepers in that they can suggest subjects for museum exhibitions.

The gatekeeping role is quite important in the production of cultural objects. Gatekeepers, such as museum directors and curators, are powerful in selecting from the vast array of art and potential art the narrow band of art that will be included in exhibitions. Corporations and government agencies influence gatekeepers when choosing the exhibitions they will fund. Funders have the opposite effect from gatekeepers on exhibitions, a broadening effect rather than a narrowing effect. Funders do not stop museums from mounting exhibitions that funders dislike. Rather, funders select exhibitions they particularly do like from among types of shows that museums would mount even without funding. Therefore, funders may encourage the proliferation of certain types of museum shows.

Whatever influence funders have on museum exhibitions is more probabilistic than deterministic (see Lieberson, 1985). Funders do not force museums to mount any particular type of exhibition. Rather, museums have a portfolio of exhibition types that they are willing to mount. Similarly, funders have an implicit portfolio of shows they are willing to fund. When museums accept external funding, the result is an increase in the number of exhibitions where the portfolios overlap. Funding increases the odds of certain ranges of exhibitions. As Becker (1982, p. 92) states:

> Available resources make some things possible, some things easy, and others harder; every pattern of availability reflects the workings of some kind of social organization and becomes part of the pattern of constraints and possibilities that shapes the art produced.

The important point of the production of culture approach is metatheoretical. Its lesson is that art is not produced solely in accordance to aesthetic conventions. Some art historians recognize that art history is a social history (Baxandall, 1972; Hauser, 1958), although many still discuss art in solely formalistic terms, as though it is produced only due to the inexorable logic of previous artistic styles. Production of culture theory suggests we view that latter scholarship with caution, and that we examine the social influences that help shape current artistic products.

Production of culture approaches often focus on easily quantifiable aspects of the cultural product while ignoring the more troublesome and arguably more interesting questions about the content or meaning of the cultural item. This is a commonly noted problem (Schudson, 1978). On the other hand, research that focuses on the ambiguity or meaning of a cultural item, although rich in interpretation, often fails to find and test generalizable propositions (Griswold, 1987). In this project, I examine artistic content in an attempt to bridge this common gap in the sociology of culture (Zolberg, 1990).

Organizational Theories

In this book, I use tools from organizational sociology to show how organizational arrangements affect culture. Organizations are not isolated entities immune from external influences (Scott, 1992). Museums are open systems that can be influenced by external pressures. To understand museums—and to understand art—we must understand how museums work as organizations. I will review three perspectives on organization-environment interactions. Institutional theory provides the linchpin for understanding museums, though I also draw upon concepts from resource dependency and strategy theories.[3] In this section, I outline these approaches to familiarize readers with the basic concepts, and I suggest what insight each approach offers for the understanding of museums.

Resource Dependency

The obvious model to start with in an examination of environmental effects is resource dependency (Pfeffer & Salancik, 1978). The key assumption of this approach is that organizations must garner resources held by other actors in order to survive. If the resources are important enough, the actor controlling the resource has power over the organization. This theory posits a power relationship between two organizations, with the stronger organization essentially extorting compliance from the weaker.

The resource dependency idea is central to understanding museum funding. To the extent that museums have become increasingly reliant on new funders, the tastes and concerns of these funders may shape the exhibition policy made by museum managers. In other words, the reward system for the museum may structure the type of art exhibited. This argument is easily recast, from an organizational perspective, into resource dependency terms. Museums cannot operate only on admission fees and small-donor memberships; consequently, they are highly dependent on other, more concentrated sources. To maintain such funding, museums must attract and appease large donors. One way museums might do this is to conform to the demands of those who supply resources—for example, to organize exhibitions around funder preferences.

Phrased this way, the depiction of resource dependency suggests that those who control crucial resources coerce organizational decision makers to meet their demands. However, influence is not always so bald. Funders can affect museums whether or not their grants come "with strings attached." Often donors give "complete freedom" to the museums' curators in the funding contract, but fund only those museums that seem to the donors to have exciting, interesting programs.[4]

Pfeffer and Salancik suggest that managers should be geared toward handling constraints created by the environment while maintaining their autonomy from such demands. The environment is not a pool of demands to be passively met. Rather, it represents an arena within which managers work to achieve specific goals. Furthermore, managers autonomously reshape demands from the environment and creatively manipulate those demands; this is more easily done when there is conflict and ambiguity in external pressures.

Strategy Approaches

Strategy models give us some insight into how managers create their organization's environment (Chaffee, 1985; Child, 1972; Miles, et al., 1978). Resource dependency models portray managers as reactive—either as being controlled by external actors or as working to avoid such control. In contrast, strategy researchers focus more on the proactive side, pointing out that managers have considerable freedom in choosing which environments are relevant to their organizations. Strategy models portray managers as actors who are able to choose a niche for their organizations as they work to position themselves better in their environment.

Strategic decision-making theory suggests that organizations try to fit into and to manage their environment. Strategic management orients museum managers to the art world. If managers are oriented outward, then they must choose which external constituencies to please. For instance, museums could choose to make exhibitions more academic to please university art historians and professional art critics. Or they may make exhibitions more popular and snazzy to entice broad audiences and funders who prefer such audiences. Museums could also try to attract a stable base of members who pay their dues every year, or they could target elite "large donors" who give a great deal of money and artwork to museums. Contributing members may be interested in different types of exhibitions than the general public or scholars. Elite donors may not be particularly interested in special exhibits at all; they may be more interested in personal, behind-the-scenes tours of the museum. Museums may choose to be less attuned to exhibitions if they wish to attract elites. External scholars may be more interested in catalogues of museum collections and in in-depth research on particular artworks published as articles in museum bulletins. Each of these strategies implies a somewhat different external orientation and internal arrangement. Though most museums do some combination of all of these activities, the particular mix of orientations dictates internal arrangements and suggests the direction of future strategies.

The main implication of strategic decision making for the environment is clear. The organization's manipulation of environmental factors, if successful, changes the environment. For instance, museums' efforts to lobby the federal government for more exhibition funding will make the funding environment more bountiful and complicated. Museums that sell postcards and scarves in the museum shop must attend to the manufacturers of those items and to the largely middle-class visitors who buy them. Less obvious, perhaps, is the fact that changing an organization's environment can affect internal arrangements of the organization (Fligstein, 1990; Pfeffer & Salanick, 1978). Implications of such changes can be far-reaching. For example, if museums are successful in lobbying for more federal support of exhibitions, then museums must hire additional administrators to manage grant-related paper flows, such as accounting records and reporting forms. Additional curators will also be needed to mount exhibitions. A shift in the numbers of these personnel can change the balance of power within museums.

Strategic contingency theory suggests that internal conflict in museums will increase with the introduction of new environments that add new factions of employees in the organization (or the strengthening of old factions). In museums, the conflict between factions is likely to affect the content of art exhibitions, since exhibitions are shaped by various "stakeholders"—curators, administrators, educators, funders, and audiences. As any one of these groups gets stronger, weaker, or changes its point of view, exhibitions are likely to change.

As suggested by power perspectives of organizational functioning, organizations are built of coalitions of actors, each coalition vying for power and resources (Child, 1972; Cyert & March, 1963). Consequently, coalitions internal to the organization strive for their own gain. Strategic contingency theory suggests that subunits within organizations best positioned to handle uncertainty from the environment tend to have more power within the organization (Hickson, Pugh & Pheysey, 1969). Research in organizational strategy highlights strategic decisions that improve the organization's efficiency or effectiveness. Not every strategic choice is made to enhance performance. In fact, the dominant coalition is often able to trade off some "performance" to obtain structures its members find personally satisfying (Child, 1972). Museum curators, administrators, and educators try to use funders to benefit their coalition, not necessarily to benefit the organization as a whole. This creates tensions in the museum.

Institutional Theory

Institutional theorists argue that organizations make decisions based on legitimacy as well as tangible resource flows (Meyer & Scott, 1992; Powell & DiMaggio, 1991; Scott, 1995).[5] Institutional theory recognizes that environments shape organizations. In contrast to resource dependency and strategy theory, however, institutional theory posits that managers will focus on maintaining the organization's legitimacy, and will pay secondary attention to resource flows. Consequently, institutional theory suggests that museums will continue to court the favor of such actors as the American Association of Museums (which grants accreditation) and art critics (who publicly review exhibitions and museum publications), even though these actors cannot provide the financial resources that exhibition funders can. This behavior happens because museums are not strictly "for profit" businesses that can drop one product line when it becomes unprofitable. Rather, a museum must maintain a good reputation to prove that it is an organization worthy of donations. Funders and philanthropists make decisions based on such considerations as: "Is it a good museum?" or "Will it take good care of that painting I donate?" or "Will it bring prestige to my corporation?"

In maintaining their legitimacy, museum managers and outside evaluators must agree on the function of museums. Most people in the museum world would agree that museums should conserve, collect, research, and teach about great art. Art museums should not be involved in entertainment or lowbrow, popular art. And they should not be concerned about fostering identities of cultural elites or ethnic minorities. Or should they? Some of the current controversies in museums focus on exactly these issues. Understandings of the legitimate functions of an organization, such as a museum, that exists in a highly institutionalized environment are forceful in shaping organizational behavior.[6] It would be inconceivable, for instance, to find a monster truck and giant tractor pull at the Metropolitan Museum of Art.

In addition to its focus on legitimacy as an important aspect of an organization's ability to garner resources, institutional theory also focuses on cultural elements and shared understandings that affect organizations. Organizational structures and procedures are profoundly shaped by external cultural elements called "rational institutional myths" (Meyer & Rowan, 1981). Rational myths are institutionalized knowledge:

> They are *myths* because they are widely held beliefs that cannot be objectively tested: They are true because they are believed. . . . They are *rationalized* because they take the form of rules specifying procedures necessary to accomplish a given end (Scott, 1992, p. 118, emphasis original).

Rational myths can be rules about missions, procedures, or the proper credentials for organizational participants. They can be drawn from folk wisdom, "common sense," and academic research. Some rational myths are taken for granted, others are consciously recognized; some are supported by public opinion, others are contested. Still others have been embodied in law. Museums are embedded in institutional arenas that specify, implicitly and explicitly, how a museum should be structured. For instance, most museum curators have degrees in art history. It would seem odd to appoint a person trained in auto mechanics or medicine to the post of curator, even if that person were an art collector or an accomplished artist self-taught in art history. Less trivially, most museums have an education department because of a generalized belief (held by museum personnel, written in museum missions, attended to by government granting agencies, and looked to by school principals arranging tours for their students) that museums should educate people about art. Museums divide curatorial departments by art historical genres established in the academic literature. It would not occur to museums to arrange fine arts departments by subject matter (the horse department, the landscape department, the nude department, the clothed department) or by color (the department of primarily pink paintings, the department of bronze sculpture and sienna watercolors). Museums are generally nonprofit corporations, as designated in section 501 (c) (3) of the Internal Revenue Code, so they can receive grants. As importantly, museums are incorporated in that way because that's how museums do it. (Museums can be government sponsored public museums, but this draws on an older model.) Managers, volunteers, and other nonprofit personnel draw upon rational myths when they make assertions about how the organization "ought to run."

Organizations are subject to the normative influence of groups that are carriers of rational myths. Institutional theory highlights the influence of professionals on organizations (DiMaggio & Powell, 1983): Professionals, socialized and trained in universities or other external settings, usually have quite strongly held notions of the proper ways to do their jobs. They import their ideas (rational myths) into organizations and continue to look outside to their professional colleagues and associations for ideas, validation, and prestige. In museums, art historically trained curators are professionals, as are many of the museums' non-artistic personnel (finance, development, education, and public relations officers, for example).

In mounting exhibitions, museum curators draw upon their own vision of museum integrity. These professionals strive to keep the museum viable and legitimate in their own eyes and in the view of other internal and external judges. What these art historians believe about museum integrity comes from their background and professional training, and such beliefs often operate without complete conscious awareness. I will call these professional influences "normative forces," following DiMaggio and Powell (1983).

To understand how museums create exhibitions, it is essential to understand that within museums a conflict exists between the visions carried by different organizational actors. In museums, curators, directors, trustees, and other personnel all hold different views that have aesthetic implications. These views vary by the professional training and the office held by the individual in question. Aesthetic views are one example of the normative views recognized by institutional theory. Some of these views are explicitly and consciously held and directly acted upon. Other visions, such as those of the financial officer who cancels an exhibition for lack of funds, are implicit or indirect.

Moreover, the decisions of external funders also imply aesthetic choices. Central to my argument is the idea that all philanthropists have goals or objectives that focus their giving. Since government agencies, corporations, and elite individuals do not have the same goals, different forms of philanthropy will encourage different types of art. Museum personnel—most notably, directors, curators, and board members—must balance the demands of each funder to keep the museum viable. Directors, curators, and board members are also "stakeholders" with their own interests, which are quite important in the decision stream.

Funders may come to museums with certain preferences and biases. When these preferences and biases conflict with the visions already institutionalized in museums, new funding creates challenges for museum personnel. Museum managers respond to this situation by trying to find ways to fund exhibitions amenable to their visions of museum integrity. In other words, museum managers strive to retain their autonomy and the legitimacy of museums in the face of resource dependency pressures. Accommodations to pressures from institutional funders will emerge from whatever normative ideas each group carries.

External influence does not necessarily reduce the role of internal decision makers. Donors may make general demands on museums for art that appeals to a broad audience or for art that is scholarly. Museums look for possibilities from old and new art to meet these demands. Thus, the sensibilities of curators and other arts professionals serve to translate and channel donor desires. But more than that, museum personnel use the opportunities posed by the array of funders to actually *create new solutions*: new definitions of art, new types of exhibitions, and different roles for museums. Their ability to find creative resolutions to the problems brought about by new funding patterns affects both the content of exhibitions *and* aesthetic definitions.

In summary, organizations literature suggests that museums become externally oriented as museum managers try to generate needed revenue. As museums focus on external funders, they orient their activities to please funders and to ensure continued income. However, museums will continue to try to please their more traditional judges, including internal constituents, to maintain their legitimacy. This bifurcation may create or strengthen coalitions in museums, and consequently, conflict and tension will increase. Various coalitions in museums compete with each other in an attempt to retain their autonomy. This competition, however, leads directors, curators, and other museum actors to innovate. The possibility of innovation helps account for aesthetic change in art worlds.

NOTES

1. Though Peterson and Berger make a good case that the concentration of the music industry affects the diversity of music, they discuss diversity and innovation as if they were the same concept. I believe, however, that innovation and diversity are analytically and empirically separable and that innovation may precede changes in market structure. Innovation, if successful, produces diversity. On the other hand, the lack of innovation does not imply a lack of diversity, merely a lack of *increasing* diversity.

2. A closely related concept is that of the "surrogate consumer" (Hirsch, 1981). These are autonomous gatekeepers such as art critics, film and literature reviewers, and disk jockeys. (The influence of surrogate consumers is not examined in this research.)

3. Each of these theories, in their pure—or is it caricatured?—form varies as to the rationality assumed of organizational decision makers, and as to the extent to which organizations are able to control environmental effects. These theories also focus on different levels of analysis. The first two concentrate on organizations themselves. These two tend to be managerially oriented. The third theory focuses on broader networks of organizations (at the societal sector level), and tends to be theoretically oriented. Many similar hypotheses can be generated from each of these theories, however. To adjudicate among these theories for museums is not the goal of the research. Instead, I will synthesize my approach from these various theories. In fact, I do not believe that it is valuable or even possible to distinguish empirically among the three theories. Proponents of these theories may disagree about metatheoretical assumptions, for instance on the "nature of man as a rational decision maker" (usually stated in non-gender neutral form). Yet the three theories explain overlapping segments of empirical reality. Further, I believe that institutional theory provides an umbrella for understanding the other two theories, and that institutional theory is strengthened by using the insights of these theories (Alexander, 1996b, forthcoming).

4. The extent that museums anticipate and respond to funders' preferences, however, indicates the level of power that is operating (Zelditch, et al., 1983).

5. It is important to recognize that institutional theory does not neglect resources, though this is a common misreading (and a caricature) of institutional theory. For instance, DiMaggio and Powell (1983) discuss "coercive pressures" on organizations. This concept implies external actors with access to sanctions, and is

identical to resource dependency in many cases. Organizational decision makers give in to coercive demands in their environment because they want the rewards associated with the demand, or they wish to avoid punishments associated with ignoring the demand. In this way, institutional theory has a lot in common with resource dependence theory, though institutional theory posits that efforts on the part of organizations to seek legitimacy are causally prior; resources are a related, but secondary, consideration.

6. A note on terminology might be useful here. "Institutional funders" means those donors who are based in a formal organization, including government agencies, corporations, and nonprofit organizations such as foundations. This terminology is a standard way of indicating such organizationally based funders. The term has the disadvantage of suggesting "institution" from institutional theory (a cultural rule or schema) along with its intended sense (a collective actor or formal organization). Though the two uses of the term are potentially confusing, I will continue to employ the standard terms "institutional theory" and "institutional funder," making my meaning clear in context. By "highly institutionalized" environment, I mean one that is highly structured with rational myths and cultural rules, not one that contains institutional funders, though the latter may also be true.

II

FROM PHILANTHROPY TO FUNDING

CHANGES IN MUSEUM PATRONAGE

Art patronage started slowly in the United States.[1] Before the Civil War, there was little support for fine arts painting, though itinerant portrait painters could make a living by traveling widely. By the 1870s, however, collecting art had become a hobby of the wealthy (Meyer, 1979), and major American museums were being formed. Although there are examples of nineteenth-century collectors who focused on American art, such as Robert Gilmore (Rutledge, 1949) and Thomas B. Clarke (Weinberg, 1976), most early American patrons preferred classical European art. Anything American created a crass and vulgar image in the minds of collectors (Rose, 1975, p. 10) who were, after all, trying to elevate themselves by associating with a European, and more aristocratic, model of art collection.[2]

The number of art collectors increased, and museums followed, modeled on European museums (Duncan & Wallach, 1980). Though American museums were like European museums in their display of objects, they contrasted with European museums, which grew out of royal and aristocratic collections. American museums, instead, were founded on the ideals of civic boosterism and cultural enlightenment. And in fact, the earliest museums in the United States grew out of the commercial spirit of P.T. Barnum and his circus. These museums were not like museums as we know them today; rather, they offered an amalgam of all sorts of objects (DiMaggio, 1982a, b; Levine, 1988). The precursor museums displayed a cupboard of curiosities alongside reproductions and paintings and appealed to both the working and upper classes. For example:

> Founded as a commercial venture in 1841, Moses Kemball's Boston Museum exhibited works by such painters as Sully and Peale alongside Chinese curiosities, stuffed animals, mermaids and dwarves. For the entrance fee visitors could also attend the Boston Museum Theatre, which presented works by Dickens and Shakespeare as well as performances by

> gymnasts and contortionists. . . . The promiscuous combination of genres that later would be considered incompatible was not uncommon. (DiMaggio, 1982a, p. 34)

A few scholarly museums were founded quite early. The Yale Art Gallery was established in 1832, and the Wadsworth Atheneum in 1842. But on the whole, the crazy-quilt model of museum contents held sway until the 1870s, when many of the nation's greatest museums were founded. The Metropolitan Museum, the Museum of Fine Arts in Boston, and the Philadelphia Museum of Art, three of the largest and most important encyclopedic collections in the United States, all opened in the 1870s.

By the 1910s and 1920s, collectors of antique art were joined by those favoring the works of living artists. This trend was highlighted by the Armory Show, which attracted enormous public attention, not all of it favorable. The move to collecting modern artists culminated in the formation of important museums of contemporary art. On Friday, November 8, 1929, just one week after the stock market crashed, the Museum of Modern Art opened its doors (Lynes, 1973). The Whitney opened in 1931, and the Guggenheim in 1937. In a span of just eight years, Depression years at that, the three most pivotal contemporary art museums in the United States were established.

Individual philanthropists were the primary supporters of museums early in this century. Most museums were founded by individual collectors, and even museums with municipal funding received that assistance as a result of pressure from the city's wealthy. Since founders usually took a great interest in the daily activities of their organizations, most early museums reflected the interests of these wealthy patrons, and of upper-class culture in general. "Created, not inherited, the American museum was animated by an unabashedly bourgeois spirit, and was brought to fruition as a local, civic institution rather than as a nest for the national spirit" (Lilla & Frank, 1988, p. 34).

The 1930's also witnessed the first large-scale federal arts programs: The government funded the Federal Art, Writers', Music and Theater Projects as part of the Works Projects Administration. Although the arts section received only two percent of the total WPA funding, the section helped establish the justification for federal arts funding; widely available art enriches the nation (Larson, 1983). The national dialogue about arts funding continued after the WPA ended in 1943. This low-key, but almost continuous, debate was based on the assumption that such funding would create a larger audience for the arts and was centered on the value of public exposure to the arts. Larson (1983) discusses the federal activity surrounding the arts in the years 1943–1965. He demonstrates that in those years, usually considered the years "when nothing happened," there was, in fact, important activity that eventually led to federal involvement in the arts.

The spirit of the Great Society in the 1960s was one of the driving forces behind the passage of legislation that created the National Endowment for the Arts (NEA) and the National Endowment for the Humanities (NEH). President Kennedy had given the arts a new recognition during his administration, and federal funding of the arts is most certainly a Kennedy legacy. In 1964, President Johnson created the National Arts Council as an unfunded advisory body. One year later, Congress established the NEA and the NEH. The endowments provide fellowships and funds for programs and performances. To museums, the NEA and NEH offer financial help for programs and exhibits, but not for maintenance, conservation, or operating expenses. The mission of the NEA is to make art available to more people, and to help cultural organizations better serve the citizens of the United States. The NEH's primary purpose is to increase humanistic understanding in America by supporting education, public programs, and scholarly research in the humanities. The picture of federal support of the arts, especially during the first decade of the Endowments' existence, is one of substantial increases. The first appropriation to the NEA, in 1966, was $1.8 million. By 1990, the appropriation was just over $150 million (National Endowment for the Arts, 1990). In real terms, however, the budget for the NEA actually peaked in the late seventies and has slowly decreased since then (DiMaggio, 1986b). The NEH also grew from an appropriation of $2.5 million in 1966 to $134.6 million in 1986 (National Endowment for the Humanities, 1966, 1986).

During the same decade, corporations began to fund the arts in notable amounts (Porter, 1981). Certainly, some corporations have been associated with the arts for a long time (Allen, 1983; Martorella 1990, Chapter 2); however, the mid-60s were a time of tremendous growth of corporate arts sponsorship. In 1965, the New York Board of Trade founded an Arts Advisory Council, and the Business Committee for the Arts (a national organization still active) was established two years later. Corporate leaders began to believe that "culture is the business of business" (Gingrich, 1969). They also came to recognize that cultural philanthropy is often a good way to improve corporate reputations (Galaskiewicz, 1985; Useem, 1984). Arts funding "provides an image for a corporation as sensitive and innovative instead of as a heartless, bottom-line company," says art consultant Tamara Thomas (quoted in McGuigan *et al.*, 1985). Interestingly, the first corporations to fund the arts on a national scale were cigarette and oil producers, the companies with the muddiest images (Ermann, 1979). Corporate patronage for the arts (including museums, dance, theater, and other arts) increased from approximately $22 million in 1965 to $150 million in 1975 (Goldwin A. McLellan, quoted in Meyer, 1979, p. 85). In

1992, 11.8 percent of the $5.92 billion given by corporations, almost $700 million, was given to culture and the arts (American Association of Fund-Raising Counsel 1994, p. 74, 77). Corporate expenditure for all philanthropic giving has grown enormously since the early 1960s. While corporate giving remained relatively constant, with adjustments for inflation, through the early 70s—between 3 and 3.8 billion 1993 dollars—it started to climb around 1975, doubling to a peak of over 7.14 billion 1993 dollars and declining to $5.92 million in 1993 (American Association of Fund-Raising Counsel, 1994, p. 74). In general, about 11 to 12 percent of total corporate philanthropy goes to visual arts, and 24 percent of the proportion given to visual arts goes to museums (Glennon, 1988).

Foundations have played a slightly different role in museums than government and corporate funders, although all three are classified as institutional funders. Foundations became important to museums earlier than the other funders, in the 1920s. Foundations then went through a period of declining influence, but became bigger players in the arts again in the 1950s (DiMaggio, 1991c, 1986c). In 1984, foundations gave 761 grants in the category "art and architecture." These grants totaled over $50 million, amounting to 3.1 percent of the total foundation giving in all categories (Odendahl, 1987b, p. 36). Despite this large contribution in the cultural arena, foundations have had a lesser impact in the transformation of museums than corporations and government during the time under study.

Increasing Prevalence of Funding

Since 1960, then, institutional funders have been giving increasing amounts of funds to cultural organizations, including museums. Figure 2-1, based on my sample of museum exhibitions from 1960–86, shows the number of funded exhibitions for all the museums in the sample combined, along with the number of unfunded/internally funded exhibitions per year. Two trends are clearly seen in this graph. First, there is a notable increase in exhibitions, and, second, there is a concomitant increase in funded exhibitions. Note that, over time, the number of funded exhibitions increases, but that after 1972 (when there is a peak attributable to a peak in children's exhibitions[3]), the proportion of unfunded exhibitions to funded exhibitions decreases. In other words, the number of funded exhibitions increasingly contributes to the total number of exhibitions. Museums appear able to garner outside support for a certain percentage of exhibitions (22 percent is the overall average of funded exhibitions), and that percentage has increased from about 10 percent in 1960 to about 30 percent in 1986.

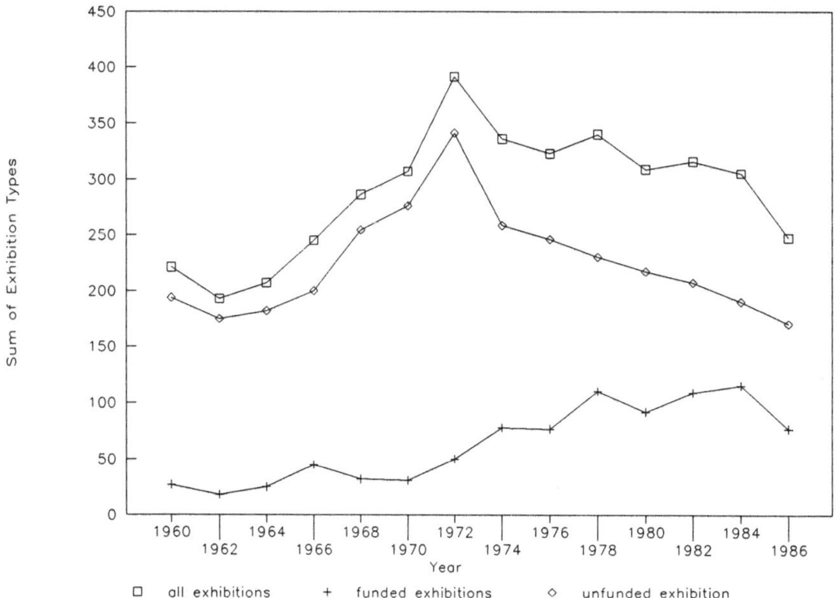

Figure 2-1. Sum of Exhibition Types over Sample Museums: All Exhibitions, Funded Exhibitions, and Unfunded Exhibitions.
Source: Annual Reports, exhibition data set.

Moreover, the character of exhibition support has changed drastically over time. Figure 2-2 shows the average number of exhibitions supported by corporations, government agencies, foundations, and individuals per museum over time. This graph shows (1) the increasing prevalence of institutional funders, (2) the stasis of support by individuals, and (3) the influence of federal administration on the level of government support.

Note first the increasing number of exhibitions funded by corporations. This finding suggests that corporations are more involved in exhibition sponsorship than they have been in the past. The picture of corporate sponsorship also corresponds with statistics on overall corporate giving to the arts. For example, corporate giving to all arts increased from $22 million in 1966 to $436 million in 1981 (Porter, 1981). Similarly, the number of corporate patrons of major museums increased dramatically. In the Whitney Museum, corporate patrons shot up from 14 in 1967–68 to 159 in 1980–81; the Museum of Modern Art's corporate patrons rose from 90 in 1965–66 to 201 in 1980–81 (Crane, 1987, p. 130).

Figure 2-2 shows a basic increase in exhibition support by government. Note, however, the fall-off during the years of the Reagan administration. This finding suggests that government agencies have become more involved in support of exhibitions. However, it also suggests that federal

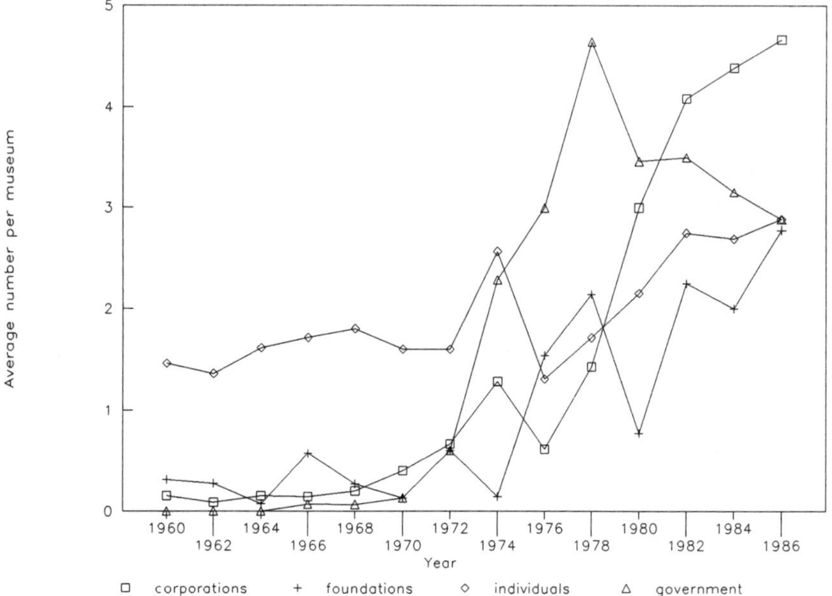

Figure 2-2. Average Number of Exhibitions per Museum, Sponsored by Each Type of Funder, by Year.

administration affects government funding. In the interviews, a few respondents noted that government funding becomes tighter under more conservative presidents. (We now know that this is true under conservative Congresses as well.) The decrease in government spending is particularly visible in this data during the Reagan years. Reagan, of course, pledged to slash—or better, eliminate—the NEA (DiMaggio, 1986b).

Foundation support for exhibitions also rises over time. This may be related to the increasing wealth of foundations (Boris, 1987) and fits with the trend of the increasing importance of organizationally based patrons in the funding of nonprofit cultural organizations (DiMaggio, 1986a). The figure illustrates the very interesting finding that there is no pattern over time in individual funding of exhibitions. This suggests that elite individuals have not changed their behavior in regard to exhibition funding in the past thirty years. The lack of change in individual giving might be a mix of two counteracting trends: an increase in the number of millionaires along with a the tendency of today's adult "baby boomers" to give less to charity than their parents' generation did (Balfe, 1989). These two trends could be combining (a smaller proportion of a larger donor pool) to create the stasis of individual funding of exhibitions.

Goals of the Funders

A key assumption of my research is that philanthropists have goals or objectives that focus their giving, and that different goals favor different art works. Thus, I wanted to know more about goals of funders to learn about the larger role of philanthropy in shaping the contents and "packaging" of art exhibitions of all kinds. To learn about funder goals, I interviewed a small sample of museum curators, directors, and educators, asking about their perceptions of funders and funder effects on museums (see the methodological appendix). Clearly, the museum respondents' views of the goals of funders may be somewhat biased. Yet their views—the museum-eye perspective—shape the decisions made within the museum.[4] Moreover, the generalizations made by museum people about the motives of various types of funders are similar to findings from studies of such funders. Here, I draw upon the interviews to paint a picture of the goals of four types of funders: the traditional individual philanthropist and the three main types of new institutional funder: corporations, government agencies, and foundations. I also present findings from the academic literature on each type of funder. The literature, by and large, supports and buttresses the views I found among museum personnel.

Corporations

As seen by museum personnel, corporations generally fund art as a public relations gambit. Corporations are interested in publicity or enhancing their reputations, rather than in art. Museum personnel say that corporations attend to the potential audience of a show and are particularly interested in audiences who consume corporate products or provide resources—including legitimacy. Corporations want to sponsor art that has a wide public appeal, either through accessible subject matter (Impressionist art and other "pretty" shows) or through well-known artists (shows of famous, "name-brand" artists). A quick survey of corporate support for exhibitions reveals many shows of artifacts, "treasures," and "material culture" (for example, shows about Dutch tile, Shaker furniture, crafts and industry of the Connecticut River Valley, and gold and silver from the Vatican). Corporations favor representational art. They are willing to fund more challenging art, like Jackson Pollock's, for example, but only if the artist has already become famous. Further, they are likely to be interested in reaching middle- and upper middle-class audiences—people who are their employees, customers, competitors and, in general, judges of the corporation. Thus, corporations may be interested in art that is noncontroversial, but that still has some claim to prestige.

Though museum personnel agree that the main goals of corporations are public relations and publicity, the interpretation of corporate donations and the attribution of goodwill to corporate donors varies greatly with museum position. Corporate funding of the arts is a great locus of controversy in museums. Curators often say, with distaste, that corporations are only interested in "what's in it for them." They don't want good art, one curator asserts; rather they want to "dazzle the eye." Directors, on the other hand, usually point to the large amount of money corporations have donated to museums, and argue that these donations have led to increased activity and vitality in museums. Directors believe that corporate dollars are indispensable to museums. Curators would love to dispense with corporate support, though they realize this would be difficult today. One director/curator, who held opinions from both camps, characterized herself as a "purist" (meaning she did not believe that museums should accept corporate funding). I asked her how one could go about running a museum with no corporate support. She answered, "You can't."

As museum respondents pointed out, corporations have no single, standardized set of application procedures and rules. Museum requests for money from corporations are not evaluated uniformly across firms (although each corporation's internal procedure might be internally standardized). The evaluations are often completed by a high-level employee who has an interest in the arts, and whose personal judgment comes into play. In other cases, corporations hire professional arts advisors who tell them what to fund. Consequently, it is difficult to generalize about how museums approach corporations for money. Some operate quite informally. One respondent told me that the head of her board of trustees has friends in business whom he approaches with her ideas, in an early and undeveloped form, until he finds someone who has some extra money. He just "calls them up, and they make a deal over lunch."[5] Other corporations have formal competitions to determine who will receive funds for a given year.

Corporation-museum relations vary greatly, as well. In one interview, two curators from the same museum met with me. One had a bad experience with a corporate funder, the other a good experience. The first curator told me that corporate representatives, who did not want to read something lengthy, limited his proposal to one page. The curator resented this limit because he felt it was not possible to do justice to an entire exhibition in one page. Although the corporation approved the grant, it did not specify how much it would give in cash and how much through in-kind services. The curator was especially concerned about the source of the publicity budget because, from past experience, he knew that when that particular corporation's people designed publicity posters (an in-kind contribution), they did not defer to art historical protocol that he himself deems essential (e.g., not failing to identify a fragment of a painting used in such a poster as a "detail"). His problems were not eased by the fact that he could not contact the corporation directly. All correspondence had to go through the museum's public relations department and had to be reviewed by the museum director.

The second curator, who was at that time working with another corporation, told me that she had prepared a ten-page brief for the corporation (a wealth of information compared to the other curator's one page). The corporate decision makers tentatively approved the project and asked the curator to give a verbal presentation to their key personnel. The corporation then put everything in writing and did not make any demands on the curator that she felt were inappropriate. These two stories illustrate the variety of behaviors that corporate funders exhibit. However, most of the stories I heard from *curators* about corporations were similar to the first one above. (Directors, on the other hand, stressed the usefulness of corporate dollars.)

Studies of corporate philanthropy agree that "corporate self-interest" is of leading importance when corporations decide to fund art (Useem, 1987; Useem & Kutner, 1986). Corporations are more interested in public relations and publicity value than they are in the art *per se*. There is a good deal of scholarly evidence that corporations donate time or money to charity in order to gain the respect of the firms' constituencies (Burt, 1983; Fry, Keim & Meiners 1982; Galaskiewicz, 1985; Levy & Shatto, 1978; Useem, 1987). Corporations prefer to fund recipients who will reflect well on them, those that are "prestigious, large, and located near headquarters or plants with large staffs," (Useem, 1987, pp. 343–4). Thus, larger and more prestigious nonprofits win more corporate funds, a finding that holds especially true for arts organizations (Galaskiewicz & Rauschenbach, 1988). As Useem (1984, p. 120) notes, "Dollar for dollar, few better investments in corporate reputation can be found than identification with the community's premier arts. It can even be more effective than explicit promotion of corporate reputation." Useem interviewed a manufacturer who heavily sponsored major museums in New York city. The company's CEO says:

> There's an indirect editorial kind of credibility to arts giving. You can take ads and say, "Look at how good we are," but if you *do* things, you get editorial attribution, which I think is more believable. The payoff is not readily discernible, but I do think it is incremental, and I do believe that over time you get a larger and larger audience that has a better opinion of you. (quoted in Useem, 1984, p. 120, emphasis original)

Useem and Kutner (1986) show that large, national corporations are the major actors in the corporate philanthropy game, with large corporate philanthropy budgets; smaller firms give a lower proportion of their (smaller) after-tax earnings and have less impact on the cultural arena.

Useem's work also shows that the CEO's personal preferences top the list of influences on where corporate money goes, regardless of the size of the corporation or its philanthropy budget. Not surprisingly, corporations give more in expanding economies, and when profits are up than in shrinking economies when profits are down (Useem, 1987, 1991).

Useem (1984) argues that the benefits accruing to corporations in terms of philanthropy are returns of good will to the business community, not to individual firms. In fact, most people can't remember whether it was Exxon or Mobil that sponsored dance programs on public television, or which of those companies is more likely to sponsor the visual arts. But the point is that, in some ways, oil companies—and all for-profit firms for that matter—appear more beneficent when they give something back to their communities.

Interestingly, some conservative economists like Milton Friedman argue that corporate philanthropy is wrong. Unless corporations can provide evidence that their philanthropy produces a direct return to stockholders, so the argument goes, the fiduciary duties of boards (which are to approve actions that will return a profit to shareholders) make it immoral, and in fact illegal, to engage in philanthropy. It is tantamount to stealing money from shareholders. The diffuse and general benefit to business that Useem points to is not good enough.

In determining their funding levels and target charities, corporations are strongly influenced by other corporations. Galaskiewicz (1985) shows that contributions by companies in Minneapolis-St.Paul are higher than the national average. This is due to a generalized sense of civic pride and community spirit in the Twin Cities and also to the rich personal and business ties among the corporate elite in the metropolitan area. Businessmen meet on the golf course or in board meetings and use social pressure to get those businesses lagging behind in giving to get with the program. Indeed, Galaskiewicz suggests that the driving force of corporate philanthropy is to enhance corporate managers' prestige in the eyes of other members of elite business groups, *not* their reputation as seen by the general public. Useem (1984, 1987; Useem & Kutner, 1986) also shows that the actions of other corporations have the most impact on where a given corporation puts its philanthropic giving, and suggests (1987, p. 344) that a good first step in garnering corporate support would be for a nonprofit to invite a senior manager of a local corporation to sit on the nonprofit's board.

The academic literature supports the impression in museums that corporations tend to fund museums whose programs attract a large, appreciative, middle-class audience (Porter, 1981). Corporations have been especially active in sponsoring blockbuster shows (Martorella, 1990; DiMaggio, 1986b). Such shows are tightly bound up with corporate advertising. For instance, Philip Morris spent $3 million to support the Vatican Show at the Metropolitan Museum, but the company spent $2 million more on advertising the show (Martorella, 1990: 17).

In a study of corporate art collections, Martorella (1990) demonstrates that corporations are conservative and that they tend to collect more easily understood pieces of contemporary art. This preference holds true for exhibition sponsorship, too:

> "Corporations are primarily interested in representational art," observed the director of development for New York's Whitney Museum, since "the masses of people relate to it more surely. The masses do *not* relate to abstract art. Corporations are interested in improving their image, and if they spent money on an exhibition which the bulk of the people do not relate to, they would in their view be doing more harm than good." (Rosenbaum, 1977, quoted in Useem, 1987, p. 355, emphasis original)

However, it is important to keep in mind that, contrary to what some critics have argued, corporations do not want to fund mindless pabulum. Rather, the art itself must retain some legitimacy if the "halo effect"—the association of sacred art with the profane corporate name—is to work its magic (Balfe, 1987).

Corporations, of course, are not all of one piece and there may be differences among corporations in specific preferences. For instance, Useem and Kutner (1986) suggest that the level of formalization in the organization's granting process, the role of the Chief Executive Officer, and the orientations of other corporate contributors known to managers of the focal firm affect both the level of the firm's giving and the types of institutions it funds.

When the goal of corporations is public relations, there are many ways to improve a corporation's image. Some corporations are more interested in improving employee or client relations, others in promoting their products or services, in polishing their image in their community, or in gaining a national reputation as a funder of the arts, and still others in building international goodwill by sponsoring American displays of art from targeted foreign countries. Corporations may sponsor exhibitions of foreign art to please particular audiences (businessmen or government officials) in the originating country. For instance, American corporations supported Chinese art about the time that the United States opened diplomatic relations with China. Conversely, foreign corporations sponsor art of their own countries that tour the United States, not merely to please the American public, but to grease the wheels of commerce by appealing to American elites.

Corporations are concerned with factors beyond just the number of people who come through the turnstiles. For instance, there are at least two types of corporate patrons: The first is the savvy corporation, perhaps one with a muddied image, that hires an art consultant to suggest the best way for the firm to invest its money, given its public-relations goals. The other kind of corporation allows a company officer to donate corporate money to the art of his choice—a kind of philanthropic perquisite. Clearly, the pattern of funding will vary between these two types of corporations. The former is more likely to base its decisions on "rational" material considerations, while the latter's decisions rest on the idiosyncratic personal preferences of the person in charge (and may thus resemble patterns of elite individual patronage of art museums).

One story, related to me second-hand, concerned the second type of corporation and the corporation's designated "philanthropist." The philanthropist told my informant that, regarding art exhibitions, his corporation funds "just the ones he likes." He does not investigate possible audiences, nor does he speak to other corporate representatives, and he does not see anything wrong with this. He knows the most about art, he says, so of course he should make the final decisions himself. (Interestingly, it seems that his art responsibilities take up only a small amount of his time; his official position is head of the advertising department.)

In arts funding, however, corporations have become increasingly formalized in grant procedures (Useem, 1991). Since the 1970s, corporations gave increasing amounts through corporate foundations, rather than directly from corporate earnings.[6] This suggests that the "philanthropic perquisite" company is currently more rare.

"Corporate altruism" isn't a big theme in corporate philanthropy, either among museum people or in the academic literature. However, firms paint themselves in a different light. In a survey of 458 companies involved in arts sponsorship (Useem, 1991) managers ranked in order of importance fourteen criteria that determine funding.[7] "Impact on the local community" and "geographic location" ranked highest, with 94 and 92 percent, respectively, of managers saying that those factors were very important. Interestingly, they ranked "artistic merit" near the top, at 66 percent. "Publicity value" ranked near the bottom, at 21 percent. The only factors ranked lower than publicity value were "matching gifts," "support by foundations/government" and "gifts from individuals."

It might be worth noting that government policy may affect corporate donations. For corporate philanthropy in general, the federal government allows tax deductions for cash and certain in-kind contributions; until 1981 corporations could write off up to five percent of their pre-tax net income and could write off up to ten percent thereafter. However, most corporations give no more than one percent of pre-tax net income to charity (Useem, 1987, p. 340). This suggests that corporate sponsorship might not be highly influenced by government tax policy, though surely the ability to write of charitable contributions does offer corporations an important incentive to give (Feld, O'Hare & Schuster, 1983). For exhibition support, many government programs work on a matching-fund basis, by supporting only 50 percent of the cost of a show. This has an important indirect effect on corporate giving, as museums must look for additional funders after receiving an NEA or NEH grant. The National Endowment "stamp of approval," however, does not necessarily encourage corporate support. For most corporations, government funding isn't what matters in corporate funding decisions, though a significant minority (30 percent) of corporations say that they pay attention to this factor (Useem & Kutner, 1986; Useem, 1991). Indeed, the evidence suggests that matching grant programs, while successful, pull corporate contributions from other potential donors rather than raising the total amount of donated funds (Rose-Ackerman, cited in Useem, 1987, p. 352; Schuster, 1989).

Government Agencies

To characterize the goals of government agencies, I will discuss the three major players in exhibition funding from the government arena: the NEA, the NEH, and state arts councils. By concentrating on only the exhibition programs of these government agencies, I do not wish to suggest that these are the only manifestations of art policy in the United States. While these programs are central to this study, there are certainly other programs that are important for museums. The NEA provides money for several other purposes, such as art purchase grants, challenge grants, and community program grants, as well as grants for conservation, construction, cataloging, intern training, and public education. In addition to exhibitions, the NEH also supports workshops, scholarly research, travel to collections, and provides fellowships for museum personnel. Additional arts agencies support museums in a variety of ways. The Institute of Museum Services grants operating and maintenance expenses to museums (A. Oliver, 1991). All 50 states have a myriad of local arts councils. The Federal Council on the Arts and Humanities pays insurance costs of objects lent to American museums from museums in foreign countries, especially supporting blockbuster exhibitions. On occasion, the government provides incidental support to museums. For instance, the Comprehensive Education and Training Act (eliminated in the early 1980s) provided salaries for secretaries working at local arts agencies and for various personnel in small museums (DiMaggio, 1986b, 1991b).

The government funding environment for museums became increasingly complex and decentralized from 1965 through the 1970s, but most government programs offering direct support to museums were eliminated during the Reagan administration, leaving only the NEA, NEH, and the IMS as the major players at the federal level. There has been a slight increase in decentralized funding during the Clinton administration, although this resurgence may be temporary. An important source of government support of museums is indirect: federal tax policy, which encourages individual, corporate and foundation philanthropy (Feld, O'Hare & Schuster, 1983).

As seen by museum personnel, the operational goals of the NEA are somewhat ambiguous. The written goals of the agency are quite clear: to disseminate art to the people of the United States. The professional, curatorial goals of the individuals who distribute endowment funds may be at odds with these written goals; peer-review panelists may be more interested in esoterica and minutiae than in broadness and massification. The NEA was founded with the explicit objective of widening the public's exposure to the arts, and many of its policies reflect this mission. For instance, museum personnel suggest that it gives preferential treatment to applicants in out-of-the-way places. (The NEA itself doesn't have an explicit "affirmative action" plan for backwater museums and denies preferential treatment). Still, the endowment aspires to further high-quality art exhibits of all kinds. The museum personnel I interviewed agreed that the NEA (or the NEH) has taken part in every high-quality exhibition that has been mounted recently. (DiMaggio, 1983, has noted this role of the NEA.)[8]

To rephrase the argument: the NEA was established with the explicit goal of bringing art into the public sphere. As time passed, the NEA appears to have been co-opted by scholars and critics who are more interested in the art itself than in exposing the public to art. There are countervailing pressures on the NEA-based scholars, of course. The conflict inherent in the NEA selection process is heightened by the fact that the NEA usually funds only fifty percent of a show. As one museum director, who had once worked for the NEA, told me, peer panels are "sort of, but not always" interested in the audience a show will attract: The review panel may believe a hard-to-sell, esoteric project is "just the sort of thing we should be funding"; it is scholarly, interesting, and no one else is funding it. Nevertheless, the scholarliness of the show may work against it: Since the NEA underwrites only fifty percent of an exhibition, the panel may decline to take on overly esoteric projects on the grounds that the organizing museum will not be able to raise the additional funds.

Museum respondents made it clear that in terms of museum reputation and in terms of concrete assistance, the NEA plays a very important role in museum exhibitions. Although the political philosophy of some curators and directors leads them to believe that big government, and therefore big federal arts sponsorship, is undesirable, all respondents agreed that government funding is essential to museum support. No respondents felt that government should discontinue its role in arts funding.

Exhibition funding from the NEA includes planning grants for exhibitions, grants for publishing exhibition handbooks, and support, on a matching basis, for mounting exhibitions. All major exhibitions are planned several years in advance; consequently, so too are most grants, whether corporate or government. One difference between corporate and government funders, however, is the stage in the project when it is appropriate to apply for the grant. The NEA offers grants for planning exhibitions, but corporations usually do not. With planning grants, museum curators can do research and collect objects, activities which otherwise would have to be paid for from the museum's general operating budget. Consequently, early NEA funding can be very valuable to museums.

In addition, the NEA has a program geared specifically to support exhibitions of contemporary artists. These are series such as *Matrix*, established in 1974 at the Wadsworth Atheneum in Hartford, Connecticut; *Projects*, which dates from 1971 at the Museum of Modern Art in New York City, or *Viewpoints* at the Walker Art Center in Minneapolis. These small exhibitions each feature one contemporary artist and often focus on works created especially for the exhibit. In 1986, there were about forty museums nationwide with similar programs. In addition to fostering small shows of interest to connoisseurs, the NEA has affected the experience of more general audiences. Museum personnel suggest that the availability of federal funds has increased activity in the museum sector; consequently, the public can choose from many more exhibits than in the past.

The National Endowment for the Arts relies on panels of art scholars to judge funding applications. Research on government funding of the arts confirms that there is a tension in peer-review panels between artistic and public-outreach goals (Cummings, 1991; Galligan, 1993; Levitt, 1991). The NEA must balance both these demands. Government panels, made up of museum curators, are caught between their professional, curatorial tastes (often for esoteric art), and their public mission, which requires that they attend to projected attendance figures, and consider the likelihood that the museum will be able to raise matching funds for the show (e.g., from corporations that focus on audience appeal). Political goals, then, require that government agencies pay attention to the potential of a show to draw large middle-class audiences, as do corporations. But government agencies must also attend to the art scholarship in a show, which is not a requirement for corporate funders. Further, the NEA is directed to support high-quality art; however, it is unclear what constitutes "high-quality." NEA panelists are likely to interpret high-quality as "scholarly"—addressing art historical questions and concerns, and conforming to art historical standards. In contrast to scholarly shows are exhibitions that cover no new territory, but which a cross-section of Americans might enjoy. These conflicts have been particularly evident in recent debates over a tiny fraction of NEA funding, for instance, art by Andres Serrano or Robert Mapplethorpe (Dubin, 1992).

To the extent that such panels are concerned only with art historical issues, the Endowments foster an "academic" art world (Becker, 1982). Such an art world is made possible by allowing a community of critics, curators, artists, and scholars to operate without concern for a general audience. In this regard, the NEA is likely to fund esoteric art and art that seems particularly exciting to curators, such as small shows of art historical interest, e.g., Italian Renaissance bronze statuettes or ground-breaking postmodern artists. At the same time, however, pressures both from within and from outside the NEA work to counteract this academicism and to tilt the funding toward education and public outreach programs.

State arts councils are a direct outgrowth of the NEA. With the important exception of the New York State Council on the Arts (upon which the NEA was modeled), nearly all the state arts councils were founded to take advantage of federal block grants offered to states with arts councils (DiMaggio, 1991b, p. 218). The state arts councils' budgets are made up of a combination of federal monies and funds designated by the state legislature.

The National Endowment for the Arts, the National Endowment for the Humanities, and state and local arts councils differ somewhat in their goals. The NEA is oriented toward the arts professions. The conventional image of state arts councils suggests that they should be particularly attuned to audiences and the public of the state in which they operate, with goals of "access, diversity, and equity" (DiMaggio, 1991b, p. 228).[9] Museum personnel saw state arts councils as particularly interested in audiences and accessibility, though not ignoring art historical concerns. The NEH, not surprisingly, requires a humanities slant to the exhibitions it funds. The message in the show, the articles in the catalog, and the speakers at the symposium must all talk about humanities issues. The NEH also requires that outside consultants be used in the preparation of the exhibit. (The NEA does not require consultants.) What this requirement means is that more people, all authorities on some subject, have input into the project. They give the exhibit a different character than a show designed by a single curator. There is a standing joke among museum people that if the wall label is smaller than the painting, the exhibition was funded by the NEA, but if the wall label is bigger than the painting, the exhibition was funded by the NEH.

As DiMaggio (1991b) suggests, stereotypical distinctions among government agencies are stronger than their behavioral differences. All government agencies are subject to political imperatives that lead them to focus on both scholarly and public goals. An essential goal of political organizations is self-perpetuation. To achieve this, they need to maintain their prestige and to garner supporters. Support must come from two quarters: from art worlds, and from the political arena. Art supporters, whose future grants are at stake, may be more active than populist supporters; on the other hand, if arts funding looks like a boondoggle for elites, government agencies are liable to come under political attack. Consequently, a judicious mix of scholarly and popular exhibits is called for, in order for the government to retain both art and political supporters (see DiMaggio, 1991b, pp. 229–30).

The goals of the government agencies pull in two directions, then. They have public outreach goals, to bring art into the public sphere, and what may be termed "professional outreach" goals, to fund the scholarly and challenging exhibitions that particularly excite the individuals who distribute funds (panelists) or who make up a lobbying constituency (museum personnel, art critics, artists, and the cultural elite).

Further, government agencies are the only funder among the four types profiled to be explicitly interested in expanding audiences beyond the traditional middle and upper classes that currently consume much art (DiMaggio & Useem, 1978). Educational components are part of most grants given by NEA, NEH, and state arts agencies. In this respect, government is likely to sponsor art of interest to lower classes or marginalized groups.

Foundations

Museum people do not talk much about foundations. It appears that museum personnel, along with academic researchers, have fewer and weaker impressions of the giving goals of foundations. In the interviews, only one curator mentioned foundation support of an exhibition, an unusual case where the foundation had approached the museum to offer funds, rather than being solicited by the museum.

Foundations are the forgotten funder in studies of arts support (DiMaggio, 1986c, p. 113). One reason for this may be that there are a variety of foundation types (Ylvisaker, 1987). Corporations often set up foundations to manage their philanthropic activity, though for the purposes of this study the activity of corporate foundations is considered synonymous with contributions that come directly from corporation coffers. Independent foundations, both large and small, are the most common type of foundation. These foundations are legally obligated to operate according to the goals stated in their charters. Some foundations are very small with no endowment (Odendahl, 1987b). These "checkbook" foundations are mainly "pass through" foundations for the individuals who set them up, and these foundations perhaps should be considered analogous to elite, individual funders in terms of the interests they serve.

DiMaggio (1986c) divides foundations that support cultural organizations into two groups. The first group is small, but is composed of important foundations—the large, well-known national foundations, such as the Ford, Rockefeller, and the Andrew W. Mellon Foundations. These foundations have been active in arts funding, and they have well-defined, formalized, highly publicized, and coherent programs. The second group contains a much larger number of smaller foundations. These mainly local foundations, DiMaggio reports, tend to be conservative in their funding patterns. They also tend to support well-established organizations that are in the foundation's own community. DiMaggio's work suggests that these foundations do not place much emphasis on audiences. Odendahl (1987b) points out that founding families retain control over most foundations, including many large ones. Consequently, foundations may have giving preferences similar to those of elite individuals. There is little information about the preferences of foundations for art scholarship, however.

Wealthy Individuals

Elite individuals are the traditional patrons of museums. They may be wealthy collectors who loan, donate, or bequeath their art , or they may be rich business women and men who donate funds for buildings, improvements, endowments, or exhibitions. As seen by museum personnel, traditional patrons are interested in art itself and sometimes in art scholarship. They may know a great deal about art and may not care about attracting audiences. Some are seen as idiosyncratic, but also educable. Thus, elite individuals are seen to care about art and to be uninterested in the type of popularizing efforts corporations and government have brought to museums. Further, unlike government and corporate donors, individual elites are not required to pay attention to public issues and concerns; unlike government agencies or foundations (family or corporate), they need not attend to accounting procedures. Museum people treat their valuable individual patrons with kid gloves so as not to drive them away over a misunderstanding or a personality conflict. The best philanthropists are very loyal to "their" museum, and the biggest concern of museum administrators regarding elite patronage is "Will their kids step into their shoes after they pass away?" In contrast, administrators worry year after year how the political and economic climate might affect government or corporate support.

Museum people—directors, curators, and educators—speak well of wealthy patrons. They highlight the selfless devotion of such patrons to the museum and point out that they are true "art lovers." Often museums have groups called the "Director's Circle" or "Collectors Forum"—an arena where patrons learn about art history (and what the museum wants by way of gifts) over lunch or cocktails with the museum director and staff. Museum personnel seem to view individual philanthropists as malleable, amateur art historians. One educator, however, noted their "snobby," anti-populist sentiments. The high esteem given to museums' individual patrons was evident in curators' comments, though some curators complained about mounting exhibitions of art owned by their wealthy patrons and trustees. Some curators feel that these exhibits can be inferior because the organizer must choose objects from an individual collection that is usually uneven and always limited.[10] Happy collectors are generous collectors, however, and many museum people are willing to sacrifice a bit of scholarship in exchange for garnering some fine art objects.

The academic literature suggests that individual collectors are indeed interested in art, or in the prestige associated with the art, both of which elicit connoisseurship (Odendahl, 1990; Moulin, 1987; Robinson, 1987). It also suggests, however, more pursuit of status honor than "selfless" interest in art (Balfe & Cassilly, 1993; Bourdieu, 1984; see also Veblin, 1934). Beyond prestige, Dauber (1993) argues that philanthropy is always tied up with self-interest and identity formation.

Weber (1946) suggests that individuals have an interest in maintaining their status through unique styles of living. Obscure or esoteric art may provide just such status. Avant-garde art, for instance, is difficult to understand without some training, and it constantly moves on to new areas of exploration. Consequently, only the most "in" members of the (post)modern art world will be able to claim status honor as true connoisseurs. Similarly, the possession of an "Old Master" work suggests extreme wealth along with good taste. Despite their different focus, the collector of classical art and the collector of modern art are both searching for status: The former's prestige derives from his possession of rare objects; the latter's comes through possession of rare knowledge, an understanding and connoisseurship of new, esoteric art.

Traditional patrons are uninterested in attracting broad audiences to museums. Indeed, individual wealthy philanthropists may prefer smaller, narrower exhibitions, both for the safety of the objects they may have personally lent to the museum, and because they are interested in gaining status as a connoisseur of rare or esoteric works. Their "target audience" is a small, elite group (Balfe & Cassilly, 1993). As Odendahl argues (1990), elite individuals tend to favor philanthropy that is beneficial to the upper classes.

These individuals often speak of their own art acquisitions in terms of furthering art scholarship and avoid discussing other, more crass interests, such as status enhancement or investment potential (Robinson, 1987). Yet, the monetary value of tax incentives and the market value of art play an important role in the philanthropic decisions of America's wealthy (Odendahl, 1987a). Income tax deductions for charitable giving encourage gifts to museums, whereas estate taxes make it expensive for collectors to pass down art to their heirs. Donors have drastically changed their patterns of donating art as tax laws have changed (Molotsky, 1993). Some art collectors are also "speculators" betting that their collections are a good investment (Moulin, 1987). Art work can vastly appreciate after it is exhibited, so collectors sometimes exhibit their artwork for such "marketing" reasons both in the nineteenth century (Zolberg 1974), and today, as in the recent Matisse show where works from the exhibition were withdrawn from the exhibition to be sold at auction.

Museums set up exhibits for "marketing reasons" when they are trying to woo an important collection from an individual or when the art is owned by a member of the museum's board of trustees. Several curators mentioned the "ethical dilemmas" in exhibiting works by living artists, as such exhibitions increase the value of the artists' oeuvres, including work that may be in the collections of museum trustees (even if those particular works are not exhibited). The curators did not, however, draw a connection between such shows and the desires of trustees for such exhibitions or pressures from trustees for them.

Wealthy donors have traditionally given money to museums for art acquisitions, donated or bequeathed artwork, and financed museum buildings, but they have generally not granted money for exhibitions—except for those of pieces they own. One goal of elite collectors who fund exhibitions, then, is to see their collections exhibited in museums—and to have museums conserve, appraise, store or otherwise help them with the care of their art objects. In addition to the advantages of exhibiting a work to increase its marketability, patrons may exhibit their artwork for other returns, such as being relieved of storage or conservation costs for the piece. Museum people did not mention these other goals; instead, they highlighted the accord that exists between the goals of such patrons and the goals of museums.

The funding preferences of individual donors might reflect the same tastes as are evident in their own collections. Some elite patrons build collections of living artists. Others have built collections of European, Classical, primitive, decorative, Asian, or other styles of art (Zolberg, 1983). Since elite individuals may know a great deal about art, they may sponsor more challenging art—art that has value to the connoisseur. This suggests that wealthy patrons will favor exhibitions of their own collections, and works of esoteric art that they may know a great deal about, or that they learn about as privileged members of museum clubs. These donors may even have had a stake in the very obscurity of the art whose exhibition they fund.

Wealthy people affect art museums in at least four other ways not covered in this book. First, personally wealthy individuals still sit on the boards of directors of museums (along with representatives of the corporate elite). Second, family foundations, established by the well-to-do, donate money to art museums. Third, museums themselves are often founded by wealthy individuals. Fourth, individual collectors often donate or bequeath their collections to museums. In this project, I do not examine newly founded or small museums,[11] nor do I study the composition of boards of directors. Family foundations come into play only in that they are included in the wider category "foundations" (excluding corporate foundations). The study focuses on exhibitions, rather than acquisitions; thus these aspects of individual philanthropy are not examined here.

The Funding Mosaic

Currently, museums draw their funds from a variety of sources. This chapter has suggested that individual philanthropists and institutional funders have disparate goals. Unlike individual philanthropists, both government and corporate sponsors are oriented toward broad audiences, though for different reasons. Corporations are counting on the "halo effect" of art to improve their image among museum visitors. Government agencies, on the other hand, do not explicitly want to improve their image in the eyes of museum-goers (though doing so increases the survival chances of such agencies). Rather, as arms of the government, these agencies want to reach a large cross-section of voters, or a disadvantaged segment in the population, in order to assert that they are doing things that government agencies should do.

It is perhaps useful to note that these funders do not calculate, formally or statistically, a relationship between the number of visitors to a museum and the contribution level. In other words, a corporation does not plan to give $100,000 to an exhibition that will attract 500,000 visitors, but only $50,000 to one attracting 250,000 people. Rather, attention to such factors as possible attendance reflects the basic outlook of the funder: Government and corporations value a broad audience. The upper-class patron does not. During the first sixty or seventy years of this century, museums were supported by wealthy *philanthropists*. But starting in the mid-sixties, museums became reliant on a mix of *institutional funders*. The difference between philanthropy (giving for the public good) and funding (grants for specific projects) indicates fundamental differences in the basic attitudes of the various donor groups. When museums rely on institutional funders, rather than on casual funding by wealthy individuals (or for that matter, on market arrangements), their operations are affected.

How do the goals of the funders mesh with museum goals? To illustrate points of convergence and divergence, I will briefly suggest, based on the discussion above, the preferences expected among the four types of funders for several types of exhibits: (1) "popular exhibitions", i.e., exhibitions attracting broad audiences (2) "accessible exhibitions," i.e., shows that are easy to understand without extensive training in art history, and (3) the traditional "scholarly exhibitions," i.e., those resting on solid art historical merit and research. (I will examine the association of funders with each of these types of exhibitions in Chapter 3).

It is easy to form hypotheses on funding patterns of corporations and government agencies. I expect that corporations tend to fund popular exhibitions (they appreciate large audiences) and accessible exhibitions (they hope to draw a broad array of middle class viewers, not just the cultural elite, and when they collect art, they collect conservative and accessible styles). But I expect that corporations tend not to fund scholarly exhibits (they have less interest in the art itself than in how they benefit from sponsoring art). Government agencies tend to fund popular and accessible exhibitions (as part of their public outreach) and scholarly exhibitions (in their professional outreach). As mentioned, government agencies are also more likely to be concerned with nontraditional audiences (they have educational programs and requirements) and contemporary art (they have programs to support living American artists).

Since there is little information, either from museums or from academic literature, it is more difficult to formulate hypotheses about foundations. DiMaggio (1986c) points out that most foundations are small, conservative and family run. But he also suggests that large, visible foundations may be especially important for large, prestigious nonprofits like the museums I study. These large foundations often have well-developed cultural programs and are much less conservative than the family foundations, thus the conservative influence of small family foundations may be less important for large museums. If this is so, foundations may tend to fund especially visible shows (popular exhibitions). If they are similar to individual philanthropists (such individuals control the many small family foundations), then foundations may be unlikely to fund accessible exhibitions and would be more likely to fund scholarly exhibits. There is little information about the preferences of foundations for art scholarship, however, so I would only tentatively suggest these latter two possibilities.

Finally, hypotheses for the funding patterns of individual philanthropists are straightforward. Individual philanthropists are not likely to fund either popular exhibitions or accessible exhibitions (they are uninterested in audiences), and they will probably sponsor scholarly exhibitions (they are knowledgeable about art). They are also likely to sponsor exhibitions of art which they own.

Museum curators are professional art historians whose prestige rests on the scholarship and quality of their work, including the exhibitions they mount. Curators do not represent the entirety of museums and the decision making that goes on within them. Directors, trustees, and educational personnel are among the other important actors. Various factions of museums are often in conflict (Allen, 1974; DiMaggio, 1991a), as I will discuss in Chapter 4. I have chosen to focus on museum curators for the time being because (a) they are directly responsible for planning and mounting exhibitions and (b) they represent traditional museum goals.

Museum curators professionalized in the 1920s and were well-established by the 1930s (DiMaggio, 1991c; Meyer, 1979). Museum curators were instrumental in institutionalizing a vision of museums that focused on conservation and scholarship, as opposed to such matters as education, public outreach, and exhibitions (DiMaggio, 1991c; Zolberg, 1981, 1974). What these art historians believe about museum integrity comes from their background and professional training. (The influence of these beliefs is termed "normative forces.")

Curators hold advanced degrees in art history, usually Ph.D. (Allen, 1974, pp. 137–139; Zolberg, 1986), and are "object oriented" and not often interested in public education (Zolberg, 1986, p 192). In this regard, I expect that curators would like to mount exhibitions that are scholarly and would be uninterested in popular or accessible exhibitions. Table 2-1 summarizes the orientation of the funders and curators, as suggested by the interviews and the academic literature. The table shows clearly that the goals of the new institutional funders do not mesh well with the traditional, curatorial goals in museums.

TABLE 2-1
Projected Orientation of Stakeholders in Museum Exhibitions (According to Interviews and Academic Literature)

Interest	*Popular Exhibitions*	*Accessible Exhibitions*	*Scholarly Exhibitions*	*Other Concerns*
Stakeholder				
Corporate Funder	yes	yes	no	—
Government Funder	yes	yes	yes	non-trad. audiences, living artists
Foundation Funder	yes?	no?	yes?	—
Individual Philanthropist	no	no	yes	own collection
Museum Curator	no	no	yes	—

Curators have had plenty of time to get used to the influence of individual patrons, whose interests overlap with their own (Zolberg, 1986). Indeed, individual funding of museums was institutionalized before the curatorial profession solidified. But the goals of the institutional funders are not the same as those of traditional museum sponsors. Moreover, the goals of corporate and government funders conflict with normatively defined goals of museum curators. Since the preferences and biases of the institutional funders conflict with the visions already institutionalized in museums, new funding creates problems for museum personnel.

NOTES

1. Patronage often takes the form of direct commissioning of art works. In such cases, art historical research shows the dramatic impact on the finished work of patrons' preferences (e.g., Baxandall, 1977; Haskall, 1963; Hauser, 1982). Patronage of the arts also refers to collecting art work that has already been produced, either independently or under the auspices of an earlier patron. In addition, patronage includes support of institutions that shelter the arts, especially founding museums, or donating money, time, or art works to existing museums.

2. American art was not completely ignored, however. In the 1840s, for example, the American Arts Union sold art through a lottery system. Individuals nationwide bought chances, like raffle tickets, and the winner took home a piece of art. This system was quite successful in supporting artists until the government declared it illegal under anti-gambling laws (Lynes, 1954).

3. There is a peak in exhibitions in 1972. The reason for this is the number of small-scale exhibitions designed for children, especially at the Metropolitan Museum. Over time, the change in children's exhibits looks like this:

Year:	60	62	64	66	68	70	72	74	76	78	80	82	84	86
Exhibits:	14	9	16	7	30	32	55	31	41	19	14	19	15	10

Total children's exhibits from all the museums in the sample rose from 14 in 1960 to a high of 55 in 1972, but declined to 10 in 1986. The change was not constant, rather, there was a peak in the number of children's exhibitions in 1972.

4. Indeed, it is possible that museum staffs' beliefs about donor goals are more important than actual donor goals, as organizational behavior is created by managers who selectively perceive and actively create their environment (Weick, 1979).

5. This example illustrates a convergence between elite individuals and corporations.

6. There are some differences between corporate giving and corporate foundation giving. Useem points out that the philanthropy budget of corporations that set up foundations is buffered from fluxes in corporate income and is thus more stable (Useem, 1987). Another difference has to do with governmental reporting procedures, which are more complex for corporate (or any) foundations than for corporations.

7. The fourteen criteria (and percentage of companies highly ranking them) are: impact on local community (94%), geographic location (92%), management

capability (80%), artistic merit (66%), employee involvement (59%), quality of application (49%), board of directors (45%), size of audience (42%), coordination with similar groups (28%), support by other firms (26%), publicity value (21%), matching gifts (14%), support by foundations/government (14%), gifts from individuals (11%) (Useem, 1991, p. 332).

8. Though, according to some observers (Useem and Kutner, 1986), corporations look more to other corporations than to the government agencies in deciding funding when external cues are needed.

9. State arts councils are also seen as supporting different types of organizations (mostly smaller and local ones) and of younger artists (in direct grants to artists) than the NEA, but these differences do not concern us here. The fact that this study focuses only on large museums precludes tapping such effects (see DiMaggio, 1991b).

10. One curator told me about three of these exhibits. Two were of private collections that, not coincidentally, the museum was hoping to acquire. The third was of art owned by members of the museum's board of trustees. The curator was not impressed by the quality of any of these exhibitions. In her educated opinion, one of the collections was "mixed"—it had some good pieces and some not very good ones—but the museum management exhibited the entire collection, rather than weeding out the weaker objects as the curator would have. The second private collection was itself "solid," but in this case, the catalog, put together in a hurry, was "flimsy." The trustees' exhibition also was not chosen carefully and the curator did not approve of it.

11. So the sample of museums examined in the research may be biased against the types of museums in which traditional patrons may still be quite powerful.

III

PICTURES AT AN EXHIBITION

THE IMPACT OF FUNDING

In this chapter, I discuss the impact of funding on changes in exhibitions. I wondered if funding increasingly influenced exhibitions and how the funder types, with their differing goals, were related to various types of museum exhibitions. I explore the association of funding with three aspects of exhibitions: the number of exhibitions, their format, and their content. After examining funding and individual exhibitions, I ask how funding is related to changes in the entire pool of exhibitions in museums. I also highlight some of the different approaches to exhibitions among museums.

The findings in this chapter rest on my analysis of archival materials, specifically the annual reports of 30 museums (see Table 3-1). I started with a list of the largest American art museums, those with operating expenditures for 1978 of approximately $1 million or more. To collect information on museums and exhibitions, I consulted annual reports of museums at the Thomas J. Watson Library at the Metropolitan Museum of Art and at the Ryerson and Burnham libraries at the Art Institute of Chicago. I used the data collected from the annual reports to build two data sets, one with information at the museum level and the second with information at the exhibit level. Neither archive had a complete collection of annual reports from all the large museums, so the quantitative data sets include only those museums for which the most complete information was available. In addition, I read every annual report in my sample before I coded it. Thus I have a great deal of textured, qualitative information on changes in museums as well as systematic, quantitative data. Though much of the analysis centers on quantitative analysis of data compiled from the archival materials, some material is presented anecdotally; other material is described in a systematic, qualitative way. In addition, the archival research is supplemented by interview data. (The collection of this data and the data sets involved are described more thoroughly in the Methodological Appendix).

I began the analysis with 1960—five years before the advent of federal funding and major corporate sponsorship of the arts—and collected data

TABLE 3-1
Museums Studied
(Annual Reports available—Even Years Only)

- Albright Knox Museum (1960–84)
- Art Institute of Chicago (1960–86)
- Baltimore Museum of Art (1970–74)
- Brooklyn Museum (1960–72, 80–84)
- Cincinnati Art Museum (1960–82)
- Sterling and Francine Clark Art Institute (1978–86)
- Cleveland Museum (1960–80, 84–86)
- Dallas Museum of Art (1976–86)
- Denver Art Museum (1978–86)
- Detroit Institute of Art (1960–86)
- Fine Arts Museums of San Francisco (1976–82); (plus, California Palace of the Legion of Honor [1960–66] and DeYoung Museum [1972–86])
- William Hayes Fogg Art Museum (1966–78)
- Solomon R. Guggenheim Museum (1978–86)
- Los Angeles County Museum of Art (1966–80)
- Metropolitan Museum of Art (1960–86)
- Minneapolis Institute of Art (1976–86)
- Museum of Fine Arts, Boston (1966–84)
- Museum of Fine Arts, Houston (1970–86)
- Museum of Modern Art (1960–86)
- National Gallery (1966–84)
- Nelson-Atkins Museum (1986)
- North Carolina Museum (1962–74)
- Philadelphia Museum of Art (1960–84)
- Saint Louis Art Museum (1960–78, 84–86)
- Toledo Museum of Art (1960, 64, 68–86)
- Wadsworth Atheneum (1960–86)
- Walters Art Gallery (1976–78)
- Whitney Museum (1960–74, 78–82)
- Worcester Art Museum (1960, 78–82)
- Yale Art Gallery (1960, 66–78, 82–86)

for the even years from 1960 to 1986. Examining data for alternate years provides a view of time trends in exhibition change while reducing coding costs. Significantly, the data set ends before the current crisis in federal arts funding, which started with the controversies over "obscene" art (see Benedict, 1991; Dubin, 1992). These controversies are not part of the research, but they render important and timely questions about the effects of funding on exhibitions.

I studied temporary, special exhibitions that change over the course of a year. These exhibitions are mounted in galleries set aside for such purposes and stay in the museum for as little as a few days to several months before they are disassembled. Permanent exhibitions, which are not examined in the study, are mounted by museums as the constant backdrop for visitors. They remain in place for years or decades and serve to anchor the viewer in the museum. In most museums, they comprise a substantial proportion of the museum's public areas. Permanent exhibitions include objects that belong to the museum or that are on long-term loan to the museum.[1] Museum annual reports rarely discuss (and I did not code) permanent exhibitions.

I coded each exhibition mounted by my sample museums into categories for artistic style and format. I noted whether the exhibition was historically or thematically organized, whether it was a traveling exhibition, and whether it was a large-scale "blockbuster." I coded each exhibition for the style of art it contained. (The fourteen style categories are described below.) I was able to identify major funders and coded the type of funders (corporate, government, foundation, individual—or internally funded) supporting each exhibition. Externally funded exhibitions receive support from one or a combination of individual, corporate, government, or foundation donors. Exhibitions termed "internally funded," have been paid for by the museum's operating budget, earned income, an auxiliary entity such as the "Ladies' Council," or small donations not directly acknowledged as exhibition support. Because I rely on museums to report their exhibition funding, the question arises as to whether museums are faithful reporters. Museums, in fact, do not thank every donor who might have given $100 to a museum auxiliary group or attended (and paid admission to) the black-tie dinner, which underwrote part of an exhibition's cost. Consequently, relying on annual reports biases my results towards the effects of large and important funders. As a group, minor funders may be comprised of middle-class individuals and small local businesses and foundations, rather than wealthy individuals and large national corporations and foundations. While it would be useful to know the effects of minor funders, the research suggests that museums are more heavily influenced by the major funders that the research design captures. More details about the coding are presented with the research findings.

Table 3-2 presents a correlation matrix of the variables indicating the external funder of an exhibit (if it had one). Interestingly, the four funder types are not highly correlated.[2] That means that the four funder types do not have a large overlap in the exhibitions they sponsor. Interestingly, there is a notable negative correlation between each of the institutional

TABLE 3-2
Correlation Matrix of Funding Variables

	Individual	*Corporation*	*Government*
Corporation	-0.384		
Government	-0.441	0.039	
Foundation	-0.256	0.050	0.039

N = 4026 exhibitions

funders and the individual philanthropists. This suggests that the new institutional funders have funding goals quite distinct from the traditional funders of museums.

Funding and the Prevalence of Exhibitions

Does the increased availability of funding for exhibits increase the number of exhibitions museums mount? How does the new institutional funding affect museum attitudes toward exhibits? These are the questions I address in this section.

Number of Exhibitions

Over the 26 years of the study, 1960 to 1986, the biggest change has been a dramatic increase in activity. For example, the Art Institute of Chicago mounted 11 exhibitions in 1960, but organized six times as many, 68, in 1986. The average number of exhibits per museum per year has steadily increased over time, just about doubling during the period (see Figure 3-1)[3].

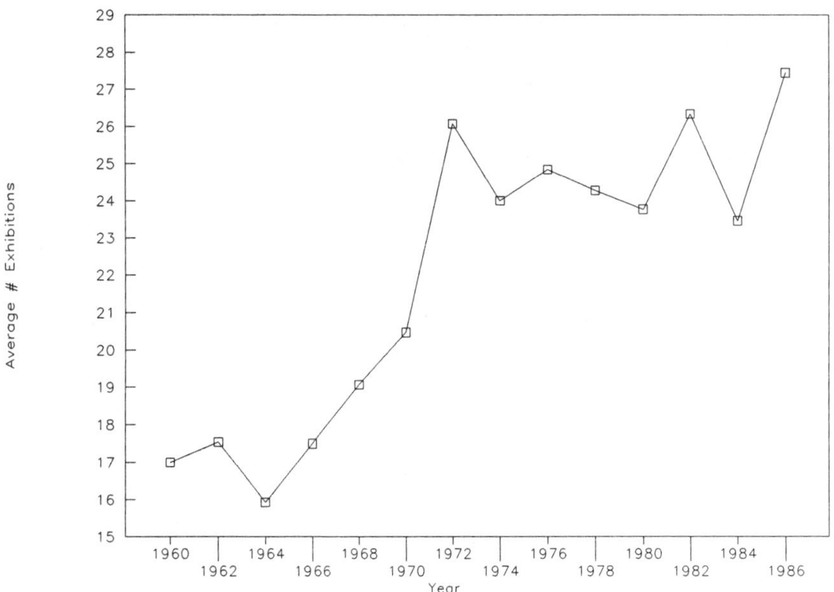

Figure 3-1. Average Number of Exhibitions per Museum per Year by Year.
Source: Annual Reports, exhibition data set.

Fitting a regression line through these points gives an estimate for the influence of time on the number of exhibitions.[4] The slope of the regression line = 0.48 (pr < 0.0001), with an intercept of 16.7.[5] In English, this means that starting with an average of 16.7 exhibitions per museum in 1960, the average number of exhibitions per museum increases by 0.48 each year. The number of exhibitions per museum, then, increases by about 13 exhibitions from 1960 to 1986.[6]

Look again at Figure 3-1. The plot does not appear to reflect a steady increase over time. Instead, the plot seems to depict three distinct curves that suggest three different eras in regard to the number of exhibitions. (This may be more visible in table format; see the first column in Table 3-3.) The first era, with no change in the number of exhibitions per museum, ranges from 1960 to about 1966. The second, with a marked increase in the number of exhibitions each year, runs from approximately 1968 to 1972, and the third, with a milder increase in exhibitions, appears after 1972.

These eras correspond to periods in the evolution of museum funding. I call 1960–1966 the *philanthropy period*, because during this time, museums were supported by individual philanthropists; institutional funding was quite rare. The middle period, 1968–1972, the *transition period*, is the time when institutional sponsorship of the arts is increasing. Institutional funding of museums was well entrenched in the later period, 1974–1986, which I call the *funding period*.

Table 3-3 shows the average number of externally funded exhibitions per museum per year along with the average number of exhibitions per museum per year supported by four types of sponsors. A regression analysis of museum years shows that, compared with the philanthropy period, the transition period has marginally more exhibitions ($b = 4.93$, $p < .075$); and the funding period has significantly more exhibitions ($b = 7.03$, $p < .004$). (See Table 3-3, note c.) Over time, the number of funded exhibitions increases, rising steadily in the funding period. In other words, the number of funded exhibitions increasingly contributes to the total number of exhibitions. Table 3-3 also shows the changing mix of individual and institutional support of museums, as well as the average number of exhibitions per museum per year that were sponsored by more than one major funder. The data show an increase in overlapping support, as museums become more adept at cobbling together a funding package for their exhibitions.

Orientation to Exhibitions

In summary, the average number of exhibitions has increased over time. The average number of externally funded exhibitions has also increased, while the number of internally funded exhibitions actually decreases in

TABLE 3-3
Number of Exhibitions,
Number of Funded Exhibitions,
Number of Funded Exhibitions by Type of Funder,
and Number of Exhibitions with Multiple Funders

(Average Per Museum)

	Average Number of Exhibitions per Museum							
			Funded by:[a]				*Multiple*	*N*
	Total	*Funded*	*Corp.*	*Gov.*	*Found.*	*Ind.*	*Funders*	*Museums*[b]
Year:								
(Philanthropy Period)								
1960	17.0	1.92	0.15	0.00	0.31	1.46	0.00	13
1962	17.5	1.64	0.09	0.00	0.27	1.36	0.09	11
1964	15.9	1.85	0.15	0.00	0.08	1.62	0.00	13
1966	17.5	3.14	0.14	0.07	0.57	1.71	0.07	14
(Transition Period)[c #]								
1968	19.6	2.13	0.20	0.06	0.27	1.80	0.06	15
1970	20.5	2.00	0.40	0.13	0.13	1.60	0.20	15
1972	26.1	3.06	0.66	0.60	0.60	1.60	0.33	15
(Funding Period)[c **]								
1974	24.0	5.29	1.29	2.28	0.14	2.57	0.93	14
1976	24.8	5.77	0.62	3.00	1.54	1.31	0.54	13
1978	24.3	7.57	1.43	4.64	2.14	1.71	1.78	14
1980	23.8	7.08	3.00	3.46	0.77	2.15	1.85	13
1982	26.3	8.67	4.08	3.50	2.25	2.75	2.83	12
1984	23.5	8.69	4.38	3.15	2.00	2.69	2.62	13
1986	27.4	8.11	4.67	2.89	2.78	2.89	3.44	9

\# $p < .10$
* $p < .05$
** $p < .01$
*** $p < .001$
N = 4026 exhibitions

Notes: [a]Funded exhibitions may be sponsored by more than one type of funder; consequently, the average number of exhibitions funded by individuals, corporations, government and foundations do not sum to the average number of funded exhibitions.

[b]The museums used for this analysis are: Art Institute of Chicago, Brooklyn Museum, Cincinnati Art Museum, Cleveland Museum, Detroit Institute of Art, Metropolitan Museum of Art, Museum of Fine Arts, Boston, Museum of Modern Art, National Gallery, Philadelphia Museum of Art, Saint Louis Art Museum, Toledo Museum of Art, Wadsworth Atheneum, Whitney Museum, and Yale Art Gallery.

[c]A regression analysis of 178 museum-years shows that, compared with the philanthropy period, the transition period has marginally more exhibitions (b = 4.93, s.e. = 2.76 [p < .075]; and the funding period has significantly more exhibitions (b = 7.03, s.e. = 2.36 [p < .004].

the latter half of the time frame. Furthermore, the character of exhibition support has changed dramatically. While individual funders have not changed much, there has been a striking increase in exhibition support by collective donors: corporations, foundations and government. Several of the museum personnel I interviewed suggested that the increase in funding has increased activity in museums. Having the money to pay for such exhibits and programs is the most likely explanation for the increase. Thus, funding is associated with the number of exhibitions mounted by museums. Though it is difficult to prove the hypothesis that the increased availability of funding for exhibits *causes* the increasing frequency of exhibits, the data are consistent with this argument. Exhibitions have also become more expensive over time. But the point is not the mundane and obvious one that exhibitions are so expensive that they must garner funding. The point is that museums mount many more exhibitions, expensive or not, and have access to external funds to do so. Does the funding allow museums to do more expensive shows, or do expenses drive museums to seek funding? Both, of course: There is a chicken-and-egg element here, but it is clear that museums, in general, are becoming more exhibition-oriented. And this emphasis represents a serious change in museum focus.

Overall, museums have increased the number of exhibitions and programs, a shift that is likely tied to increased levels of funding. This sounds straightforward—more money, more exhibits—but its impact has been profound. The shift represents a substantial change in the focus of museum operations. Special exhibitions have played a variable role in museums throughout the century, but starting around the 1920s, as university-trained art historians gained control of museums, exhibitions have been only a small part of a museum's activities (DiMaggio, 1991c; Meyer, 1979; Zolberg, 1974). Museums concentrated instead on their permanent collections. Although accessions to the collection are still of tremendous importance to museums, this facet of museum life is rivaled more and more by the planning and installing of special exhibitions.

Interestingly, though, the curator-dominated museum has been a reality for only about a half century. The image that this is the "correct" way for museums to be (and that they have always been thus) has gained a strong foothold. This is similar to the process of defining "high art" as sacred, and seeing it as more challenging and of better quality than popular art. This division has been recently challenged, but we mainly take this distinction for granted, even though as DiMaggio (1982a, b) and Levine (1988) convincingly demonstrate, it was a late nineteenth-century invention.

Currently, museum personnel expect to mount several special exhibitions each year and many believe that cutting back on the number of such shows would be detrimental to the museum. Indeed, the Wadsworth

Atheneum in Hartford Connecticut tried to cut back on special exhibitions in the mid-1970s. Their attendance plummeted, and they reinstituted a more vigorous program including large, traveling exhibitions. The Atheneum did not admit that their policy had reduced attendance. It was clear, however, that attendance did fall off after the no-loan exhibit policy was put into place. In 1970, 215,447 people visited the Atheneum, and 183,745 came in 1972. In 1974, 121,937 visitors attended the museum and, after that, the Atheneum did not report attendance again until 1979. (The Atheneum does recognize that exhibitions increase attendance, as their lament reported below demonstrates.)

Along the same lines, the Fine Arts Museums of San Francisco's Department of Exhibitions reports (1978–80, p. 28):

> After the closing of *Treasures of Tutankhamen*, this department began to return to normal, although it is clear from the activity and interest expressed by the Museum's visitors and members, that they will continue to demand a varied program of exhibitions of high quality, including major international special exhibitions which bring great art of the world to San Francisco.

Museums also recognize that exhibitions keep membership levels up. For instance, the *Picasso* exhibit increased the Museum of Modern Art's membership by 14,000 (Museum of Modern Art, 1980–81, p. 8).

> So great was the response that new membership sales were suspended twice during the run of the show so that the demand to see it by current members and those who had joined early in its run could be satisfied. (Museum of Modern Art, 1980–81, p. 41)

And museums like to remind their members of special exhibitions, especially the most popular ones. In its April 1990 solicitation letter, the Art Institute of Chicago pointed out that the Institute has been exhibiting, and visitors enjoying, Impressionist art for the past 95 years.

Museums noted the membership and attendance benefits of special exhibitions over and over. For instance, the Art Institute of Chicago launched an extensive marketing campaign to attract as many visitors as possible to *Pompeii, A.D. 79*, and attendance was high—489,018 (Art Institute of Chicago, 1978–79, p. 21). Smaller, special loan exhibitions also attract audiences. As the Wadsworth Atheneum (1979, p. 13) notes:

> Ironically, in a time when the strategy of presenting exhibitions from our own collections is continuing to demonstrate its effectiveness, general gallery attendance was down during the year by almost precisely the number attributable to a loan show of the previous year—that of the work of Duane Hanson in the MATRIX series.

Clearly museums are oriented, to some degree, to their audience. This orientation may be due, in part, to the pressures from corporate and government funders to attend to audiences. Indeed,

> Nancy Hanks, Chairman of the National Endowment for the Arts, observed that "the Endowment is especially pleased with the way in which its Museum Program has been able to assist the nation's museums in their growing awareness of the desires of the American public." (Quoted in Baltimore Museum of Art, 1972.)

This serious attention to audiences did not always exist in museums. Museums were started as protectors of culture, oblivious to the breadth of their audience and interested, if at all, in "educating" rather than pleasing the masses. Although museums have always been pulled between populist and elitist conceptions of their duties, the curatorial model, which views the museum as a place for quiet, scholarly contemplation has been dominant.

In 1962, the director of the Brooklyn Museum wrote:

> The endless parade of borrowed exhibitions is contrary to the wishes of many people: the objects of art to which they are devoted unfold their powers slowly and without end; they are to be explored and re-explored, offering more as the viewer grows in experience and sensitivity. The four-week, two-hundred-piece special exhibition descends like a horde of someone else's children shattering the quiet evolution of the family, occupying its places, demanding time and eating up resources which might have produced a publication, refurbished a gallery or made an acquisition possible. (Brooklyn Museum, 1962–63, p. 76).

Brooklyn's Curator of Oriental Art obviously agreed with this sentiment, and in 1966 he described his department as "serene and exhibitionless since 1964." (Brooklyn Museum, 1966–67, p. 16). Yet the dominant attitude in the museum changed. In 1984, the Director stated:

> In the area of exhibition funding, the Museum received one of the largest grants ever awarded by the National Endowment for the Humanities, $340,000 toward the exhibition *The Machine Age in America, 1918–1941*, scheduled to open October 1986. The matching portion of this grant was met by $100,000 from the J.M. Kaplan Fund.
>
> Major exhibition support has also been received from the National Endowment for the Arts, the New York State Council for the Arts, and the corporate sector. Most notable among the last is a grant of $230,000 from IBM to mount a retrospective of the work of Gustave Courbet that will open in 1988. (Brooklyn Museum, 1982–86, p. 13).

The Director went on to thank American Airlines, Atlantic Richfield, Chase Manhattan Bank, Manufacturers Hanover Trust, Morgan Guarantee Trust,

Federated Department Stores, the Pfizer Foundation, Philip Morris Companies Inc., and Warner Communications for exhibition support.

The shift shows a drastic reorientation of museums from internal matters (art historical research and conservation) to external matters (exhibitions and audiences).[7] It also represents a re-conceptualization of the museum's aesthetic mission. If funders, in general, push museums toward broader exhibitions, this shift also represents a move from a more elite mission to a more populist one. The new focus on exhibits is not universally welcomed, however. To paraphrase the Director of Art Institute of Chicago, exhibitions are the lifeblood of great museums, but the staff thinks of them as tails that wag the dog (Art Institute of Chicago, 1974–75, pp. 12, 14).

Funding and the Shape of Exhibitions

There are two different ways to explore the question of how changes in funding are related to the presentation of art. First, are funders associated with the method by which shows are *packaged*? For instance, do funders prefer certain formats such as "blockbuster" shows? Second, are funders associated with the actual *content* of shows? Are shows of certain types of art work more likely to get funding than others?

Format of Exhibitions

Exhibitions occur in various formats. Special exhibitions can be drawn from the museum's permanent collection, or borrowed from the collections of private patrons or other museums. In the latter case, the exhibition is a "loan exhibition." Museums distinguish between major exhibitions, usually loan shows that require a great deal of effort to plan, and medium and smaller shows that take less effort.

In addition, museums host exhibitions that are arranged elsewhere, and circulate exhibitions that they themselves organize. Exhibitions shown in more than one museum are called "traveling exhibitions" for obvious reasons. These exhibitions are less common than other types of exhibits due to the trouble and expense involved in shipping artworks. "Blockbuster" exhibitions are large-scale exhibitions designed to attract sell-out crowds and are defined in terms of reaching the public.

In this section, I explore the connection of funder type with several variables indicating format. I have coded exhibitions as (a) popular, (b) accessible, or (c) scholarly. I also examine exhibitions composed of works from private patron collections. *Popular exhibitions* (those attracting broad audiences) are indicated by two variables: blockbuster shows and traveling exhibitions. Blockbuster shows attract a large audience in (at least) one venue, whereas traveling shows multiply their potential audience by the number of cities in which they appear, hence their designation as popular shows.

Traveling exhibitions were easy to code. These shows appeared in more than one city or were developed at a museum other than the one where it appeared when I coded it. In contrast, there is no easy, established definition of a blockbuster. Consequently, I must mention reasons for choosing the indicators I did and the effects of this choice. Blockbusters are shows designed to reach large audiences. Not all blockbuster shows travel, but many do. Also, blockbusters are not always large in terms of the number of objects. For instance, the famous blockbuster *Treasures of Tutankhamen* was composed of only 57 objects. Art historian Albert Elsen cynically defines a blockbuster as "a large-scale exhibit, which people who don't normally go to museums will stand in line for hours to see." (quoted in Glennon, 1988, p. 42) Some people say that "blockbusters" are by definition shows that have corporate support. This last definition is not helpful in trying to gauge the effects of corporate sponsorship on exhibitions.

I chose three blockbuster indicators, present in exhibition write-ups in annual reports, (1) the use of advance ticketing, especially by Ticketron, (2) high attendance figures, or (3) mentions in the annual report of long lines of people waiting to get into the exhibit. These factors indicated expected large audiences (advanced ticketing) and actual large audiences (high attendance figures and long lines). These choices have several effects. First, I am more likely to find *successful* blockbusters through this scheme. Large-scale, international traveling exhibitions that were supposed to, but did not, attract crowds would not necessarily be captured as blockbusters in my coding.

Second, I also captured *surprise* blockbusters, exhibitions that no one in the museum guessed would be as popular as they were. These exhibitions might not have had the corporate backing that many expect of today's blockbusters. The Art Institute of Chicago notes:

> It is quite impossible to predict what will succeed and what will not in the case of a loan exhibition. The totally unexpected success of Renoir went some distance . . . to offset the popular failure of Braque, which failed quite beyond the most pessimistic expectations. To borrow from an early Shaw title, *You never can Tell* (1972–73, p. 14).[8]

Both shows were organized by the Art Institute and neither traveled. The Renoir attracted 354,000 visitors, the highest exhibition attendance ever reached up to that point by the museum (p. 4). The attendance figure for the Braque exhibition was not noted.

Third, though the blockbuster phenomenon developed in the late 1960s, the roots of the phenomenon can be traced back at least 50 years (Balfe, 1987, p. 198). For instance, the Armory show of 1913 was certainly a blockbuster. Many of the surprise blockbusters I coded were mounted during the philanthropy period, and might not have had external support. The Albright-Knox museum, for instance, had two hit shows during the early 1960s. The first was in 1962, an exhibition of Andrew Wyeth. The museum reports: "By the time the exhibition had closed on December 9, almost a quarter of a million people had viewed the work of America's foremost realist. As many as 27,000 guests crowded the Gallery in a single day, and traffic tie-ups threatened to turn Elmwood Avenue into another Times Square," (Albright-Knox, 1963, p. 20). In 1965, "Art Today" which was part of "The Buffalo Festival of the Arts" attracted 186,640 people in the two weeks of the festival, and 313,042 total visitors (Albright-Knox, 1966, p. 8). The annual report has a charming photograph of people waiting in a line winding around the corner on what looks like a pretty chilly day (Albright-Knox, 1966, p. 7). The festival was externally supported by the New York State Council on the Arts. The main point is that my coding scheme does not come up with a perfect correlation between shows I deem as blockbuster and the externally funded, international loan exhibitions that might come to mind with the term.

Accessible exhibitions are shows that are easy to understand without extensive training in art history, and are indicated by both format and content variables. An accessible format is the "theme show." Such exhibitions are organized around a theme, rather than around a traditional art historical category. These are shows such as "The Window in Twentieth Century Art," which included only paintings and drawings incorporating windows (Newberger Museum, 1986–87), or "A Day in the Country: Impressionism and the French Landscape," which organized paintings by their subject matter instead of by the more traditional categories, such as the artist or the chronology of the work (Art Institute of Chicago, 1984–85, pp. 14–15).

Scholarly exhibitions are shows resting on solid art historical merit and research. A show can be designed in a way for scholars to learn more about the art in the show. A survey, which shows the development of a style or series of styles, and a retrospective, which shows the development of a single artist's oeuvre, are art historically based formats for exhibitions.

The categories that comprise the format variable mostly overlap. Theme shows and scholarly shows are mutually exclusive; a show cannot be both. But a show can have one or all of the characteristics: traveling, blockbuster, and theme, or traveling, blockbuster, and scholarly. The format data also address an additional concern of funders. To test whether individuals tend to sponsor their own art works, I coded the source of art for exhibitions. The variable "patron collection" indicates that all or virtually all of the art in a given exhibition came from the collection of the individual or corporation who sponsored the exhibition.

Table 3-4 shows the relationship of funder type with exhibition format. This table shows the number of exhibitions of each format type sponsored by each funder type, the number of each type of exhibition funded internally, the total number of exhibitions of each category, and the total number of exhibitions supported by each funder type. The table also reports the statistical significance levels of the difference between the proportion of exhibitions sponsored by a given funder as compared with the pool of exhibitions that are supported by other funders or that are not funded by any external funder (i.e., those exhibitions that are internally funded in one way or another). Statistical significance indicates a non-random difference between the proportion of exhibitions sponsored by a given funder as compared with those sponsored by other funders or those that are internally funded in one way or another. Significance levels are determined using logistic regressions (see the Methodological Appendix).

TABLE 3-4
Format of Exhibitions Sponsored by Four Types of Funders

	N Exhibitions Sponsored by				*N Internally Funded*	*N Format (Total)*
	Corp.	*Gov.*	*Found.*	*Ind.*		
Format:[a]						
Traveling Exhibition	101+***	121+***	53	58	386	604
Blockbuster Exhibition	25+***	23+***	15+*	5	27	57
Theme Show	47+***	25	18	16-***	269	344
Art Historical	97	176+***	81+**	70-***	944	1258
Patron Collection	26	8-***	19	269+***	48	346
Total by Funder Type	259	303	171	362	3171	—[b]

* $p < .05$
** $p < .01$
*** $p < .001$
N = 4026 exhibitions

Notes: [a]Asterisks indicate whether a type of funder sponsored a significantly greater or lesser number exhibitions of a given category as compared to internally-funded (unfunded) exhibitions.

Significance levels were determined by logistic regressions of 4026 exhibitions. The variables Individual, Corporation, Government and Foundation are 0,1 variables and are not mutually exclusive. The omitted category in this case is exhibitions not funded by any of the four categories of funder. All variables for exhibition characteristics are 0,1 variables where 1 indicates the presence of the trait.

[b]More than one sponsor can support a given exhibition, and each exhibition can be classified into more than one format; consequently, figures do not sum by row or column.

Here we see very interesting effects of funding. Institutional funders sponsor more than their share of blockbuster exhibitions, and both corporations and government disproportionally sponsor traveling exhibitions. This has to do with the fact that both government agencies and corporations are concerned with broad audiences, and what better way to reach those audiences than though media-hyped, large-scale, and traveling exhibitions? Foundations also funded more of one type of popular exhibition, blockbusters. This suggests that the large, visible foundations DiMaggio (1986c) spoke about are important for museum funding, at least for the sponsorship of popular exhibitions.

Table 3-4 also demonstrates that corporations sponsor more exhibitions of accessible art, as indicated by their sponsorship of theme shows. Individuals fund fewer accessible exhibitions than other funders. Government and foundation sponsors have no statistical relationship to accessible exhibitions. Art historical exhibits are disproportionally favored by government and foundation donors; both sponsor more of these formats. Corporations do not sponsor particularly more or particularly fewer exhibitions that are art historical. Individuals, however, sponsor fewer shows that are organized along art historical lines.

In addition, Table 3-4 demonstrates that individuals fund a great deal of their own collections. Government funds disproportionally fewer patron collections; no surprise, since government does not usually own art. The findings that individuals sponsor their own collections but not scholarly (or accessible) shows may indicate that individuals are connoisseurs but not scholars (or educators). The findings that individuals sponsor fewer theme and art historical formats may be artifactual, however, a result of the way the data was coded and not a true difference. Because individuals are strongly associated with exhibitions of their own collections, they are sponsoring a good number of exhibitions that are usually of a "mixed" layout (a variety of styles not otherwise ordered). This variety of styles lowers the proportion of both art historical and theme layouts they support.

The logistic regressions control for the overlap in funding but do not demonstrate the existence of coalitions among funder types. Using cross-tabulations, I checked for significant overlap in funder types for each exhibition variable. This is important, since the NEA and most other government agencies fund exhibitions on a matching basis. So an important overlap may exist in government and other types of funding (although the matching funds can come from internal or quasi-internal funds as well as from other major donors). Two variables had a notably high degree of overlapping funding: 40 percent of blockbusters had multiple funders, as did 14 percent of traveling exhibitions. Government and corporations together sponsor 33.3 percent of blockbuster exhibitions, while 9.9 percent of traveling exhibitions share both corporate and government funding. Just about a quarter of blockbusters are supported by a combination of corporation and foundation dollars (although only 5 percent of traveling shows are supported by this combination of funders). Similarly, just over a quarter of blockbusters are supported by governments and foundations (and just over 5 percent of traveling exhibitions are thus supported). No combination of institutional and individual funders sponsored more than 3.5 percent of either traveling or blockbuster exhibitions. In general, institutional funding is associated with popular exhibitions and indicates a broadening of audiences for exhibitions.

Style of Exhibitions

Museums exhibit art of various styles. The style of a given exhibition is independent of the format by which it is arranged. Exhibits are coded into 14 different categories for the "style" of art presented (see the Methodological Appendix). The first three categories—"modern," "European (medieval through nineteenth century)," and "classical" art—represent the traditional canon: "the" history of art (e.g., Janson, 1986), which is now called the history of Western art. The traditional canon has the most detailed style categories. Postmodern and contemporary styles are those new styles, considered a continuation of the canon, that emerged in the sixties, seventies, and eighties. I coded exhibitions as "postmodern" if they contain art in postmodern styles and "contemporary" if they contain art by living artists working in styles other than postmodern, such as modern or traditional, or if they mixed work by artists working in both postmodern and modern styles. (Craft art appears elsewhere, even if the artist is living.) Most of the contemporary and postmodern artists coded here were living at the time their art was shown, so for the purposes of this analysis, "living artists" are indicated by the combined style category for postmodern and contemporary art.

"American old masters" refers to artists—such as Grant Wood, Thomas Cole, Andrew Wyeth—who worked in the United States prior to the advent of modernism or, if contemporaneously with it, clearly in the older tradition. I coded an exhibit as "American ethnic" if the description of the exhibit made a point that the works were created by historically disenfranchised groups in America. "Asian art" refers to art from any epoch (except modern and postmodern) and from any region of Asia, including India. Some "style" categories refer to media of the art, without further reference to style, for instance, "photography," "commercial art," or the decorative arts that are coded under "craft/costume." The category "local artists" is for shows explicitly billed as including artists living in or coming from the museum's home city. "Child/community" exhibits include exhibitions of art by children, exhibitions specially geared toward children and those specifically designated as community outreach. "Mixed styles" includes shows of *fine arts* (such as painting, drawing, and sculpture, as opposed to crafts, photography, or musical instruments) which overlap more than one style category. I coded exhibitions into several additional styles, which are lumped together under the rubric "Other styles." These styles include primitive art (art made by so-called primitive peoples, native to Asia, South America, Mexico, Africa and Oceana, regardless of date of origin), architecture (all styles and eras), film (films that are presented as art, but not films that accompany exhibits of other subjects, documentary films, or filmed lectures), South American, Mexican and African art (art from these regions that is not otherwise primitive, modern, or postmodern—Diego Rivera, for example), exhibitions with unidentifiable contents (such as the show "Oom Pah Pah" at the Metropolitan that was listed by title but not further described) and, finally, exhibitions designated to a residual sub-category called "other" (referred to here in lower case). The subcategory "other" in Other styles was generally used for objects not part of the traditional or current canons of art.

The variables in this analysis examine funding and its association with both accessible and scholarly contents. (I do not examine popular exhibitions here, because this term refers to format only, whereas the other two terms can indicate either format or content.) Several styles of exhibition indicate *accessible* contents. Though there are more accessible and less accessible artists within each style category, I assume that American old masters, craft and costume, commercial art, local artists and child/community exhibits are more accessible than other style categories. In terms of content, *scholarly* shows are indicated by the traditional canon. Postmodern art, a conglomeration of styles that draws upon, reacts against, or plays with the conventions of modern art, also indicates art historical contents. Two content variables address questions about government funding of living artists and art of interest to non-traditional audiences. Sponsorship of American ethnic art demonstrates an interest in non-traditional audiences. "Living artists" are indicated by the combined style category for postmodern and contemporary art.

Funders may have preferences for certain types of art, for instance, for art that is accessible to broad audiences or art that is scholarly. Table 3-5 explores the association between type of funder and style of exhibitions. This table reports the number of exhibitions in each style category sponsored by each funder type. Again, statistical significance levels, determined by logistic regressions, help with interpretation of the table.

Table 3-5 shows, first of all, that each of the funder types is associated in some degree with most of the art styles. But, this said, it is more important to note the varying patterns among funders. Individuals sponsor a disproportional share of modern art, classical art, American old masters, Asian art, crafts and costumes, and mixed styles. When sponsored by individual philanthropists, mixed styles are overwhelmingly a patron's own collection from varying epochs or locations. Similarly, all styles sponsored by individuals perhaps represent those that philanthropists collect for themselves. Individual philanthropists sponsor significantly fewer exhibitions

TABLE 3-5
Style of Exhibitions
Sponsored by Four Types of Funders

	N Exhibitions Sponsored by				*N Internally Funded*	*N Style (Total)*
	Corp.	*Gov.*	*Found.*	*Ind.*		
Style:[a]						
Modern	34-*	79+***	25	66+*	434	596
European, Med - 19th C.	30	41	30+*	40	331	440
Classical	5	6	3	9+*	31	47
Postmodern/ Contemporary	17	44+***	6-*	16	100	162
American Old Masters	21	16	12	35+**	182	247
American Ethnic[b]	4	5	0	4	42	53
Asian	12	10-*	17-**	39+***	174	232
Photography	20	28	11	7-***	229	282
Craft/Costume	20	12-*	8	42+**	250	317
Commercial	12+*	6	5	7	100	124
Mixed Styles	29	20-*	17	55+***	304	402
Local Artists	6	9	7	7-**	180	201
Child/Community[c]	4-*	2-***	2-*	0	305	312
Other Styles	45+*	25-***	28	35-**	507	611
Total by Funder Type	259	303	171	362	3171	4026

* $p < .05$
** $p < .01$
*** $p < .001$

Notes: [a]Asterisks indicate whether a type of funder sponsored a significantly greater or lesser number exhibitions of a given category as compared to internally funded (unfunded) exhibitions.

Significance levels were determined by logistic regressions of 4026 exhibitions. The variables Individual, Corporation, Government and Foundation are 0,1 variables and are not mutually exclusive. The omitted category in this case is exhibitions not funded by any of the four categories of funder. All variables for exhibition characteristics are 0,1 variables where 1 indicates the presence of the trait.

[b]During the period sampled, no foundations sponsored an exhibition of ethnic art; consequently, significance levels cannot be calculated.

[c]During the period sampled, no individuals sponsored an exhibition of children's or community-oriented art; consequently, significance levels cannot be calculated.

of photography and local artists. Thus, individuals sponsor a mix of both scholarly and accessible styles.

Corporations show an interesting pattern. They sponsor disproportionally fewer modern art shows, but disproportionally more commercial art and Other styles (within the Other category, the subcategory "other" makes up the lion's share of corporate sponsorship). Corporations also sponsor few children's and community exhibitions, as do all funder types. This suggests that corporations are less interested in art, like modern art, that is part of the traditional canon. Styles that were classified in the subcategory "other" were done so precisely because they did not fit in well with traditional and contemporary classifications. Note that individuals and government agencies—those funders who claim to judge exhibitions using some measure of artistic scholarship—fund fewer exhibitions in the category Other. Overall, only corporate sponsors seem to prefer to fund predominantly non-canonical, accessible art.

Government encourages both modern art, and postmodern and contemporary art, and consequently supports shows of living artists. Interestingly, both of these styles are either part of the traditional canon or are current styles drawing on the traditional canon. Both styles are created largely though not exclusively by Americans, as well. Government has a strong negative association with Asian, craft/costume, mixed, child/community and Other styles. Thus, government seems especially supportive of scholarly contents, avoiding the more accessible styles. Foundations sponsor more European art, and less postmodern, Asian and child/community art than is funded internally.

Interestingly, most styles of art are disproportionally favored by one or another type of funder. The exceptions are American ethnic art, photography, local artists, and children and community exhibits. Ranking the styles according to percent funded yields four groups: first, the heavily sponsored postmodern and contemporary (38 percent of exhibitions are externally funded), and classical art (34%); second, the solidly funded modern (27%), American old masters (26%), Asian (25%), European (25%) and mixed styles (24%); third, moderately supported craft/costume (21%), American ethnic (21%), commercial (19%), photography (19%), and other styles (17%); and the sparsely funded local artists (10.4%) and child/community (2.2%). The overall percentage of funded exhibitions for the entire sample is 21 percent.

Funding and the Pool of Exhibitions

So far, I have investigated whether funders are associated with particular formats or contents of exhibitions. This provides a baseline for understanding the next phase of the analysis, the change in the entire exhibition pool and the possible influence of funders on the pool of exhibitions as a whole. To learn about this level, I compare the exhibition pool before and after institutional funders increasingly enter the museum arena.

Museum Autonomy

Organizational theorists suggest that managers seek autonomy from demands from the environment (C. Oliver, 1991; Pfeffer & Salancik, 1978). Further, because they operate in an institutional environment, museum managers must maintain the legitimacy of their museums. Indeed, to the extent that external demands conflict with curators' ideas of what grants them legitimacy, they may actively resist external pressures. Table 3-6 summarizes the findings of the analysis of funding and the shape of exhibitions, comparing these to the orientation of curators.

TABLE 3-6
The Orientation of Stakeholders in Museum Exhibitions (According to Findings on Exhibition Funding)

Interest	*Popular Exhibitions*	*Accessible Exhibitions*		*Scholarly Exhibitions*	
	(format)	*(format)*	*(content)*	*(format)*	*(content)*
Stakeholder					
Corporate Funder	Y	Y	y	—	n
Government Funder	Y	—	N	Y	Y
Foundation Funder	y	—	—	Y	y
Individual Philanthropist	—	N	y	N	y
Museum Curator	no	no	no	yes	yes

Key:
- Y Strong positive association in quantitative analysis
- y Moderate positive association in quantitative analysis
- — No association in quantitative analysis
- n Moderate negative association in quantitative analysis
- N Strong negative association in quantitative analysis
- yes Likes this type of exhibition (evidence from interviews)
- no Dislikes this type of exhibition (evidence from interviews)

The analysis so far has shown that funders do have preferences, and these preferences affect their choice of exhibits to fund. How does this fact affect the mix of exhibitions that museums mount? Are museums mounting more of certain types of exhibits than others? One way to view this would be with a resource dependence model, which suggests that shifts in funding will change the overall mix of exhibitions as funders disproportionately sponsor exhibitions they prefer. In other words, as museums become more reliant on external funders, the exhibition pool will include more exhibitions that reflect the tastes of the funders. This model implies that museums complyingly accept external resources by mounting more exhibitions of the type that funders prefer. However, museum curators may endeavor to retain both autonomy and legitimacy through two strategies: buffering and resource shifting.

Buffering: Museum curators may be more interested in the actual content of exhibitions than in the format in which those exhibitions are mounted. Organizational theorists suggest that managers shield the most central and crucial aspects of an organization (its technical core) from environmental pressure, a process called buffering (Thompson, 1967). Consistent with the idea of buffering, we might expect that the format of exhibitions will change more than the content of exhibitions. This model suggests that as museums become more reliant on external funders, the exhibition pool will change more in format than in content.

Resource Shifting: Since museums have discretion in mounting exhibitions paid for internally, however, it is possible that they rely on external funders to sponsor exhibitions of the sort the funder prefers. This may shift the mix of externally funded exhibitions. But museums may "make up the difference" by mounting (and paying for) more of the excluded types of exhibitions. Thus, the mix of internally funded exhibitions may shift as well, with the result being that the entire pool of exhibitions does not shift. Museum curators suggest this is true:

> "Our more scholarly projects do tend to get funded internally," admits Diana Duncan of the Smithsonian. . . . "If something is not a sexy project, the inside tracks are much more important. But lack of corporate sponsorship doesn't mean we don't do those things." (quoted in Glennon, 1988, p. 42).

In other words, museums would like to mount certain types of exhibitions—a mix of popular, scholarly and accessible. They endeavor to "sell" some of them to funders, and mount the rest with internal funds. Over time, they may have found more exhibits agreeable to external funders, but may not have changed the mix of exhibitions they wish to mount. If this is true, then as museums become more reliant on external funders, the exhibition pool will not change.

The Mix of Exhibitions

To test for changes in the exhibition pool, I divided the sample into two periods, 1960–1972 and 1974–1986. This division separates the philanthropy and transition periods from the funding period (i.e. the time when institutional funders had less impact from the time when they had more impact on museums, as can be seen in Figure 3-1, above).

Table 3-7 shows the number of exhibitions in each format and content category analyzed in the previous sections. Once again, I ran logistic regressions to see whether the *proportion* of exhibitions from a given category increased from the philanthropy and transition periods to the funding period. Small changes are considered random fluctuations and are listed as no change.

The most important finding presented in Table 3-7 is that the format of exhibitions has changed substantially in the latter period. The proportion of blockbusters, traveling exhibitions, theme shows, and art historically arranged exhibitions increase. Patron collections decrease as a proportion of the total. In terms of content, three styles increase; exhibitions of classical art, postmodern and contemporary art, and photography. Shows of local artists, exhibitions of children's art, and community-oriented shows have also declined significantly. Nevertheless, the content seems to have changed less than the format, which lends support to the idea that museum curators have some autonomy and discretion in choosing exhibitions.

Though it was not a new invention during the funding period, the blockbuster format nevertheless grew due to increased availability of funding coupled with the specific concerns about audience carried by the new institutional funders. Corporations, government agencies, and foundations fund a large share of blockbuster exhibitions. Most blockbusters are just too expensive for a museum to mount without outside support. The fee for the King Tut exhibition, for example, was $2 million per exhibiting museum. Such fees were often paid by a corporation. In 1983 Philip Morris supported *The Vatican Collection: The Papacy and Art* at the Metropolitan Museum to the tune of $4 million (Martorella, 1990:15). The price of insuring all art, and especially art from other countries, is very high. The insurance tab was often picked up by the Federal Council on Arts and Humanities. Consequently, external funding is quite common for such exhibitions. Overall, 54 percent of blockbusters receive external funding.[9]

The increase in traveling exhibitions is also related to the preference of corporations and government for this type of exhibition. Theme shows are also not a new type of exhibition (Coleman, 1939, p. 288). However, theme exhibitions became more ambitious as it became possible to attract outside funders for them, especially corporations. Scholarly formats—surveys and retrospectives—increase over time. Government and foundation

TABLE 3-7
Changes in the Format and Style of Exhibitions From the Philanthropy and Transition Periods to the Funding Period

	Number of Exhibitions			
	1960–1972 (Philanthropy & Transition)	*1974–1986 (Funding)*	*Increase/ Decrease?*	*Total N*
Format:[a]				
Travelling Exhibition	252	352	Inc.*	604
Blockbuster Exhibition	17	40	Inc.*	57
Theme Show	129	215	Inc.***	344
Art Historical	508	750	Inc.***	1258
Patron Collection	190	156	Dec.***	346
Style:[a]				
Modern	280	316	—	596
European, Med - 19th C.	194	246	—	440
Classical	14	33	Inc.*	47
Postmodern/ Contemporary	42	120	Inc.***	162
American Old Masters	115	132	—	247
American Ethnic	21	32	—	53
Asian	97	135	—	232
Photography	82	200	Inc.***	282
Craft/Costume	156	161	—	317
Commercial	60	64	—	124
Mixed Styles	229	173	Dec.***	402
Local Artists	134	67	Dec.***	201
Child/Community	163	149	Dec.*	312
Other Styles	263	348	—	611
Total by Time Period[b]	1850	2176		4026

* $p < .05$
** $p < .01$
*** $p < .001$

Notes: [a]Asterisks indicate whether there is a greater or lesser proportion of a given format or style in the exhibition pool in the years 1974–86 as compared with the omitted category, the exhibition pool from 1960–72.

Significance levels were determined by logistic regressions of 4026 exhibitions. All variables are 0,1 variables where 1 indicates the presence of the trait.

[b]This row indicates the total number of exhibitions for the time period. Note that the categories for style are inclusive and mutually exclusive, so the column sums to the total. The categories under format are neither mutually exclusive nor inclusive of all exhibitions; consequently a summing of these columns would be meaningless.

funders are particularly associated with this format. The decrease in the proportion of patron collections reflects the decreased influence of individual philanthropists in museums during the funding period.

Exhibitions of postmodern and contemporary art have increased. This is not surprising, as postmodern styles developed during the period studied. As we have seen, however, government funds a great deal of these types of art. Though one would expect more postmodern and other contemporary styles in museums as these styles are invented it is not possible to know if the availability of government money has increased the proportion of these styles in museum exhibitions more than would have occurred without such funding. Crane's (1987) study of the avant-garde in New York City demonstrates that New York museums were much more conservative in exhibiting postmodern styles as they emerged than the same museums were decades earlier when modernism was on the cutting edge. (Regional museums, however, provided some alternative outlets for postmodern exhibits.) Crane argues that various changes in museums led them to exhibit fewer of the available postmodern artists, compared to the proportion of modern artists they exhibited a generation earlier. She suggests that government incentives for displaying contemporary art might be an important factor in museums' continuing commitment to the avant-garde. In addition, the avant-garde has grown enormously since the middle of the century, and the pool of postmodern artists is larger than the pool of modern artists. Crane attributes much of the growth of the avant-garde to increased corporate and government support of and involvement in the art world in general. So government funding may have both indirectly and directly spurred the production and institutionalization of postmodern styles.

Mixed exhibitions have declined, in step with patron collections (these categories overlap). The big losers seem to be local artists, though it is possible that museums exhibit local artists under the rubric of contemporary artists more during the later period. Interestingly, exhibitions that are mounted less frequently are comprised mostly of contents that have been peripheral to museums (e.g., children's art). Contents that are mounted more frequently appear to be more accessible styles, though not all the change seems to be associated with funding. For instance, photography, generally an "accessible" style, has increased as a proportion of the exhibition pool. Individual philanthropists sponsored disproportionally fewer photography exhibits. Corporations, foundations and government agencies all sponsored some photography exhibitions, but not out of proportion to such exhibitions mounted without such sponsorship.

Why have funder preferences translated more directly into changes in format but not in content? I argue that curators use a combination of buffering and resource shifting strategies to maintain their own interests in exhibits. The fact that the content of the exhibition pool does not change much after the advent of the institutional funders suggests that museums may retain autonomy from their environment through a strategy of resource shifting. They may "sell" exhibitions they want to mount, but which also have funder-appeal to external grantors, and may then use resources left over to mount exhibitions that also appeal to curators but not to funders.

The research demonstrates that museums are faced with pressures for increasing popularity and accessibility of art exhibits. However, museums have not responded, in general, by mounting masses of low quality, but snazzy shows. This is because museums must maintain their legitimacy as houses of high culture. I suggest that curators allow the format to change more, to protect the "core" of museums, shows containing a variety of artistic contents.

Resource shifting may be an important strategy for donative nonprofit organizations (Alexander, forthcoming). For instance, in a study of donors to a university, Stout (1992) found that university officials used internal and unspecified grant funds to subsidize departments underfunded by external entities, leveling the playing field between them and more richly supported departments. The evidence I have for resource shifting in museums is more anecdotal than systematic; consequently, this interpretation is tentative and more research will be needed to understand the phenomenon. I conducted interviews with museum directors, curators, and educators as part of the study. I did not ask the respondents about resource shifting or their strategies for avoiding external influence; rather, I asked how exhibitions were funded and what influences funders might have on museums and exhibitions. Nevertheless, some of what the curators said supports my contention that museum managers react strategically to environmental pressures. For instance, the director of a large, encyclopedic museum told me that funding in the museum is a "matching process." Curators plan exhibitions and then go looking for funding. At the same time, the development department tries to find funding possibilities and then look for exhibitions that curators are planning. This process has some affinities to the garbage can decision model (Cohen, March & Olsen, 1972). The director, however, keeps a general mix in the exhibition schedule, which is planned several years in advance:

> I try to shape shows on a yearly basis. That is, strike a balance between large and small shows, shows with a broad audience and those with a small audience, those [shown only in the museum] and those for outside travel.

Funding usually happens after these decisions are made. In a telling glitch, the museum found itself short of funding (and time) for a Chagall exhibit. The museum managers had anticipated easily obtaining support for the show, and was quite surprised when several possible funders turned them down. But the show went on as scheduled, and the museum used an "internal" source for underwriting the show: They charged a hefty fee for the opening dinner.

A curator in a second museum avoided funder pressures by avoiding funding. The modern art department he ran did not pursue corporate funds, but as a result, also did not mount major exhibitions in modern art and had reduced opportunity for scholarship published in the catalogues that accompany such exhibits. The curator said to me:

> It's a trade off. Contemporary art here is a low-budget operation. It was a very conscious trade off.

In addition, my reading of the annual reports of 30 museums suggest two other strategies museums use to retain autonomy: "multivocality" and, relatedly, "creative enactment." Museums have mounted many more shows that are multivocal—that appeal to different audiences on different levels. Museum curators innovate to find art that is both accessible and can be viewed with a critical eye. Since corporate funders of large, traveling blockbusters may be less interested in the art, per se, than they are in the press coverage, some writers have argued that blockbusters are just low-quality pabulum designed to bring in mindless crowds (Balfe, 1987). It is important to recognize, however, that many blockbuster and traveling exhibitions solve the problems posed by multiple stakeholders pulling for different sorts of exhibitions. Curators, along with NEA panels, are interested in the art historical merit of exhibitions. These stakeholders often have input into popular exhibitions. Popular exhibits, especially blockbusters, attract large, middle-class audiences, many of whom are not particularly schooled in the intricacies of art history. Along these lines, popular exhibitions also attract corporate sponsors. The resources of a large, traveling, blockbuster exhibit, however, can also finance advantages for scholars: (a) well-researched and nicely designed exhibits often bring together a large number of objects from overseas museums, objects that have not been seen together before, or that have not been seen in the United States, (b) blockbuster catalogs, chock-full of new scholarly analyses alongside the pretty reproductions, or (c) an opportunity to conserve and repair art works, obtain display cases or otherwise improve a museum's holdings. That some blockbuster exhibitions can have a scholarly component points to the ability of curators to use funding to meet their own ends.[10] It is notable that institutional funders (government and foundations) are associated with art historical formats and that such formats have increased in the funding period. This suggests that curators are able to draw on these funders to do more of the types of exhibitions they prefer (scholarly) along with more of those they do not prefer (popular and accessible).

For instance, a traveling exhibition appearing at the Art Institute of Chicago offered a valuable opportunity to its curators:

> The superb survey of "Master Drawings by Picasso," organized by the Fogg Art Museum, gave us both an insight into the private decisions behind many of the artist's public statements and a better understanding of how works from the Institute's superb holdings and those of a number of private Chicago collections—which were added to the Chicago showing—related to his entire oeuvre. (Art Institute of Chicago, 1980–81, p. 10)

The exhibition also provided a scholarly and beautiful catalogue and attracted quite a few viewers. In addition to the Art Institute and the Fogg, this show traveled to the Philadelphia Museum of Art. The exhibition was supported by the NEA, the Ministry of Foreign Affairs of Spain, and the Alsdorf Foundation, as was the catalogue, which mentioned each of the 102 objects displayed in the show (plus an addendum on items appearing at only one venue). The exhibition was indemnified by the Federal Council on the Arts and Humanities.

Museum personnel also appear to creatively enact their environment as they seek external funding (Pfeffer & Salancik, 1978; Weick, 1979). Enacting is the process by which managers interact with the environment to actually *create* opportunities or constraints.[11] The Fine Arts Museums of San Francisco used a strategy that "was creative, fulfilling needs beyond those of the immediate exhibit" (Fine Arts Museum of San Francisco, 1983–85, p. 13). The museum expanded its temporary exhibition space to accommodate a large traveling blockbuster—art from the Vatican. Funds for the gallery expansion came from donations supporting the special show. The Vatican show was installed in the special exhibitions galleries and the newly created space; but after the exhibition was over, the American Galleries, which were adjacent to the temporary exhibition rooms, were expanded and installed in the new rooms.

Recently, serious scholarly attention has been paid to newly-recognized art forms, such as folk art (Metcalf, 1986) and American masters (Corn, 1983; Wallach, 1981). This may be evidence for the ways funding encourages curators to locate art historical merit in objects that have more popular appeal. Both corporations and government may be particularly interested in American art: government because of its necessary focus on American society, and corporations because of the figurativeness and accessibility of the art forms. The Bicentennial provided a nationalistic focus on all things American, and museums found ample support from corporations and government for bicentennial exhibitions, on which planning began in the early parts of the 1970s. During that decade, scholarship on American arts proliferated, much of it in the form of museum catalogues funded by organizationally-based benefactors. While the public thrilled to the array of American exhibits, scholars argued that the earlier lack of attention to these styles was lamentable and wrote academic articles suggesting art historical reasons for the resurgence of interest in these forms.

Museum managers may think of clever ways to attract funding for an exhibition they wish to mount, perhaps by appealing to an interest a corporation might have that is not ordinarily associated with art. For instance, the Philadelphia Museum mounted an exhibition of seventeenth century Dutch art sponsored by Mobil Oil which owns offshore drilling rigs in Dutch waters. Theme exhibitions sometimes have theme sponsorship. For instance, Polo/Ralph Lauren sponsored the show titled *Horse and Man*, filled with hunting pictures, other canvasses of people and horses, and hunting apparel (see Silverman, 1986). *Undercover Agents: Antique Undergarments from the Costume Collection of the Fine Arts Museums of San Francisco*, was supported by Victoria's Secret, the lingerie firm. Folger's has sponsored traveling exhibitions of its silver coffee pot collection. And Fisher-Price Toys underwrote *Jouets Américains*, an exhibition of American toys, organized by the Musée des Artes Décoratifs in Paris, which toured the United States.

Museums continue to mount exhibitions of more esoteric art, past and present, but these shows tend to be funded by museum sources, sometimes supplemented by government grants, rather than by the combination of government and corporate monies that support the more popular exhibits. For instance, in 1987 the San Francisco Museum of Modern Art started a program for small, flexible exhibitions that would compliment its main program of larger exhibitions that are planned well ahead. An auxiliary group, the Collector's Forum (in this study, considered an internal funder) supported the program, which was later also subsidized by the NEA:

> The *New Work* concept was to give the Museum a program that could be reasonably nimble in responding to new ideas and opportunities, in contrast to a large museum's usual scheduling, which occurs several years in advance. It consists of a series of five or six serious but modestly scaled projects annually that are intended to provide West Coast museum audiences with a timely opportunity to see and consider some of the most interesting and important artistic accomplishments—regional, national, and international—of the day, by both younger and established artists. (San Francisco Museum of Modern Art, 1988, p. 11)

This may suggest that unfunded exhibitions represent true curator desires. Though curators most likely value exhibitions that are internally funded (they would not be mounted otherwise), curators may equally value at least some of the funded exhibitions as well. Further, if museums plan ahead and shift resources, then it is important to recognize that to a considerable degree, unfunded exhibitions should be seen as a residual category, not just as art for curators' sake. The fact that the *New Work* series was able to pick up government funding highlights this point.

Turnstile Triumphs

The funding mosaic has made curatorial innovation possible, and allowed for more scholarly format exhibitions as curators manage to buffer and resource shift. Nevertheless, funding has clearly encouraged museums to mount shows accessible to broad audiences. This has been the big change in museums in the past two decades.

Museums are often proud of their blockbuster exhibits. Many museums (the Albright-Knox Museum, the Art Institute of Chicago, Museum of Fine Arts in Houston, the Whitney) printed photos in their annual reports of the long lines of people waiting to get into the popular shows. Other museums report the community benefits of blockbusters, notably the tourist revenues attracted by the show. For instance, in 1978–79 (p. 6), the Metropolitan Museum of Art hired a public opinion firm to estimate the money spent in New York from out-of-town visitors to the King Tut show—the total: $110 million flushed into the New York system! The Vatican exhibition in 1982–83 (p.7) was slightly less successful in boosting tourism; the Metropolitan's figures suggest that $101 million was spent "on travel-related expenses like hotels, restaurants, entertainment, and transportation, as well as for shopping." The Met goes on to note: "These surveys offer solid evidence of the very considerable degree to which the Metropolitan contributes to the economic well-being of all New Yorkers and reinforce the argument that the Museum is a sound and profitable investment for New York." The Met's action demonstrates the creative efforts on the part of museum managers to demonstrate their value to the community, and highlights the fact that blockbusters are not important just in terms of big audiences, but in addition, they shore up general support for the museum (Balfe & Cassilly, 1993, p. 123).

A theme in the interviews was that a big impact of the shift from philanthropy to funding was the new emphasis on popular exhibitions designed to appeal to a large, broadly-based audience. Blockbusters, due to their fiscal benefits, have had a notable effect on the aspirations of museum personnel, especially directors. One set of curators told me that their director was "salivating for numbers," that is, he was hungry for the sell-out crowds of the blockbuster. The director, according to curators, was not particularly concerned with the content of the show, so long as it was financially successful.

The blockbuster does put a lot of pressure on museum directors: First, directors are sometimes disappointed by big crowds because they were expecting even larger ones. Second, directors must always strive to do better and to get even more people in next year. Third, museum visitors use blockbusters as a yardstick for all subsequent shows, even of lesser scope and ambition (one museum director overheard a woman at an exhibit exit: "It's OK, but not as good as King Tut"). And fourth, museums are criticized for trying to attract broad audiences rather than focusing on scholarship, as this Art Institute of Chicago defense shows:

> A great museum must mount a variety of exhibitions, both major and minor, and it is this distinction which makes the museum everyone's Aunt Sally. What are major and minor? The Monet exhibition, a serious examination of the career of a very great and most influential artist, was criticized for not being serious enough, for not including certain key works, and, God forbid, for being "too popular", which meant too many people saw it. There *were* major gaps; there always are in such an exhibition, but there were also major presences, one or two not seen in America for many years or ever. Armchair critics seldom know how a major exhibition is organized, nor do they believe the stated purpose of an exhibition. In this case, it was to bring to a glorious close the great series of exhibitions begun over thirty years ago which examined in depth the works of the great Impressionist and Post-Impressionist painters. . . . Because the museum is a center of nineteenth century French art, it quite properly will continue to examine the nineteenth and early twentieth centuries and their antecedents. (Art Institute of Chicago, 1974–75, p. 14)

Despite the potential drawbacks, blockbusters are attractive to museums. Successful blockbusters are very kind to museum coffers: Often, admission receipts are put into the museum's general operating budget, relieving strains there. Dramatic exhibitions also encourage people to become members of the museum, (a) because the visitor may be so pleased with the exhibit that she cannot resist joining, and (b) because museums give preferential treatment to members when distributing tickets to sell-out events. Blockbusters can spur unanticipated gifts of art work, usually from the exhibition itself or in a similar theme, from collectors who are impressed by the exhibition. Such benefits to the museum appear to accrue even from blockbusters that are not initiated by the museum itself. The success of the show often exceeds the large fee that the museum pays to get the show. For instance, the *Treasures of Tutankhamun* drew over 1.3 million visitors in San Francisco (a world record for attendance at an art exhibit), and museum membership "soared" to more than 77,000 people during the exhibit (The Fine Arts Museums of San Francisco, 1978–80, p. 9).

Blockbuster shows represent a significant departure from the traditional image of a museum exhibit involving quiet contemplation of art objects. Indeed, blockbusters often attract a milling crowd, which fills the exhibition rooms to capacity, so the viewer does not have time to sit and look at the paintings. There are long lines outside, and the exhibits are crowded inside, with people piled up three or four deep in front of particularly striking or famous objects. In addition, museums often provide acoustiguides for a modest fee. These individual tape recordings act to keep the traffic flowing; at the same time, they restrict the audience's experience of the show, focusing attention on a few easily described highlights. For instance, the acoustiguide tape for the Degas show at the Met in October 1988 ran 40 minutes. The exhibition contained 300 works; consequently, the tape allowed the viewer to spend an average of eight seconds/picture. Certainly, no one played the tape straight through, and the tape did not discuss every object in the show, but it clearly functioned as an aural traffic cop by keeping its listeners moving.

One interesting facet of the blockbuster is that it offers a more accessible, less elite way to look at art. The viewer does not need detailed knowledge of the subject—it is chosen precisely for its accessibility. The viewer merely walks through the rooms, and at the end, she can say she has been there. One way to interpret this facet is to say that blockbusters are more "middle class" than traditional exhibits. It is also, to use a different term, "middlebrow" (Lynes, 1954)—accessible to large audiences, yet with some claim to prestige.

As mentioned, theme shows focus on a motif, rather than on art-historical categories. Some further examples of theme shows are: *A Woman's Place: Changing Perceptions, The American Cowboy*, and a show at the Museum of Fine Arts, Boston in 1970, composed of masterpieces expressing the philosophy of Zen, which, as the museum wrote, "attracted a large yet very discriminating audience in which young people were conspicuous" (Museum of Fine Arts, Boston, 1970–71, p. 21). More recent was the traveling exhibit *Diamonds are Forever*, a show of baseball-oriented art and memorabilia, which was popular with both adults and children.

I think that these exhibition titles are amusing, and I assume that museums and sponsors hoped the shows would be entertaining. But museums do not want to be laughed at. Many museum curators still view museums as, ideally, halls of scholarship, and curators are much like academics, very serious, not appreciating the apparent frivolity of theme shows. Recently, the Metropolitan Museum of Art refused to mount an exhibit—Andrew Wyeth's Helga paintings—citing the poor scholarship of the exhibition and its unfortunate tendency to pander to the masses. A number of museums rejected this very hyped show. The National Gallery, under Carter Brown, did accept it, however. The exhibition proved to be controversial precisely because many members of the museum world thought it lacked scholarship (but the public couldn't have cared less and attended in droves).

It is important to recognize that the situation in museums today is not simply the result of constraints imposed by the new funders. Instead, a different set of funders (and attached opportunities, as well as constraints) has come to rival an older set of donors. It is important to recognize that the changes are related to the shift in the funding environment, the institutional funders versus the traditional philanthropists. Museums have always mounted popular and accessible exhibitions (see Coleman, 1939; Meyer, 1979; and Zolberg, 1974); today these "middle brow" exhibitions take the form of funded blockbusters, traveling exhibitions, and theme shows, rather than the small, unfunded shows of local artists, children's exhibits, and community-outreach contents of the earlier era.

Still, this new emphasis on blockbusters, theme exhibitions, and popular subject matter does not please most curators (McGuigan et al., 1985). They often assert that corporations and government have "distorted" the types of shows that museums put on. A general theme among curators (but not among museum directors) is a belief that corporations, especially, constrain and flaw exhibitions. However, museums clearly have some discretion in balancing large, crowd-drawing exhibitions with much smaller ones that lack external support. Museums attempt to balance mass-appeal shows and smaller, more academic shows. Indeed, I believe that the new funders have given curators *more* freedom than they have had in the past. One piece of evidence for this is the increase in art historical formats of exhibitions. If museums are primarily funded by wealthy, elite donors, then curators are limited by the ability and desire of those patrons to fund their ideas. Additional funders create more options. Each type of funding has its own limits, but now there are several types of limits from which to choose. Nonetheless, questions of discretion and constraint are analytically complex. Clearly, even if curators are free to choose within a set of possibilities, the *universe of possibilities* is determined by funding.

Museum Effects

To explore trends in the average number of exhibitions per museum, I again ran a regression analysis. Ordinary Least-Squares (OLS) Regression of the number of exhibitions against year and dummy variables for each of the museums (with the Detroit Institute of Art as the "omitted category," i.e., the comparison museum) shows that year is positive and statistically significant (see Table 3-8). I am not suggesting here that *time* causes the number of exhibitions. Rather, I suggest that time is a proxy for an unobserved variable, namely some measure of the increase in funding. Time is only a rough stand-in for growing external funding, and it is not the only relevant factor, but the regression clearly shows that, in general, museum exhibitions increase. Note some museums have significantly more, and others significantly fewer exhibitions than Detroit. The Art Institute of Chicago and the Metropolitan Museum mount more exhibitions than Detroit. Cincinnati, the National Gallery, St. Louis, Toledo, and Yale all mount fewer exhibitions than Detroit. Brooklyn, Cleveland, the Museum of Fine Arts in Boston, the Museum of Modern Art, the Wadsworth Atheneum, and the Whitney Museum all mount about the same number of exhibitions as Detroit.

TABLE 3-8

Regression Model of Number of Exhibitions per Museum per Year as a Function of Year, Expenses, and Museums

	Model 1:		Model 2:	
	b	(s.e.)	b	(s.e.)
Independent Variables:				
Year[a]	0.525***	(0.098)	0.503***	(.157)
Expense[b]	—	—	0.001	(.000)
Museums:[c]				
Art Institute of Chicago	17.284***	(3.334)	11.393*	(4.837)
Brooklyn Museum	-0.660	(3.751)	-1.057	(4.191)
Cincinnati Art Museum	-16.385***	(3.625)	-16.253***	(3.860)
Cleveland Museum	-2.006	(3.417)	-4.592	(3.951)
Museum of Fine Arts, Boston	0.933	(3.755)	-1.277	(4.092)
Metropolitan Museum	11.070**	(3.334)	4.221	(5.816)
Museum of Modern Art	4.641	(3.334)	2.484	(4.137)
National Gallery	-10.468**	(3.623)	-20.428**	(7.293)
Philadelphia Museum of Art	1.309	(3.417)	-0.195	(3.709)
Saint Louis Art Museum	-7.470*	(3.749)	7.301	(7.947)
Toledo Museum of Art	-16.744***	(4.124)	-16.673***	(4.604)
Wadsworth Atheneum	2.284	(3.334)	3.393	(3.652)
Whitney Museum	-3.835	(3.626)	-1.874	(4.805)
Yale Art Gallery	-16.010***	(3.623)	—	—
Intercept	17.385***	(2.302)	17.177	(2.780)

	Model 1	Model 2
* $p < .05$	N = 198 museum-years	N = 144 museum-years
** $p < .01$	$R^2 = 0.51$	$R^2 = 0.47$
*** $p < .001$		

Notes: [a] Year is indicated by calendar year minus 1960 (i.e., 1960 = 0 and 1986 = 26).

[b] Expense is expressed in 1,000s of 1967 constant dollars.

[c] Museums are indicated by dummy variables. The excluded museum is the Detroit Institute of Art. Yale Art Gallery is not included in the second model as no expense information was available.

Museum dummy variables act as a proxy for other factors affecting the frequency of exhibits. There are several possibilities for these hidden factors. Perhaps differences in museums' annual budgets account for some of this heterogeneity. Expenses for museums are one measure of the size of the museum, and also an indicator of the money available for exhibitions, though in a second regression, this variable was not significant beyond the impact of the museums themselves.[12] (For this second analysis, I needed to leave out Yale, as they did not report their annual expense information.) Nevertheless, expense does make a difference. Controlling for museum expenses, the Metropolitan has about the same number of exhibitions as Detroit, and so does Toledo. Ignoring expenditures gives different results for these two museums.

The average number of exhibitions per year does not behave uniformly across museums, as can be seen from the regression results in Table 3-8. It is possible that museum dummy variables capture the exhibition-orientedness of individual museums. Though the focus on exhibitions has increased in the aggregate, some museums are historically less inclined to mount exhibitions. I have no independent measure of this factor. Indeed, an increase in the number of exhibitions is striking in some museums (e.g., the Albright-Knox Museum, the Art Institute of Chicago, the Metropolitan Museum of Art), while other museums (e.g., the Brooklyn Museum, the Cleveland Museum) appear to change little in numbers of exhibitions over time. These figures do not necessarily indicate the level of emphasis the museum places on exhibitions, as the above discussion of problems in using the raw number of exhibitions suggests. Museums may mount the same number of exhibitions over time, but focus more attention on those arranged in the later period.

Other possible explanations of differences over museums in the number of exhibitions mounted include fundraising ability (i.e., skill of the staff), potential audience, size of home city, financial viability of home state, and floor space dedicated to exhibitions. Size of the museum may play a role, e.g., small museums may not have the administrative capacity or monetary reserves to mount a steady stream of exhibits, so the number of exhibitions from year to year may be uneven.

Number of Exhibitions

In the aggregate, the number of exhibitions mounted in museums may be a reasonable measure of the attention all museums pay to exhibitions. Within individual museums, however, this measure can be difficult to interpret. The number of exhibitions a museum can mount is limited by the amount of floor space the museum has available for exhibits. Museums must divide this space into that reserved for permanent exhibits (which I did not study), and that dedicated to temporary exhibitions. This decision is usually zero-sum. Permanent exhibits are changed occasionally, but they are rarely removed to make way for special exhibitions, unless the permanent gallery is converted, for the foreseeable future, into a temporary gallery. Further, when a museum builds more square feet of exhibition galleries, the number of exhibitions initially declines, because during construction, museums tend to close at least some of their galleries. When the new galleries open, however, the number of exhibitions again increases. (Construction also clouds the relationship between museum expense and the number of exhibitions: Construction increases the museum's expenses at precisely the time that the number of exhibitions drops off due to gallery closure.)

In addition, the size of exhibitions affects the number of exhibitions. One very large blockbuster may take up most of the exhibition space in a museum, but only counts as one exhibit. For instance, the complex installation of *The Splendor of Dresden* (and a museum renovation making it possible to house the exhibition) closed the Legion of Honor building (part of the Fine Arts Museums of San Francisco) for 9 months in 1978 and 79 (Fine Arts Museums of San Francisco, 1978–80, p. 9). More striking, the phenomenal 1980 *Picasso* exhibit, viewed by more than one million visitors to the Museum of Modern Art in New York, used the entire MoMA building. This enormous exhibition of 923 works—the most extensive exhibit of Picasso ever—opened in May and closed September 30. It took 4 weeks to dismantle the exhibit and reinstall the galleries (Museum of Modern Art, 1980–81, p. 5). In other words, one exhibition tied up the MoMA for 6 months (not including the time it took to install the exhibit, a factor which was not mentioned in the annual report).

Although I attempted to collect data on the size of the exhibition, the number of objects in the show was reported for only 25 percent of exhibitions. I suspect that this quarter of the sample is not representative. Museums are likely to report the number of pieces in an exhibition when the number is somehow notable. Further, how big the exhibition seems depends on the type of object. An exhibit of 50 large-scale, industrial-sized modern sculptures would be a *huge* exhibit, an exhibit of 50 oil canvasses would be fairly large, but an exhibition of fifty works on paper would be considered a medium-sized show. The age and rarity of the items also change perceptions of size.

Further, the number of exhibits does not reflect the amount of effort going into exhibits, since one large exhibit might take as many personnel hours to plan and mount as several small exhibits. Loan exhibits drawing from many collections, especially those in foreign countries, take more time to arrange than exhibitions of museum works or exhibitions of works from one external collection (such as a trustee's collection). For example, in

1964, The California Palace of the Legion of Honor packed and unpacked 11,700 objects that were loaned to or borrowed from other institutions. The effort this took in terms of recording and packing is astounding, let alone the work that went into arranging loans with other museum, insuring them, and handling related details.

For these reasons, some kinds of fancy funded shows might decrease the total number of exhibitions mounted in a given year. In contrast, large-scale blockbusters organized at other museums may take relatively little effort on the part of an auxiliary museum because the effort is geared only toward installation, not exhibition planning. Finally, museums sometimes alternate small and large exhibitions in some regular way. After mounting the successful *Paintings by Renoir* in 1972—attendance was 355,000 in just two months—the Art Institute of Chicago concluded:

> A major exhibition of paintings organized by this museum can be done only in alternate years. To supplement this we must share exhibitions with other institutions and make more of the contents of our own collections, both for educational purposes and for the pure pleasure of seeing familiar things in new ways (Art Institute of Chicago, 1972–73, p. 12).[13]

The exhibition took almost four years of "intensive" work to bring to fruition. These facts help explain why the number of exhibitions is so variable from year to year for many museums.

Discussion

The chapter reports some evidence of resource dependency pressures on museums. Museums have become increasingly oriented toward exhibitions and larger audiences. Moreover, it is easy to see the general orientations of funders translated into exhibition outcomes. Funders have goals that shape their giving. But the goals of the funders conflict with one another, and more importantly, with normative visions of museum integrity held by curators. Museums must continue to garner legitimacy from actors external to the organization, not only funders, but also critics and scholars who are oriented to the art historical merit of a museum's operation. According to traditional views, museums are assumed to be in the business of collecting, conserving, displaying and teaching about elite art. They are not in the entertainment business nor are they supposed to focus on "lowbrow" or "popular" culture. Though these views are being challenged, most museums make an effort to keep their highbrow legitimacy. One ramification of this is that museums attract exhibition support for mainly canonical art forms, styles that have built-in legitimacy. However, I believe that curators also innovate in terms of the art styles they focus on in exhibitions.

The results suggest that an increase in funding has led to an increase in the number of all types of exhibitions. A striking shift has been the increase over time in the impact of funding on the content and especially the format of art exhibits. Government arts policy has had two notable and opposite effects on art exhibitions. Government desires for large audiences along with policies which require matching grants has led to bigger, more popular exhibits. Museums, however, want to demonstrate that they are scholarly, and that they keep up with current trends in art. Consequently, museums mount exhibitions with art historical formats and small exhibitions of contemporary artists. This type of exhibition is more difficult to fund, but the NEA encourages this type of exhibition through its living artist programs.

Corporations encourage blockbuster and traveling exhibits which draw large audiences, and accessible exhibits such as theme shows. The styles that corporations fund more—commercial and "other" styles—also indicate a popularizing effect of corporate support. Easy-to-understand, "popular" exhibits have been given a boost by corporations.

Individuals and foundations favor various styles. Individuals do not sponsor popular or large-scale exhibitions, though foundations do sponsor blockbusters. Individuals overwhelmingly support their own collections, and thus they legitimate their own, elite tastes.

Overall, it is clear that changes in funding go hand in hand with changes in exhibition format. Corporate and government funding has especially increased blockbuster and traveling exhibitions. Effects on style are less clear. Though government does sponsor a disproportional share of post-modern and contemporary art, new styles falling under this category emerged during the funding period. There is no way to know how much government funding contributed to the increase in such styles.

This chapter also highlights differences among museums in the number of exhibitions mounted. Possible explanations for the differences were suggested: the level of exhibition-orientedness (which may capture such factors as the conservativeness of the trustees or director), availability of funds (either internal solvency and level of endowment, or skills for and success at attracting outside support), and floor space for exhibits, among others. Furthermore, sudden changes in the number of exhibitions in some museums indicate changes in general exhibition-orientedness, perhaps in response to new opportunities. What accounts for these differences is a fascinating issue that deserves further research.

Funders have goals that are readily apparent in their funding patterns. Still, the new institutional funders of museums have also given curators leverage and flexibility, allowing them to pick and choose funders and to play them off one another to reach their own goals, and have spurred curators to innovate in order to maintain their autonomy. This argument has something in common with economic approaches to museums, which argue that museums will innovate and mount appealing exhibitions when there are monetary incentives to do so (Frey & Pommerehne, 1989). But this chapter argues that the engine is different: Curators do not innovate because they are interested in financial incentives. Rather they are constrained by the need for external funding, so they innovate to keep as much autonomy and legitimacy as possible.

To the extent that museums legitimate and signal current definitions of the artistic canon, museum exhibitions influence artistic boundaries. Along these lines, the research suggests that art is shaped by mundane organizational processes. The research suggests as well that funder pressures for accessibility is mainly handled by changes in exhibition formats. And due to the actions of professional museum curators, the basis for inclusion of art works in exhibitions remains art historical merit, rather than popularity.

Still, there is evidence for a broadening, popularizing effect of institutional funders. How do curators feel about these trends? How do directors manage the increased demands made on museums? These organizational ramifications of funding-induced changes are the topic of the next chapter.

NOTES

1. Works loaned on a long-term basis are usually from a patron's collection and often are intended gifts to the museum.

2. The correlation matrix also shows that there is no problem with multicollinearity among the four funder variables.

3. This is the raw average, including museums which were closed for part of the exhibition year (thus having a lower number of exhibitions).

4. The variable YEAR - Z (equal to YEAR - 60, i.e. 1960 = 0) was used rather than YEAR in all the regression analyses to facilitate the interpretation of the parameter estimates.

5. Table not shown. R^2 for this regression = 0.85, though this statistic is relatively meaningless, since the dependent variable is the *average* number of exhibitions per museum per year. Thus, much of the variation in the number of exhibitions was removed prior to the regression.

6. Using the formula for simple regression: $Y = a + bX$, where a = the intercept, and b = slope for Y = average number of exhibitions, and X = year.

7. It is perhaps useful to point out that audiences also became more attuned to museums as museums became more attuned to audiences. Blau (1989, p. 36) reports that, between 1975 and 1980, museum attendance increased from 44 to 60 percent of Americans.

8. Here, museums resemble for-profit culture industries, where best-sellers of all types are similarly difficult to predict (Hirsch 1981).

9. This number may seem too low given an image of blockbusters as externally funded major loan exhibitions mounted during the funding period (1974 and beyond). Remember, my definition of blockbuster captures a somewhat different

definition of blockbuster—shows that were popular any time in the sample period. Note, too, that the overall percent of exhibitions funded for the entire sample is 21; the popular, "blockbuster" shows I've coded are funded at a much higher rate.

10. Not all popular shows solve the stakeholder dilemma, however. The exhibit must contain a scholarly as well as a public component to resolve the conflicts involved, and to gain art historical legitimacy for the museum.

11. Enactment blurs the distinction between organizational actors and environments. In Weick's view, environments are not tangible entities to which organizations respond; rather, environments come into organizations only through managerial enactment:

> Managers construct, rearrange, single out, and demolish many "objective" features of their surroundings. When people act, they unrandomize variables, insert vestiges of orderliness, and literally create their own constraints. This holds true whether those constraints are created in fantasy to justify avoided tests or created in actuality to explain tangible bruises (p. 164).

Enactment can embody bracketing, deviation amplification, self-fulfilling prophecies, and the social construction of reality. See Weick (1979; chapter 6).

12. The variable "expense" was the museum's annual expenditure on operations. Expenses may also be related to construction costs, some of which are used to build exhibition space. I attempted to collect the actual exhibition expense. Unfortunately, this information was reported sporadically. Moreover, what each museum counts as exhibition expense, in a line-item under the operating expenses, appears to vary considerably from museum to museum. Museums sometimes included only the fees associated with externally organized, traveling exhibitions, rather than costs, such as curator time associated with in-house exhibits. Data on exhibition income was even more problematic.

13. At first glance, it appears that choosing a coding scheme that looks at every other year is unfortunate given that the Art Institute of Chicago and other museums attempt to alternate years with a big exhibition. However, this turns out not to be problematic; since no museums were successful in keeping to a biennial schedule, the coding scheme tapped both blockbuster years, and non-blockbuster years for all these museums.

IV

FROM SCHOLARSHIP TO MANAGEMENT

CHANGES IN MUSEUMS AS ORGANIZATIONS

This chapter looks at the changes in art museums that relate to the increasing structure of the museum field. The museum environment has become increasingly organized and formalized, especially regarding funding. This process is known as rationalization.[1] The rationalization of the museum environment leads to increasing rationalization within museums. I examine how the shifting funding environment of museums has led to changes in museum missions and management. Further, within museums, two institutional logics or visions have collided. The first logic is the art historical, conservation and collection-oriented vision of museums held by curators. The second is the logic of business and of modern capitalism, which entered museums through several channels and is maintained by administrators, board members and, to a large degree, by museum directors. These conflicting institutional patterns lock their adherents into pitched battles, where participants vie for ascendancy of their view. This chapter addresses the organizational ramifications of the funding environment, using data from both interviews and annual reports. I address questions at two levels of analysis, the museum level (the organization) and the museum industry level (the organizational field).

Museum Missions

Chapter 3 demonstrated that the number of exhibitions mounted in museums has increased, signaling an important change in museum missions, which now include exhibiting along with collecting and conservation. The interviews and the text of the annual reports suggest several other important changes in the orientation of museums.

Tensions of Mission in the Past

Museums have long been pulled between populist and elitist conceptions of their responsibilities. Indeed, in many ways these "tensions of mission" (Zolberg, 1986, 1981) antedate the institution itself. The precursors of today's museums (in the first half of the nineteenth century) were oriented toward audiences. At the time, the distinction between high art, popular arts, crafts, and curiosities was not clearly drawn (DiMaggio, 1982a; Levine, 1988). A wide range of for-profit enterprises mixed what we now call "high art" with other objects to create smorgasbord shows designed to entertain a wide enough audience to make money. For instance, rhino horns might be exhibited in the same room as a Thomas Cole painting.

In the late 19th century, museums institutionalized an uneasy alliance between educational and curatorial functions. Though they defined most curiosities as outside their purview, early U.S. museums contained a large number of reproductions and plaster casts, objects used only for didactic purposes, as well as original works of art. The goals of the upper-class founders were as much to educate and uplift the masses as to gain status. A prime example is Boston's Museum of Fine Arts, which was established in 1870 as a direct result of threats to the primacy of the elite (DiMaggio, 1982a, b). As Boston's immigrant population grew, the new arrivals began to challenge the Brahmin's political control of the city. Stung by these attacks, the elite sought to reestablish control (albeit cultural rather than political) over the community and to develop a new basis for its claim to status honor. The Museum of Fine Arts was established in 1870 for precisely this purpose. The elite framed high culture in such a way that it became equated with morality, nobility of spirit and social status. In other words, in addition to collecting art objects, the elites "were collectors of what Bourdieu has called 'cultural capital', knowledge and familiarity with styles and genres that are socially valued and confer prestige upon those who have mastered them." (DiMaggio, 1982a: 35)

Nevertheless, the elite did not set out to exclude the lower classes from the museum. Indeed, the movement to establish the Museum of Fine Arts explicitly included the ideal that the museum would help to educate the masses and improve the whole society. This illustrates the general proposition that while status-enhancement and mass education may pose disparate challenges, the latter is essential to the former:

> As Weber noted, mastery of the elements of a status culture becomes a source of honor to group members. Particularly in the case of a dominant status group, it is important that their culture be recognized as legitimate by, yet be only partially available to, groups that are subordinate to them. (DiMaggio, 1982b: 303)

The Museum of Fine Arts was funded privately, yet the same tensions of mission are also found in public museums. The Metropolitan Museum, for example, was founded (also in 1870) by New York businessmen, with substantial municipal assistance in the form of building funds and land. The founders secured this assistance partly by claiming that a museum would bring prestige to the city and provide a public service (Tomkins, 1970). But this public service was clearly not the primary goal of the museum. For instance, the museum kept short hours and was open only on business days, so working people could not easily visit; and the subdued, church-like atmosphere intimidated many outsiders (Meyer, 1979).

By the turn of the century, the ambiguities of museums' missions had engendered a heated scholarly debate. John Cotton Dana (1856–1929) epitomized museum populism while Paul J. Sachs (1878–1965) championed elitism (Meyer, 1979). Dana believed that museums should be educational bodies like public libraries, with branch offices oriented to a mass audience. Located in convenient areas, these satellites would feature frequently changing exhibits and would loan educational objects to the public. In contrast, Sachs, who trained two generations of museum curators at Harvard, urged universities and museums to join in developing professional standards in the arts (Museum of Modern Art, 1937). An advocate of connoisseurship, he believed that museums should be in the business of identifying and collecting only the finest examples of art. DiMaggio, (1987a) describes how, during the 1920s and '30s, the Sachs model triumphed as curators professionalized and gained more control over museums.

The curatorial model of museum functioning has recently been challenged once again by a more populist, educational vision of museum goals. The belief that museums should appeal to large, popular audiences resurfaced dramatically in the 1960s with the growth of institutional funding. Not only did the arts suddenly gain the attention of the nation (especially in Democratic circles), but during the egalitarian 1960s, all institutions, including arts institutions, were exhorted to help humanity by actively seeking out the poor and disadvantaged as beneficiaries of what the institution could offer. In a study of the Art Institute of Chicago, Zolberg (1974) shows that at the turn of the century, the museum mounted a large number and variety of exhibitions, but as curators gained control and status in museums, the number of exhibitions declined. This low level of activity remained the norm for forty years, from the 1920s to the 1960s, after which the number of exhibitions in the Art Institute increased once again.

Orientation toward Funders

Chapter 3 showed the increasing importance of funding over time and suggested as well that museums have become more oriented to funders.

To learn more about this issue, I coded whether the annual reports mentioned funders in the text of the report (excluding acquisitions pages, but not excluding acquisitions, if thanks for those were given in the main text). I also noted whether museums kept separate lists, usually at the end of the annual report, of museum members or benefactors for each category of funder. Over time, museums are more likely to mention all types of funders, corporations, governmental units, foundations, and individuals, in the text of their annual reports (Table 4-1). Museums also increasingly provide lists of individual and corporate donors in appendices to the annual report (Table 4-2) though they rarely list foundations or government agencies separately. (Foundations are often listed with individuals and government units are not numerous enough to require separate lists). This suggests that museums are increasingly aware of funders and increasingly try to please funders by acknowledging their good deeds. Indeed, during the funding period, a major function of annual reports is to thank donors publicly.

In addition, the orientation to funders is evident in the tone of the discussions concerning them. The Whitney Museum was the first to manifest a markedly pro-funder stance. In 1967–68, it published as part of

TABLE 4-1
Percent of Annual Reports with Mentions in the Text of Corporate, Government, Foundation, and Individual Support Over Time

	Corporations	*Government*	*Foundations*	*Individuals*
YEAR				
1960	15.4	33.3	23.1	38.5
1962	25.0	33.3	33.3	50.0
1964	16.7	8.3	25.0	36.4
1966	28.6	21.4	35.7	35.7
1968	30.8	8.3	30.8	46.2
1970	25.0	31.3	18.8	46.7
1972	35.7	46.7	28.6	42.9
1974	46.2	64.3	38.5	61.5
1976	58.3	81.8	66.7	61.5
1978	53.8	92.3	69.2	61.5
1980	64.3	64.3	46.2	53.8
1982	85.7	71.4	64.3	71.4
1984	72.7	80.0	63.6	72.7
1986	85.7	85.7	71.4	71.4

N = 16 museums.

TABLE 4-2
Percent of Museums with Separate Lists of Corporate and Individual Members or Patrons Over Time

	Corporation	*Individual*
Year		
1960	15.4	23.1
1962	33.3	41.7
1964	50.0	58.3
1966	53.3	66.7
1968	46.7	60.0
1970	46.7	73.3
1972	43.8	62.5
1974	53.8	69.2
1976	53.8	69.2
1978	58.3	83.3
1980	69.2	84.6
1982	78.6	85.7
1984	81.8	90.9
1986	88.9	100.0

N = 16 museums

its annual report a one-page statement titled "Business and the Arts, New Patterns of Cooperation." This statement described the cooperation between Philip Morris, Inc. and the Whitney, RCA's financial intervention to save a Whitney exhibit, and Whitney's efforts to help corporations with their art questions. Other museums moved in this direction. In 1970, the Metropolitan Museum designated Olivetti its first "Corporate Benefactor" for support of the *Before Cortés* exhibition. In the same year, the Met's president and director together wrote:

> The Museum's first priority is to expand income. In addition to the new admission policy, many other measures are being undertaken, to broaden membership, to attract corporate support, to keep governmental agencies alert to their financial responsibilities to the Museum, and to improve the income from our related business activities. (Metropolitan Museum of Art, 1970: 4)

In the same year, the Art Institute of Chicago's President stated:

> We are indeed indebted to the legislators of our State for their sympathetic understanding of our financial plight, particularly because *funding will have*

> *to come more and more from public and corporate sources* to enable museums in this country to meet their constantly soaring operating costs and to raise the staggering amount of money needed for new facilities. (Art Institute of Chicago, 1970–71, pp. 4–5, emphasis added.)

After 1970, not only do acknowledgments of external benefactors increase, but museums suggest more and more often that one of their roles is to seek such support. In the mid-1970s museums begin to establish (or mention for the first time) development departments. In 1976, Cincinnati hired a consultant to create a development plan for the museum and, in 1977, hired a part-time development officer. The Albright-Knox Museum established a full-time Development Office in 1978, and "also sought, for the first time, corporate underwriting of major exhibitions" (Albright-Knox, 1978–79, p. 7). My interviews demonstrated that, in the funding period, museum people thought about funding a great deal. Though both curators and directors felt that external funding was necessary for the survival of the museum, curators were likely to view institutional funding as a necessary evil, while directors stressed the many benefits such funding brings to museums.

Orientation toward Management Rhetoric

One of the better-documented changes that the shift from patronage to funding has engendered concerns accountability. As the number of funders has increased, so too have demands from funders for accountability and for services from museum personnel. Consequently, as museums seek funding, having staff knowledgeable in development and fund-raising becomes helpful. This has increased the number of non-art specialists on museum staffs.

Museums have not always been good record-keepers. Peterson (1986) reports that an "impresarial" management style characterized museums until federal and corporate funders began to require accountability in the 1960s. Private donors to the arts did not have the desire, or perhaps did not have the authority, to review museum books and records. They did not require an accounting of every penny and were often unconcerned if some of their money went to uses other than the project for which it was originally intended. Public and corporate funders, however, are quite concerned about these issues. [2] In fact, the new funders may have fostered the general trend toward professionalization in the arts.[3]

Pressures from funding organizations for accountability have increased the number of non-art specialists, such as accountants, fund-raisers, public relations experts, and lawyers on museum staffs (Peterson, 1986). There is ample evidence of the addition of such personnel in the annual reports; the proliferation of reports from non-arts departments (public relations, membership, development) is one example. Mentions of new accounting procedures, or a first financial report is another. This suggests that museums will move their organizational focus from scholarship to self-management.

Given the professionalization of nonprofit management, it will be interesting to note the changes in strategic management over time. One interesting issue is the influx of business school graduates into arts management. At this point, business school graduates and other non-arts professionals, are entering art museums, but very few have made it to the director level yet. Certainly, museum boards of directors now contain representatives from business, in addition to wealthy individuals. The presence of individuals sophisticated in management techniques may affect the running of museums.

Have these new professionals shaped the missions of museums? For example, how much evidence of professionalization and management-orientation is notable in museum decision-making? In regard to financial solvency, museum personnel keep in mind possible funders as they make decisions about art shows. In some ways, this is true in all museums, because a museum that does not stay in the black can not continue to operate. Many museums operate at a deficit for years running, but ultimately, they must raise the money necessary to continue operations.

Some museums handle exhibitions and funding formally, by requiring that each show be funded before the museum will commit to mounting it. If the show does not have enough backing, the project will not go forward. (It appears that large museums are most likely to have such requirements.) In addition, some museums have written guidelines for accepting corporate and other outside funding.

When does the issue of funding arise? Must curators have an idea of potential funders in mind before proposing, even informally, exhibition subjects? Or do museums handle the potential for funding informally, as directors and peers either encourage or discourage curators as they float their ideas? Or do museums handle potential funding formally, by allowing curators to suggest any topic, by writing a formal proposal to solicit funds, and by canceling those that fail? All three of these situations occur, but the mix of the three is very difficult to determine: Museums do not keep good records about the formally rejected shows, and curators may be reluctant to admit their own failures.

Not all museums have instituted such formal policies, however; museums still mount exhibitions with no external funding, usually smaller exhibitions funded from the general operating budget. Children's and didactic exhibitions are often not funded, nor are smaller, art historically oriented exhibits. I asked directors to tell me how projects receive funding. They described a "matching process" in which projects are initiated by curators (who are often helped by planning grants from the NEA or NEH), and then the development office approaches funders who may have an interest in such projects. Overall, museums tend to approach funders rather than vice-versa (though this is not always the case).[4]

One museum director, whose curators compose their shows before funding is obtained, mentioned a downside to the procedure: Occasionally, the development department is unsuccessful in obtaining outside funds, and the show is canceled. The director was not overly concerned about this, however: "That's life," she said. But, as I discuss in Chapter 3, this is how the mix of exhibitions in museums can change, (and why curators complain).

Some museums carefully plan each year's exhibits, seeking to strike a balance between mass-appeal shows and smaller, more academic shows. For instance, the Wadsworth Atheneum implemented a program in 1980 of "at least two major presentations a year underlaid with several kinds of 'micro-exhibitions.'" (1981 p. 10) The Museum of Fine Arts in Boston also tries to keep a balance, but is more blunt about the reasons: "Shows that do not project a good attendance should exist only if balanced by 'winners,' for the expenses involved make operations of moment only to a few connoisseurs . . . a patent luxury" (1972–73, p. 15).

Note, however, that museum policy and actual practice do not always fall into line. For instance, the Fine Arts Museums of San Francisco made a commitment to mount shows of local living artists, but in 1978–80 said, "Exhibitions showcasing the work of Bay Area contemporary artists were sporadic . . . because of the disruptions caused by work surrounding the two international exhibits" (p. 28). (The two exhibits were *The Splendor of Dresden* and *Treasures of Tutankhamun*.) Also, museums changed their policies fairly often, most likely reflecting the turbulent nature of their environment.

How much evidence is there that museums use sophisticated business tools? For instance, do museums engage in "strategic decision making?" In as much as they take their environment into account and try to meet future contingencies (Middleton, 1986), many museums appear to use strategic management, large museums more so than small. The staff of large museums believe that they are able to plan for the future and explicitly state that their museums have advantages in such planning over small museums. The latter have less slack in their budgets and have fewer alternative resources. Their employees told me that they experience shifts in funding with each new presidential administration. They do not believe that there is much that they can plan; they just try to get as much funding as possible each year.

I talked with an educator who told me a story illustrating that his museum engaged in strategic decision making. His story accords well with Middleton's (1986) suggestion that appealing to new audiences is a form of strategic management. When this educator joined the museum, his department had a poor reputation. The state funding council thought that education at the museum consisted of "rich ladies talking at children." The educator went to the state council, talked to them, and came back to the museum to rewrite a mission statement for the education department. In the statement, he took into account the museum's perceptions of the community, the community's perceptions of the museum, and the museum's resources— "basic business school stuff." The museum offered a variety of programs to appeal to different members of the community and within five years, the museum's education department was considered a model for the state.

Museums have also picked up the concept of "marketing"—making their product appealing to funders and audiences. Indeed, some of the larger museums (the Metropolitan, the Art Institute of Chicago, the Whitney) appear to be quite sophisticated about it. For instance, the Detroit Institute of Art formed a long-range plan in 1982 (Detroit Institute of Art, 1983, p. 5) that "outlined sixteen priorities for the museum, including capital improvements, museum staff organization, the development program, marketing, community relations and public relations, art acquisitions, review of the financial system and controls, etc." Also in 1982, the Art Institute of Chicago hired a marketing consultant to propose ways of reaching their many constituencies. This move grew out of a two-year "Self-Study and Long-Range Plan." Interestingly, however, over-use of business terms can cause a backlash; for instance, the Metropolitan Museum has banned the word "marketing" from all their meetings.[5]

If for-profit ventures—cafeterias, restaurants, book and souvenir shops, mail-order sales—indicate strategic management (Middleton, 1986), then many museums engage in it. These activities tend to be concentrated in medium to large museums that have the resources to fund bookstores or restaurants, which have relatively high start-up costs. Museums vary in how well they manage these businesses. In addition, museums must carefully consider decisions concerning their in-house profit-makers. These enterprises are initially expensive, sometimes fail, and cause internal political problems, (because money put into restaurants means less money put into restorations). But at their best, these enterprises can be quite lucrative. The Metropolitan Museum's merchandising revenues topped $25 million in 1982 and the Smithsonian Institution grosses more than $10 million in restaurant sales each year (Skloot, 1987, pp. 381–2).

To some extent, all museums plan poorly for the future. Most museums operate on a break-even or deficit basis and do not plan for more than a few years in advance. Someday, according to worried observers, arts giving may no longer enhance corporate images. In addition, many museum personnel expressed concern over the 1986 tax law changes and were afraid that the changes would reduce their revenue. They did (Molotsky, 1993). Unfortunately, museums have not developed plans to handle such events. In other words, there is evidence that museums engage in both proactive (strategic management) and reactive (resource dependency) behaviors. Nevertheless, there is no question that museums have become more attuned to business jargon and to the profit-making (or at least break-even) mentality of other businesses.

One mechanism for this change, as previously mentioned, is the need to be accountable to business and government funders and the subsequent entry of business professionals into art museums. In addition, being in contact with and closely observing other museums stimulates some of the increase in business orientation, as museums learn from each other. DiMaggio and Powell (1983) suggest that organizations copy each other, especially under conditions of uncertainty, thereby gaining legitimacy. Through copying, they also come to resemble one another, a process known under the shorthand "mimetic isomorphism".

Yet there are differences among museums, notably between large and small museums. In part, the ability of large museums to implement business strategies stems from the fact that large museums have bigger endowments and therefore can sustain greater losses at any one time. Large museums, especially those in cities with a high concentration of corporate headquarters, have a more complex funding environment than do small museums. Large museums have a greater number of potential funders from which to draw. They are also more likely to have the internal resources necessary to engage in strategic decision making. For instance, the Detroit Institute of Art's executive vice president and chief operating officer noted, in 1984, that he had been a businessman his entire adult life and suggested: "I am fully convinced that the application of many business management practices to this museum will significantly aid in its long-term development" (Detroit Institute of Art, 1985, p. 25).

Institutional theory suggests that organizations seek legitimacy. One way to do this is to import organizational practices legitimated elsewhere. Interestingly, museums appear to have become attuned to *management* (short-term, handling internal complexities) and *strategy* (long-term, dealing with external factors) at the same time. In contrast, for-profit firms invented management first and only much later discovered strategy. Further, it is commonly noted around business schools and in for-profit firms that management and strategy can pull in conflicting directions (Miller, 1992). And it is true that attempts to solve external problems often have a detrimental effect on internal arrangements, and vice-versa. This suggests an institutional component to museums' discovery of management and strategy: Museums got both tools in a kind of "business savvy kit" given by trustees, or borrowed from other museums.

Using business procedures in museums is a strategy to make museums appear better managed to corporate funders who are concerned with the quality of management in organizations they sponsor. This is a strategy used by other nonprofits dependent on corporate donations. Powell (1988) reports that New York's WNET, the nation's largest public television station, underwent an internal reorganization from a unitary to a multi-divisional form, a form which has been institutionalized as a more efficient form for business organizations (Chandler, 1962; Fligstein, 1990; Palmer, Jennings, & Zhou, 1993). The reorganization was a conscious effort by WNET to copy rational myths from the for-profit sector in order to gain legitimacy with business executives. Even though WNET managers were unsure about the technical benefits of the reorganization, they believed the reorganization would send a strong signal to their business patrons that WNET was well-managed.

Orientation to Audiences and the Local Community

The interviews suggested another shift in museum missions, a focus on education and on reaching out to local audiences. Traditionally, museums have concentrated on building their collections, paying much less attention to mounting exhibitions. Moreover, museum programs, the educational projects a museum undertakes either in collaboration with or independent of exhibits in the museum, were largely overlooked by both the public and by curators during the middle part of this century. Indeed, many education jobs in museums have been created in the past thirty years; and current positions are more important than the traditional minor jobs of arranging tours for school children. There is some evidence that education departments grew during the transition period; for instance, the NEA (1974, p. 42) reports that 61 percent of art museums increased their educational activities between 1966 and 1974, 34 percent remained the same, and only 3 percent decreased such activity.

Museum education is not a new phenomenon. Museums have always had education staffs and early museums used education as a justification for their existence (see DiMaggio, 1982a, b). However, it was not until the 1960s—when all institutions were under pressure to become less elitist—that museums began to broaden their programs. At first, the changes involved programs for school children. Such programs tried to bring under-privileged children to museums, and unlike earlier programs, tried to bring them back for several sessions so that they could really soak up the arts. Later, in the 1970s, educators began to wonder if their changes should sweep even wider, and they began to try to attract broader audiences of adults into museums.

Museums are also in the process of redefining what should be provided to museum visitors to create an aesthetic experience. An educator described a seminar her museum planned for its curators. Curators were asked what they thought would constitute a perfect exhibit. They imagined a single painting hanging on the white wall of an empty room. There would be a chair or a bench so that the observer could sit and contemplate the work. There would be no wall label, not even a tiny one, to distract from the painting.

Then the same curators watched ordinary people in an exhibit. People like wall labels and spend a good deal of time in galleries reading, rather than looking at art. The standard wall label in museums includes the artist's name, the title and materials of the object, and information on patrons who donated the piece or funds to buy it. Ordinary people read these labels, but find them incomplete. They prefer descriptive panels, many of them with plenty of didactic information that help them put the art into context. This exercise gave curators a better understanding of how people who come to art without a strong art historical background approach exhibits. It also reduced some of the tension (in this museum at least) over disagreements about exhibition design.

As exhibition designers come to understand how audiences relate to art, and how they enjoy background information and aesthetic instruction, they create "rational myths" about how to organize exhibitions. Woodcome (1995) describes how curators and educators in the Museum of Fine Arts in Boston used these new rational myths of exhibition design when they reinstalled a permanent exhibit of Nubian art. The exhibit contains detailed panels on Nubian customs and identity. The exhibit also includes a *model* of an ancient Nubian burial pyramid. This model was built by museum designers, yet it is enclosed in an exhibition case and takes a prominent place in the gallery. Inclusion of this object blurs the boundary between aesthetic and didactic objects.

Are these changes related to institutional funders? Certainly they are to some degree. State arts councils are very interested in funding museums that bring in a diverse audience (DiMaggio, 1991b). This is true for federal agencies as well (DiMaggio, 1991b): One educator told me that she was often overlooked in grant applications sent out by other departments. She asked the director to include education in their grants, and the museum agreed to her request when it lost an important NEA grant because the museum did not have a related public program. Currently, she asserted, education is another "line item" on their NEA and NEH grant applications—a practice that she said is common in many museums.

Another educator believes that museums have come to recognize their "responsibility to the community," and have offered more programs, lectures and community events. She believes that museums should express care and concern for the community, but that many museums are concerned with public programs "for the wrong reasons," that is, because their funding depends on it.

Have such programs been effective in broadening audiences? Educators answer with a conditional affirmative. The programs have reached "pockets" of individuals, one educator explains, but the people who come to the American Indian show one week do not come back the next week for the Irish music festival. Her personal justification for the pocket approach is that in the 1980s "we are moving away from the melting pot" and toward an understanding that it is important for individuals to retain their ethnic heritage. (See Garfias, 1991; Yoshitomi, 1991.)

Here, once again, the interviews suggest that curatorial interests conflict with new foci in the museum, in this case, the museum's commitment to the public. The effort to broaden audiences has changed the content of programs. For instance, museums have increased the number of exhibits designed to appeal to minority groups. One curator expressed concern about this trend: She believes that it is an important step for museums, but in their "rush" to appeal to minority groups she feels that museums have overlooked art historical concerns. If a curator objects to a minority-oriented show, even on the curatorial grounds that it does not enhance the scholarship in this area, he will be labeled "narrow minded, snobbish and elitist."

In addition, she believes that such shows do not really broaden audiences; for instance, a show on African art attracted "yuppie blacks," not those who live in poor areas. The curator's objection embodies another intraorganizational conflict, this time between educators and curators, and is further evidence of the tension between elitist scholarly concerns and efforts to broaden the museum's public.

Choice

Over the past twenty years, then, museums have dramatically increased the number of exhibitions they mount. In addition, they have implemented larger and more ambitious education programs and have widened their role and responsibilities to the community. All of these changes have led museums to focus more on attracting audiences. DiMaggio (1991a) argues that museums have become increasingly oriented toward not one but three different pairs of museum personnel and outsiders: curators and patrons, education and outreach staff and disenfranchised publics that would not visit museums without encouragement, and marketing and membership personnel and the general museum-going public. DiMaggio points out that the first two have existed—and have been in conflict (Zolberg, 1986, 1981)—in museums since at least the 1920s, but that the third "submuseum" has emerged only recently. DiMaggio calls the first pair the *patron's submuseum.* This coalition is at the core of the museum and revolves around acquisitions, conservation, and research. The second pair is the *social submuseum.* Here, education and outreach departments try to engage people who don't attend museums (the *non*-public?). The goal of this submuseum is to teach, at a rudimentary level, art appreciation, which can uplift the masses. The social submuseum was institutionalized in the earliest American museums, along with the patron's submuseum. The third pair, the *marketing submuseum* involves the marketing and membership departments and colleagues in other departments, especially those who plan exhibitions and programs. These groups are oriented to the museum public, people who have the propensity to attend museums, and who may be regular visitors or members. The goal of the marketing submuseum is to lure the public to the museum. This may sound like the social submuseum, but there is an important difference. The social submuseum thinks of its public as an educational target, as people who would benefit by learning about art. The marketing submuseum, by contrast, thinks of its public as a sales target. The key is to "market" the museum's "products" to the pubic, so they will buy admissions and memberships. This submuseum developed in the era of institutional funding, as museums drew upon organizational ideas from the business world.

Museum managers redefine museum missions. Museums become less elitist, more popular institutions that are increasingly geared toward income and funding. Further, external funding encourages professionalization, changing museums from scholarly to managerial organizations.

During the period in this study, directors and trustees have redefined their museum's role in the community. I will quote two passages at length to show the similarity of the demands on two museums, the Cleveland Museum and the Metropolitan Museum of Art, and the different solutions each set of directors and trustees has suggested. The differences here reflect museum focus, size, location, and funding mix (Cleveland is well-endowed), the social structure of the two cities (Cleveland has a cohesive business upper class and New York has much more fragmented elites), and most importantly, differences in time (1964 versus 1970). There is a degree of organizational choice involved in defining an organization's responsibilities, and the directors and board members have some leeway in trying to meet external demands. In 1964, Sherman E. Lee, director, and Emery May Norweb, president of the Cleveland Museum noted that museums were coming under increasing pressure because of the "cultural explosion" of the 1960s. Their solution was to propose that museums avoid the shrapnel of demands bursting from the explosion:

> There are numerous current signs that more than art museums are needed for art. . . . If we insist on the museum being all things to all people—being completely representative of the new, and yet properly conservative of our heritage; a place of contemplation where the essential private dialogue between the object and the beholder can occur, but also a place of humming activity whether primarily concerned with the visual arts or not—then we insist upon something we cannot afford in matters of quality and excellence—the package deal, the all-purpose pill, an art supermarket.
>
> There are those who might prefer just that. Indeed the fantastic technology of our age may well have convinced many that what was is "dead and gone"; all that remains is to come. But the very existence of such a viewpoint, however right or wrong, is just the most powerful reason for the museum to reaffirm and perform its fundamental responsibility—the presentation, display, and elucidation of man's heritage. . . . For the current increased needs of art and of man for art, for the instruments of the much-desired and now inevitable cultural expansion, we need more and varied institutions and organs. Especially, we need, as a beginning, adequate visual education in our schools. But above all, *we shall need the art museum, dedicated to the conservation of those sources of artistic power which history and criticism have indicated to be essential parts of our still-living past.* (Cleveland Museum, 1965, p. 142, emphasis added.)

Thus, the leaders of the Cleveland museum assert that the way to handle multiple pressures is to stay the course. Their conservative approach keeps the museum in its traditional role.

Thomas Hoving, director, and Douglas Dillon, president of the Metropolitan, write of similar pressures, but a different solution:

> One hears on various sides voices of criticism and dissent about museums. . . . Often these voices are responsible, seeking appropriate changes in institutions not generally known for their desire to change. Sometimes these voices are irresponsible, calling for the abandonment or even destruction of museums. . . . On one side, one hears that the dignified Metropolitan Museum should be of the most elite intellectual character, without involvement in education—a place removed, staid, and quiescent where nothing experimental, social, or political should be tolerated. On another side one hears that the Metropolitan must never fall into the mistake of catering to the uninformed middle class. On still another side it is proclaimed that the Museum should cut off all vestiges of elitism and be purely a living cultural service, with no old-fashioned concepts of collecting impeding its social significance. Still another view proclaims that the proper role of the Museum is to be merely a community center, with primary emphasis upon dealing with the problems of local neighborhoods.
>
> *The truth is that the Metropolitan must be all these things —but in the right balance.* It must embody intellectual elitism at least in one of its missions, namely, in the acquisition and preservation of the greatest works of art available. In refining our collections, neither committees, not community

> groups, nor laymen can be of much help in deciding what is great or good, lasting or ephemeral. Only the gifted and well-trained connoisseur can do that. But the Museum's need for the highest specialization in one part of its complex existence does not mean that it should shun what pleases the public in other parts of its being. The Metropolitan must also be a community-oriented organism, eager to teach, amuse, and relate to a wide audience. (Metropolitan Museum of Art, 1970, pp. 6–7, emphasis added.)

As Zolberg (1986, p. 186) writes, museums increasingly experience external demands and the "dissatisfaction that these demands reveal represents both internal dilemmas and the changing environmental pressures that impinge on art museums."

Internal Conflict

The introduction of staff with specialties in business, accounting, education, fundraising, and public relations bring those different perspectives into the museum. In combination with a larger choice of funders, these different perspectives have created conflict within the organization as business-oriented administrators and art historically trained curators pursue divergent goals. As I have shown, different types of funders have different goals or objectives in funding museums. Museum personnel—most notably, directors, curators, and board members—must balance the demands of each funder to keep the museum viable. Further, within the museum, directors, curators, administrators and board members vie for the ascendancy of their own perspectives.

That the addition of new types of organizational participants has created conflict is not surprising. Many theorists view organizations as coalitions that make disparate demands on corporate resources (Child, 1972; Cyert & March, 1963; Pfeffer & Salancik, 1978). In the case of the museum, at least two internal coalitions battle for control over exhibitions: the curatorial faction and the administrative faction. Curators demand that exhibitions have scholarly merit (a traditional yardstick of exhibition quality and also a key determinant of curatorial reputation). Historically, this group has been dominant in the museum. The administrative faction—now coming into its own, but not usually recognized as "in charge" of the museum—tries to keep the museum's books in the black, allocates resources, distributes press releases, and handles the demands of the funders. These two groups have never been fully in accord (Allen, 1974), but the rise of new funders has created more options for museum personnel, and thus more conflict between the two coalitions. The history of museums is replete with conflicts between populists and elitists who clashed over the central mission of museums, between elite patrons and curators, and among trustees who did not see eye to eye.

I interviewed a variety of museum decision makers—directors, curators, and educators—who did not always agree with one another. This tendency to disagree indicates the level of consensus within the museum itself. In other words, if curators and directors belong to different, and perhaps conflicting, subcultures in the museum, they will be likely to view the impact of funding from different angles and will report disparate opinions on the funders. .

Internal conflict is clearly evident in the interviews. Although curators, directors, and educators held disparate views of each type of funder, the differences were not manifested in the substance of the comments as much as in the interpretation of the substance. The interviews suggest a tendency among curators to perceive corporations as bad for museums, and for directors to see them as good. Museum personnel mentioned government as a very useful, if nontraditional, patron of museums, and they believe that upper-class, old-money individuals are natural allies of the museum world. These beliefs suggest that the elite roots of the museum are still strong, especially for the curators.

In the interviews, curators were particularly likely to take aim at corporate funding, noting its "distorting" effects. Indeed, it is safe to say that most curators are hostile to corporations, accusing corporations of malicious self-interest. Directors are more receptive to and accepting of corporate funders. Directors are concerned with financial aspects of the organization; thus they recognize that museums could not stay open, at least at their current level of operations, without the new funders. Directors point out how much corporate funding has allowed them to expand and grow and offer more services to the public than ever before. Curators argue that this is exactly the point: museums have grown in the wrong direction, focusing too much on the public, at the expense of art and scholarship.

The new emphasis on blockbusters, theme exhibitions, and popular subject matter does not make most curators happy. Curators disparagingly refer to theme shows as "The Dog in Art" shows. The broadening of exhibition audiences is viewed not as evidence of the "democratization" of culture, but rather as a treacly distortion of the true function of museums.

Curators talked frequently about the demands of corporate funders. They felt that corporations make especially heavy demands on art museums. For instance, corporations want to have their names first and in large print on catalogs, even if they give less money to the show than other contributors. Corporations can do this by sponsoring the production of the catalog. For instance, the 1988 Degas show at the Metropolitan Museum was funded by United Technologies and the National Endowment for the Arts, and indemnified by the Federal Council for the Arts and Humanities. The beautiful exhibition catalog was funded just by United Technologies, however, so the only exhibition funder mentioned in the catalog was United Technologies.

Corporations have designed advertising posters naming only themselves as funders and have made posters in "poor taste" (according to curators) or that "do not match the spirit of the exhibition." Curators felt that corporations are insensitive to the needs of individuals and to professional standards. For instance, one corporation forced a museum to break a contract with a catalog designer so that the corporation could handle the design of the catalog with its own choice of personnel.

The government makes very different demands on museums than do corporations, according to museum personnel. Directors and curators rarely mentioned restrictions or impositions from the federal government, especially compared to the frequency of their comments about corporate funding. Interestingly, curators seldom discussed the fifty percent of the project not covered by Endowment funds, even though the NEA and NEH require museums to find matching support for most exhibition grants. The Endowments also require museums to submit receipts or vouchers before payment, and, just like corporations, they now require that their names be put on all documents connected with the exhibit.

Museum personnel liked the NEA, although some conservative respondents suggested that big government, which includes arts funding, is wrong. There was very little conflict in museums over government funding. Chapter 3 demonstrates that government has been as responsible for fostering popular exhibitions as corporations. That government agencies are interested in art scholarship seems to mitigate government's interest in audiences. All museum personnel also tended to regard wealthy patrons favorably.[6]

Why did respondents speak of individual donors so favorably and corporations so unfavorably? Though there are several possibilities, I believe that it is because traditional elites are perceived as less of a threat to museum autonomy than are corporations. This perception is particularly interesting because the elite funder is more likely to wish to "be a part of" the museum. Hence, elite funders make more demands on the museum than other funders, although in some ways elite individuals may be more pliable, in the curator's view, than other funders. Since elites are driven by their desire to gain status from their knowledge of, not just their association with, art, they often rely on information from curators and directors. Patrons seek advice from museum experts on collecting new pieces and conserving those they own, and they often learn about art at museum functions, such as public lectures or private receptions. Elite individuals often sit on museum boards. One might expect less criticism of funders so closely connected to the museum. Though again, this lack of criticism may have more to do with curatorial perceptions of who is currently the greatest threat to museum autonomy.

The curatorial perception that corporations have no business in museum funding is a particularly interesting one. The managerial revolution of the twentieth century has changed corporations from firms controlled by charismatic and wealthy individuals to firms controlled by upper-middle class professionals. Yet, early patrons of the arts—the Rockefellers and Mellons, for example—were America's captains of industry. And some turn-of-the-century elite individuals had notoriously bad taste. Mrs. Leland Stanford is one example: She commissioned a life-sized painting of all her jewelry before she sold the collection and donated the proceeds to Stanford University. Early industrialist philanthropists and today's corporate representatives occupy similar organizational positions, and one wonders why museum curators see such a difference between the two. Indeed, it is relatively easy to think of corporations, or especially corporate representatives, as analogous to elite funders: Both have a lot of money, fund art to increase their status, often know little about art (this may have been especially true about the elite funders a century ago), and act either on whim or on expert advice. And increasingly, corporate representatives are replacing wealthy philanthropists on museum boards.

One solid, practical reason for concerns about corporations was mentioned by one museum director. The new corporate patrons are less stable than the old individual patrons. In the past, museum directors worried whether the children of benefactors would carry on the family tradition. Today, museum directors wonder whether economics will allow for continued corporate support from year to year. (This was not a reason curators cited, however.)

In the interviews, I asked some curators about the "professionalization" of museum management. I received a very cool response. One curator subsequently told me that she "bristles" at the use of the word professionalization. She explained that curators, usually trained in art history, find those with business or other outside training to be lacking in "professional standards." For instance, public relations personnel may not understand the value art historians attach to identifying objects used in advertising posters or of labeling "details" as such (important, given art history's concern with composition and balance). A curator reported conflicts over these very issues with his public relations representative. Although the representative was an "expert" at his job, he had not learned the standards and conventions important to art historians. In advertising posters, as in any reproduction of an art work, one must identify what the object is, its title, artist, size, and materials (to put it into a context) and the museum or private collection to which it belongs (to enable one to study it in person, should one desire), and it is "common courtesy" to identify the donor of the piece if it is part of a museum collection. Note that all these criteria are important to art historians, museum curators in particular, but that they may not be important to the general public.

A story related to me concerned a poster that a corporation was preparing. In their first poster mock-up, the corporate designers took a pair of sixteenth-century gloves and made "ears" out of them—"distorting the gloves beyond recognition" and removing their intrinsic beauty, in the curator's view—and drew a "Matisse face" around the ears. A public relations officer from the museum gave a tentative approval of the poster, but at the urging of the curator, he checked with the museum from which the gloves were borrowed. The lending museum declined to allow the use of their gloves in that manner. In the corporation's second-draft poster, the designers took an enlargement of an "exquisite" piece of lace and put a section of it on the poster. The corporation didn't want to identify the piece (nor, by implication, the donors of the lace). In fact, the corporation did not even want to identify the piece of lace as a detail. All of this information clutters the poster, but is "essential information" in the eyes of art historians. Again, the public relations officer gave his approval of the poster. The curator was not pleased that the corporation did not understand art historical issues, but said that was perhaps understandable enough. The curator's real worry about these incidents was that a museum representative did not understand them.

Along the same lines, an educator told me that a local newspaper ran a story from a press release from the museum's public relations department, and that the release referred to the artist's works as "paintings" when they were really "watercolors." She told me that she knew the public would not notice but she said, "It's irritating, well, because it just isn't accurate."

These curators were using the word "professional" in a different manner than I had been. I had meant "professionalization" to refer to academic credentialing, whatever the subject (Collins, 1979; Larson, 1977). The curators, however, meant two things. First, they used "professional" to refer to the careful adherence to specific art historical standards that curators observe. Second, they understood "professionalization of museums" to mean the introduction of outsiders who specialize in fields other than art history. Trained art historians consider themselves professional (and have done so since the 1920s). It appears that most curators today are required to have advanced degrees, usually a Ph.D. in art history, whereas just 20 years ago, individuals with B.A. or M.A. degrees could become curators through, essentially, an apprentice system. Nevertheless, the curators' reactions are evidence of the increase in the number of "outsiders" on museums' staffs and the ensuing competition between two groups of highly trained individuals—the classic conflict between craftsmen or engineers (quality-oriented) and management (profit-oriented). In this case, art historians are competing with business specialists for occupational prestige and organizational power.

Conflicts often occur over "marketing" decisions. As curators' "horror stories" about public relations departments and advertising posters illustrate, many curators feel that they are being undermined by their own institutions. (Staff in three out of five museums where I conducted interviews complained about advertising posters.) Further, museum directors are not always trying to please curators. In one museum, the staff complained about a series of posters, and the director responded by telling the staff, "Look, they aren't for you!" The director asserted that the posters were designed for a particular audience less sophisticated than curators, and "that was that." The director refused to hear further complaints from curators.

Boards of directors must mediate between these two groups. Changes in the composition of boards, especially the trend to include more business people (who may have less sympathy for curators), may also have heightened the conflict.

Conflict Embodied in Organizational Structure

The organizational structure of museums illustrates the conflict between administration and curatorship functions. I use the organizational charts, described in interviews, of two museums to demonstrate this point. In one museum, the "business" side of the organization is separate from the "art" side. The president presides over the public relations, development, membership, and finance departments. Ten curatorial departments, conservation, education and the registrar report to the director. A small liaison department, Exhibitions, handles communication between the two sides of the museum, assisting curators in their interactions with the development department.[7] (See Figure 4-1.)

In the second museum, the organizational chart had changed recently. Before the change, the director presided over the curatorial department. All the other departments—development, accounting, and grounds and maintenance—were considered "support departments" and were under the curatorial department on the organizational chart. After the change, the director presided over four equal departments: development, curatorial, accounting, and grounds and maintenance. Between the four departments and the director were two associate directors: One was associate director of collections and exhibitions from the curatorial department and the other was associate director of programs and marketing from the development department. In addition, the education department was moved from the curatorial to the development office. The curator who told me of these changes, a "sad ballet" in her words, claimed that no one in the development office had ever worked in an art museum before (Figure 4-2). This is happening in other types of museums as well. See Honan (1990), who describes how the Department of Public Programs has been placed above curatorial departments in the Field Museum of Natural History in Chicago.

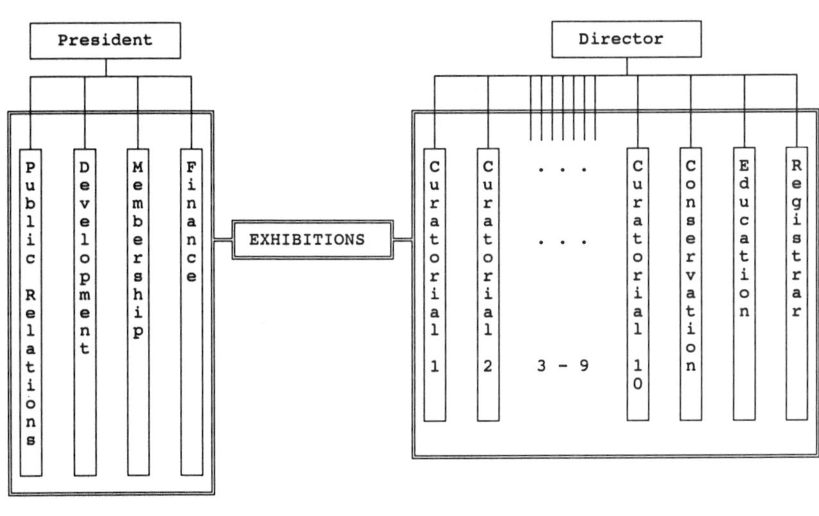

Figure 4-1. Organizational Chart of Museum A.
Source: Interview, Director Museum A

The change in the organizational charts can be seen as an effort to "buffer" the core of the organization (Thompson, 1967), that is, to protect the core personnel—curators—from fluxes in external conditions by separating and setting aside departments, such as development, membership, and public relations that handle actors in the environment. Further, the changes represent organizational isomorphism with the *environment* (as opposed to that with other organizations) described by Meyer (Meyer & Rowan, 1981; Meyer & Scott, 1992)—as the museum's external environment becomes more complex, the internal arrangements become articulated to deal with more environmental complexity.[8] Nonprofit organizations often come to mirror the complexity in their environment (Alexander, forthcoming).

The organizational structure of each of these museums also embodies the conflict over power and resources between the business professionals and the art professionals. An interesting parallel may be drawn to Fligstein's (1987, 1990) strategic contingency research: In the mid-1900s, American industry shifted from recruiting upper management primarily from production departments to recruiting upper management mostly from marketing departments. Fligstein argues that this change was rooted in a shift of power within organizations, as marketing departments sur-

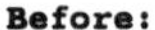

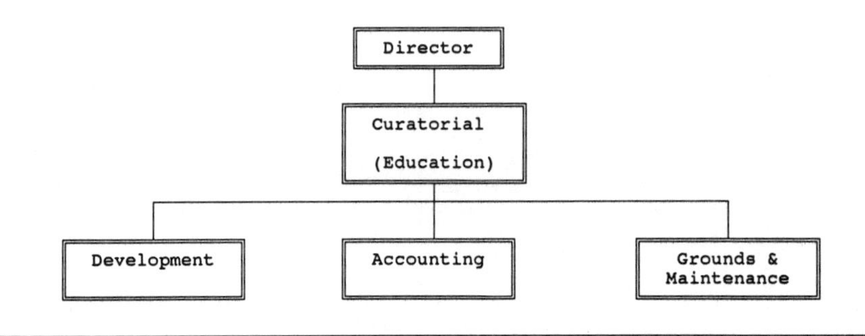

After:

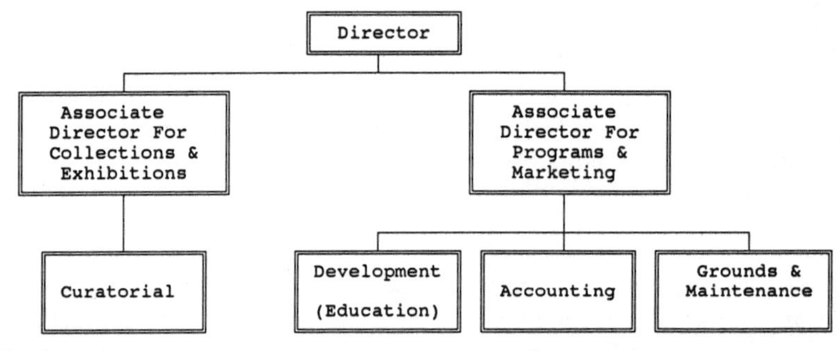

Figure 4-2. Change in the Organizational Chart of Museum B
Source: Interview, Curator, Museum B

passed production departments in their ability to understand and control environmental uncertainty. American museums may now be experiencing a similar change. As museums become more dependent on outside funding, uncertainty shifts away from concerns about the authenticity of a painting or the history of a sculpture to concerns about financial resources and financial solvency. As a result, directors and administrators will become more valuable than curators in handling environmental uncertainty for museums, and curators will lose power as compared to these other coalitions.

Pfeffer and Salancik (1978, Chapter 9) also suggest that organizational environments affect the selection of executives. They argue that the environment affects the distribution of power within the organization. The dominant coalition controls the organization and selects or influences the selection of new managers. These managers, in turn, make decisions about strategy and structure. Museums have only recently been in a position where alternative funders are available to them. Museum directors have become increasingly business oriented; they are currently drawn mainly from the ranks of art historians, but in the future may increasingly come from non-arts tracks, perhaps from development departments. Business backgrounds are already noticeable in the lower rungs of museums and among museum presidents (who are often trustees drawn from the business world). Curators still study art history, but many other museum personnel have their specialties elsewhere: in public education, accounting, and public relations, to name a few. Indeed one might predict that in the future museum directors may even be found to hold M.B.A. rather than M.F.A. degrees. Thomas Krens at the Guggenheim is an example. His degree is an M.P.P.M. (Masters of Public and Private Management) from Yale. Most holders of this degree go into finance or for-profit consulting. Krens is a maverick, and he is shaking up the museum world (see Prod'homme, 1992).

Institutional Carriers of Conflicting Visions

The conflicts described above pit actors with different institutional and aesthetic visions against one another (Zolberg, 1981). Each faction carries a vision of museums; these visions actually represent different models of museums—what they are, what they are supposed to do, how they should be "constructed" as organizations. These are powerful cultural ideas, rooted in an individual's background, training, and organizational position. Normative visions held by various actors in museums—a curator's orientation to art history and scholarship, for instance, or the bottom-line mentality of an administrator—are institutionally composed. These actors compete for the privilege of defining what a museum is, a quiet place for study and conservation or a busy place for marketing a product to an audience.

This internal conflict between curators and directors is most certainly an organization level effect of funding. I believe that the heightening of tension between the art and administration camps arises from assaults on curatorial autonomy. Curators, as a group, are losing power in the museum to other parties. Indeed, in interviews, some curators painted a picture of an idealized past world where scholarly curators worked under the benign care and feeding of nice, rich patrons, and where commercial pressures had no impact. Elite funders symbolize idyllic past museums where curators were kings (They were mainly men.). Though this past world certainly never existed, its power as symbol is quite real.

Becker (1982) discusses the vehemence with which aesthetic choices are argued:

> The heat in discussion of aesthetics usually exists because what is being decided is not only an abstract philosophical question but also some allocation of valuable resources (p. 135).

The conflict between curators and administrators, however, is not merely a conflict over organizational resources. Rather, curators and administrators hold different beliefs about *what a museum is*, how it should operate, how it should relate to the public. Curators view museums as places for scholarship, quiet and subdued. Acquisitions should be of primary importance alongside conserving those pieces already owned by the museum. Museums should spend money on research leading to scholarly catalogues. Museum visitors should respect the dignity of the art on the walls. Preferably, these people will already know a great deal about art and will come to gaze upon the same objects again and again. The perfect way to display art is on a plain wall with only a small plaque containing identifying information. The room should be devoid of all didactic information since the extra words will take away from the direct interaction of the work with the viewer.

Directors are articulating a different vision: a place of lively activity, with special exhibits designed to draw in varied audiences and occasionally even crowds. Didactic information, including wall essays on historical context, is seen as a way of attracting a variety of visitors, including those with little background in art. Funding is extraordinarily important in maintaining this frenetic level of activity. Directors do not disparage traditional concerns of collecting, conserving, and cataloguing; however, given the emphasis on additional functions, such as education, audiences, and funding, the traditional concerns are no longer first priority.

Curators and directors are drawing on different normative visions of museums. Moreover, the rational myths each party draws on are situated in a different institutional logic. Institutional logics are "both supra-organizational patterns of activity through which humans conduct their material life in time and space, and symbolic systems through which they categorize that activity and infuse it with meaning," (Friedland & Alford, 1991, p. 232). Institutional logics are systems of rational myths; there are several logics in American society. Friedland and Alford (1991) list five broad logics: the state, the family, religion, the market, and democracy. In museums, the new visions empowered by shifts in the environment draw upon a business logic, one geared toward managing an organization with the bottom line indicating success. The older, curatorial vision draws upon a professional, scholarly logic, analogous to the vision professors in universities hold. In the scholarly vision, professionals should be free to pursue truth and beauty and to perform their jobs as they know best, without interference.

DiMaggio (1988b) calls for an understanding of institutional and political models as complementary tools. DiMaggio believes that rational myths arise through "institutional projects" analogous to "professional projects" (Larson, 1977).

> Put simply, the argument . . . is that institutionalization is a product of the political efforts of actors to accomplish their ends and that the success of an institutionalization project and the form that the resulting institution takes depends upon the relative power of the actors who support, oppose, or otherwise strive to influence it. (DiMaggio, 1988b, p. 13)

Fligstein (1990) studies the changes in the background, and hence, the normative visions, of managers in large business firms in the United States since 1880. He argues that change is precipitated by a crisis at the field level, often accompanied by state action. The crisis, in other words, affects all organizations of a certain type, not just particular individual organizations. This crisis shifts the balance of power within individual organizations and sends field-level leaders scurrying for new strategies and structures—and rationales to legitimize them. In this way, business leaders institutionalize new rational myths: new organizational forms and procedures.

These new rational myths are based on ideas held by participants in the organization, and are shaped by a particular world view, a "conception of control," which is a totalizing view created by the positions those individuals hold in the organization. Managers' perspectives are

> bounded by the internal logic of their organizations, what those actors know, how they perceive the world, and what they define as appropriate organizational behavior. . . . Actors are assumed to create rationales for their behavior on the basis of how they view the world. Their goals and strategies result from those views. . . . The construction of courses of action depend greatly on the position of actors within the structure of the organization, which form the interest and identities of actors. (pp. 10–11)

Normative visions (a conception of control, in Fligstein's terms) are institutionalized rational myths that shape interests (Scott, 1987). But interests shape rational myths as well, when actors endeavor to institute organizational structure that is based on their conception of control. The process is profoundly dialectical (Sewell, 1992).

This research suggests that there are profound struggles within museums over underlying justifications for museums and over museum roles. Structural features adopted by museums to signal their legitimacy are hotly debated by curators and administrators. In museums, the administrative faction has been empowered and has been working to institutionalize its vision in museums. Curators, however, are not toothless (yet). These situations suggest that institutionalization is shaped by powerful actors who are sometimes quite cognizant of the implications of their efforts.

Funding and Conflicting Normative Visions

The growth of corporate and government funders represents, symbolically, and is in fact responsible for, the curators' loss of power. This is not true for educators—just the opposite: They have gained power and legitimacy in museums as a result of government pressures for education programs. Directors, too, are still powerful, but they are now, as Peterson (1986) notes, administrators rather than flamboyant impresarios.

Curators see the new funders, especially corporations, as almost *evil.* Corporations represent service to Mammon by directors and development officers. Curators are scholars, art historians whose prestige rests on the quality of their written work and the art historical merit of the exhibitions they mount. Their prestige does not rest on how many people come to their exhibits, or whether the exhibits finish in the black.

In the past, curators had a great deal of power within the museum. Today, even though there are more curators, and they have more work to do, curators must share power with administrators, sometimes as actual subordinates to public relations and accounting personnel. Curators are, in many ways, better off today than they were in the past: better paid, with amplified roles and numbers, more insulated from conflict with external parties, and less subject to the whims of directors and patrons. Yet curators no longer "call the shots" and there is some evidence that today's museum directors are less often culled from the ranks of curators (DiMaggio, 1987a), indicating that fewer people holding curatorial views run museums.

Although curators have not been losers on an absolute level, they certainly hold less power and authority than they used to have relative to other museum factions. Indeed, curators have become "deskilled" as some of the jobs they used to do in museums (e.g., most of the administrative work) have been given to other specialists. Curator career stability may have fallen off. Although museums still hire staff curators, some museums have decided to hire curators on so called "soft money," money received from grants for specific exhibitions. When that money runs out or the exhibition is completed, the curator will be out of a job unless more external funds can be found to pay his or her salary.

Museum directors usually view corporations and government as valuable resources for the museum. And indeed they are: Museums are bigger, more active and more viable than they have been in the past. Curators, however, view the new funders dimly because these funders symbolize—and are literally responsible for—the reduction of curatorial power within the museum.

As mentioned, these findings fit with strategic contingency theory, which suggests that subunits within organizations that are best positioned to handle uncertainty in the environment (in this case, sources of money) are the units that tend to have more power within the organization. On a grander scale, however, the loss of curatorial power is evidence of a general social trend in which power based on social connections is replaced by more organizationally based and specialized—hence limited—power. In a study of arts organization directors, DiMaggio (1987a, pp. 14–16) shows the change from appointments based on social background to hiring based on educational attainment. In art museums, relatively few people who became directors before 1963 held advanced degrees. A large proportion of these older directors had graduated from Ivy League colleges, and most of their grandparents were born in the United States, suggesting they came from established, elite backgrounds. Younger cohorts of directors (those appointed after 1968) tended to hold Ph.D.s (55 percent, three times the Ph.D. holders in the older cohort). The younger ones also came from a wider variety of colleges and fewer had grandparents born in the United States.

The roots of this shift were first noticed by Weber (1978) who described rationalization in western society, the replacement of traditional authority with rational-legal authority, and bureaucratization in organizations. The change is also related to changes in the structure of elites, from local families to a geographically mobile managerial elite (Dahrendorf, 1959; Domhoff, 1967; Useem, 1980). Rationalized and specialized roles reduce the capriciousness of people in power, but as Weber points out, well-defined roles also constrain the actors occupying the roles.

As Gans (1974) argues for popular culture, displaced elites vilify the symbols of their perceived loss of status. Curators disparage corporations and corporately sponsored art as a way of expressing discontent over their loss of power and status in museums relative to other factions. The reactions of curators are similar to the reactions of intellectuals against popular culture:

> The existence of the critique has less to do with changes in high and popular culture than with the position of the intellectuals in society . . . over time, the critique has appeared when intellectuals have lost power and the status that goes with the power, and it has virtually disappeared when intellectuals have gained power and status. (Gans, 1974, p 7)

Interestingly, it is corporations that bear the brunt of curators' ire. Yet it is the *system* of institutional funding that has led to many of the changes in museums, and government orientation toward audiences is as strong as the corporate focus, when measured by support of blockbuster and traveling exhibitions. So the hostility toward corporations is not the result solely of the deskilling of curators. It also has to do with the fact that corporations' fundamental goals do not overlap with those of curators. In contrast, curators are not opposed to exhibitions funding by the NEA, an organization which, at least on some fronts, shares the art historical values of great art and scholarly exhibitions.

Compare this with the situation of teachers in schools. In the early 1950s, teachers' colleges and teachers' groups began to commission what became a series of occupational status studies. These studies were propelled by the perception that teachers were losing status. None of these studies, however, showed a decline in status. The problem for teachers was that schools were becoming rationalized and included as a part of formal organizations (school districts), rather than existing as single units in the community (one room schoolhouses). Formal organizations protect teachers, pay them more, reduce conflict with the local community, and insulate teachers. But teachers did not recognize these advantages. The insulating effects of rationalization were experienced as stifling effects, and teachers believed they were losing status.[9]

Innovation

The changes in museums are related to changes in their environment. But change is not a passive process. On the contrary, what strikes me is the *opportunities* that new funding has given museum decision makers to *rewrite* museum missions, to *change* the museum's role in the community, and to *establish* new exhibition formats and subjects. The multiple constituencies involved in the funding environment allow decision makers to innovate in order to sustain their own vision while satisfying the demands of their funders. These instances of innovation are not adequately addressed by resource dependency theory. This book considers an important management question: "How do museums use conflicting pressures as an opportunity to innovate and improve the organization?"[10] This poses the issue of "strategic choice" (Child, 1972).

What happens in museums is not simple acquiescence to funder pressures. Instead, funders offer inducements to museums to which managers adapt in a context of internal dissension, by fashioning the most palatable redefinition of missions that is consistent with their organization's needs and the resources available to it. Chapter 3 suggested that museum personnel innovate when it comes to exhibition design and funding. Though funding encourages larger, more popular exhibitions, museums clearly have some discretion in balancing large, crowd-drawing exhibitions with much smaller ones that lack external support. Museums may thus be able to strike a balance between mass-appeal shows and smaller, more academic shows.

Organizations have greater autonomy when more than one actor controls a crucial resource. In museums, a larger variety of funders allows museum personnel to pick and choose constraints in order to broaden their choices. For example, if a curator wanted to mount an exhibition of American art, but needed funding, she might approach the federal government for a grant (arguing that the exhibition will appeal to a wide variety of the American people), a private individual (arguing that several pieces of his personal collection would be invaluable to the exhibition), or a corporation (arguing that sponsorship will provide a patriotic image). Contradictory pressures permit curators to innovate aesthetically, directors and board members to redefine museum domains, and museum managers, in general, to establish shared assumptions that are part of the museum field.

In absolute terms, curators may not lose, and may actually gain from the influx of new funders. Curators' relative loss causes them to view new funders negatively, (especially corporations who rarely have the art critical concerns that the NEA sometimes shares with curators). More importantly, it also spurs them to work to discover forms of art that satisfy these external funders but allow them their curatorial vision. Their ability to find creative resolutions to the problems brought about by new funding patterns affects both the content of exhibitions and aesthetic definitions. Curators make innovative aesthetic choices, incorporating new ideas of three aspects of art: (1) New ideas of what art is, (2) new ideas of what scholarly questions can be addressed to an existing, recognized body of art, and (3) new ideas of what existing art has been ignored or what unrecognized or undervalued art should be elevated into the canon of high art. Curators use these innovations to resolve the conflicting interests of the different funders, and at the same time they use the innovations to reclaim autonomy they might otherwise lose to external constituents. This ability may appear to increase their importance to the core functions of museums, though curators may not receive the recognition they deserve for their innovations.

Museums in Organizational Fields

Institutional theory examines organizations not only as units but also at a network level called a "societal sector" or an "organizational field."[11] An organizational field is a network of organizations from the same industry or centered on a core domain. A field constitutes a shared environment for the organizations within it. The field of interest here includes: museums; their funders, patrons and members; art schools; museum associations; galleries; critics; artists; and a wide variety of other interested parties. This network of organizations and actors is tied together in complex ways.

But a field is more than a network of organizations; a field also encompasses cultural and historical features (Scott, 1983). Networks of organizations that interact frequently—those within the same sector—tend to coalesce around a common perception of their core domain. Common understandings of how things operate, how to view a problem, and other shared assumptions, such as perceptions of what is the "right" number of exhibitions to mount each year, become part of the field. The cultural aspect is crucial to the definition of a sector: A network of organizations does not comprise a field unless a cultural component exists to some degree. (There can be various degrees of consensus on cultural elements, and fields can enclose subcultures, just as networks can vary on the tightness or density of their links.) Further, the array of network features and the character of cultural elements are shaped by the particular historical development of the system.

Organizational fields become organized, rationalized, and recognized as distinct through a process called "structuration" by DiMaggio. This entails:

> (1) an increase in the level of interaction among organizations in a field; (2) an increase in the load of information on organizations in a field; (3) the emergence of a structure of domination; (4) the emergence of a pattern of coalition; and (5) the development, at the cultural level, of an ideology of the field. (DiMaggio, 1983, p. 150)

As sectors become more structured, organizations within them develop common understandings of how things operate, how to view a problem, and other shared assumptions (DiMaggio, 1983). Over time, organizations within a sector come to look alike through a variety of homogenization processes.

The infusion of new funders in the museum environment in the mid-sixties changed the museum field in two ways. First, institutional funding fostered a more articulated structure at the field level. Second, institutional funding helped to transform some of the shared beliefs of the museum sector. For instance, the newcomers may have spurred the acceptance of popular formats for exhibitions in museums. Other aspects of museum structure, such as the incorporation of certain professional groups (certified accountants and art historians) or the format of annual reports, become more similar as the museum sector becomes more structured. Professionals increase the legitimacy of museums in the eyes of their new funders: Not only do professionals come to museums knowing standard business procedures (such as accounting or public relations), but their credentials signal to outsiders the museum's efforts to manage itself well.

During the period under study, museum environments have become increasingly rationalized. I have noted three major areas of changes associated with the environmental change. First, museum missions have profoundly changed, as evidenced by several shifts in orientation; most notably, museums mount more exhibits and become increasingly exhibitions-oriented. Museums also increasingly attend to audiences and their local community. Second, the external changes in funding represent a rationalization of the museum environment that leads to structuration in the museum sector. The rationalized, structured environment leads museum staffs to become more professionalized and increasingly oriented toward funders, which furthers the structuration of the museum sector as professionals and funders create linkages within the field and provide common understandings across museums. Museums become more oriented toward business tools and jargon, as they struggle to "market" their exhibitions and to handle "the bottom line" more effectively.

The museum sector employs uncertain technologies. Art, after all, is not standard nor is it standardizable. Judgments about what art is great and has lasting value are difficult. And what museums should be doing is socially defined, not given *a priori*. This means that museums will focus on legitimacy, and they will be judged on the basis of institutional standards, "rational myths," about how they should organize (Meyer & Rowan, 1977). This situation leads to structural similarities as organizations incorporate rational myths (DiMaggio & Powell, 1983), such as new kinds of specialists or new management techniques. There are three mechanisms that lead toward increasing isomorphism, all three of which are evident in museums. Coercive isomorphism is caused when holders of resources (the national and state government funders) require certain structures as a condition of granting the resources. Mimetic isomorphism results when organizations copy each other's structures and procedures. And normative isomorphism is the structural similarity that comes from relying on professionals who share the same visions and conception of control across different organizations.

In museums, requirements by funding agencies for accountability, leading in turn to the adoption of standard procedures, is an example of coercive isomorphism. In addition, the emphasis on legitimacy is likely to lead to intra-sector ties as administrators read, talk to each other, or hire consultants to learn what the guiding myths are (mimetic isomorphism). Professionals, including art historians, often put professional identity ahead of loyalty to their particular place of employment. Ties to professional culture are important in creating links across organizations, as well as being a source of normative isomorphism across museums.

The extent to which business school graduates or other non-arts professionals have entered a museum (as employees, consultants, or trustees) surely influences the museum's sophistication concerning management techniques. The structures of museums can to a significant degree be traced to the environment in which they operate. These are instances of isomorphism: normative, in the case of business school and other non-art professionals entering the museum; coercive, when funding depends on it; and in many cases, mimetic, when museums look to each other for solutions to management and strategy problems.

Although museum people always talked to each other to some degree, a community of museums did not really develop until the late 1960s (Larson, 1983). The museum sector went through an initial burst of structuration in the 1920s, as museum curators professionalized (Meyer, 1979) and as an external institutional funder, the Carnegie Corporation of New York (a philanthropic foundation), donated money for studies of museums (DiMaggio, 1991c). The next burst of structuration in the field came with the formation of the National Endowment for the Arts, which focused museums' attention on funders and on each other. DiMaggio (1983) has shown that the presence of the NEA brought museums into an increasingly structured field. In this case, state and federal arts councils and endowments, artists' associations, arts lobbies, theaters, museums, orchestras, and other interested parties make up the organizational field. DiMaggio shows that the "more centralized . . . the resources upon which organizations in a field depend, the greater . . . the degree of interaction among organizations in that field" (p. 149). DiMaggio finds that the centralization of arts funding under the National Endowment for the Arts led the arts field to become more closely linked. Further, new organizations that link arts organizations arose, among them the state arts councils, trade associations and "agency watchers" who publish newsletters about NEA activities.

The presence of the NEA fostered these new organizations and interorganizational links in several ways: First, the NEA increased the amount of information arts organizations needed to operate effectively. This led to the establishment of several trade associations and agency watchers. Second, the NEA reinforced the shared ideologies and commonalities among organizational participants. Although museums undoubtedly had ties to each other prior to the introduction of the NEA (see Larson, 1983)[12], the presence of centralized funding tended to increase commonalities, and hence, bases for interorganizational ties. Third, the NEA actively built a constituency to help itself survive.

Format of Annual Reports

Interestingly, the trend toward professionalization of museums was highly visible in the format of annual reports. Some big museums had slick, business-like annual reports dating well before 1960. Yet some other museums did not publish reports at all until the late 1960s or early '70s.

The Guggenheim Museum's first annual report appeared quite late, in 1977, on their 40th anniversary. Other early reports were informal, incomplete, did not put the museum in a good light, did not contain financial information, or were even typewritten. Toledo, for instance, did not present income and expendative accounts in its "annual report"—called "Museum News: Your Museum Reports"—until 1970. By the late 1970s, though, all museums in the sample had relatively polished reports. Notably, the change from rough to polished reports was abrupt, usually occurring in one annual report (or occasionally a few), rather than a gradual change over the entire period. This indicates that the museum had made a conscious decision to change and is evidence of an institutional diffusion pattern (Tolbert & Zucker, 1983).

The change in annual reports most likely reflects pressure exerted by the museum community. The formation of the National Endowment for the Arts, as mentioned, focused museum attention on funders and on each other (DiMaggio, 1983). Participants in societal sectors may come to share common definitions of their situation. And in the museum sector, perceptions of what an annual report should look like have certainly coalesced around one vision. Even museum professionals have noted that annual reports now look "exactly" like one another. (This observation was made by the interview respondents and also in several annual reports themselves.) For instance, the director of Art Institute of Chicago wrote in 1969:

> The Annual Reports of most of the major art museums in the United States these days bear a striking resemblance to each other, not only in format, but in content. The format developed seems to have proved its value to general readers, art historians and scholars, in that the acquisitions, exhibitions, activities, and publications are set forth for posterity. Even the content of these reports are frequently alike, for as mentioned in last year's report, we all have the same dilemmas of rising costs, increasing demands for services, and a sense of frustration due to lack of funds. (Art Institute of Chicago, 1968–69, p. 4)

Other evidence of the increased structure the museum field includes the fact that museums have adopted external assessment criteria (Meyer & Rowan, 1981, p. 541). Since 1972, museums have been accredited by the American Association of Museums.

Uniqueness of Museums

There is a flip side to the pressures from the development of a societal sector, which may lead not to isomorphism, but to diversity. As museums are drawn into the museum sector, they become part of a community ecology (Astley, 1985). Growing out of the work of population ecologists (e.g., Aldrich, 1979; Hannan & Freeman, 1977, 1984; McKelvey, 1982), community ecologists are concerned with succession of organizational forms and the structure of organizational communities (usually business communities).[13] Community ecologists employ a level of analysis that, to my eyes, is notably similar to the societal sector.[14] In the case of museums, although external funding has led to certain kinds of isomorphism, the competition for external funding has also spurred museums to become different from other museums. This differentiation allows museums to hold slightly different niches than one another, thus increasing their competitive advantages.

Museums applying to the same national or regional funders want to appear distinct, so they specialize, or emphasize their own uniqueness: For instance, the Albright-Knox Museum, which today is considered a very good modern art museum, exhibited in the 1960s several shows of art that were not modern, or even from the twentieth century. These exhibits included *Religious Art from Byzantium to Chagall* in 1964, and *Paintings, Sculpture and Drawings from the Fogg Art Museum* in 1966, which was composed of 59 works from five centuries. Many museums stress that they have a collection of a particular type of art uniquely suited to some purpose. Museums claim this even when other museums have collections of similar art.

In other words, museums must find a niche. For some museums, the niche is that of a generalist, but other museums must specialize. The slot that museums choose is, in part, determined by their closest competitors. The Fogg Museum, which is part of Harvard University, trains potential curators. In 1966, the Fogg stated that it also was obligated to serve the general community (p. 9). In 1974, however, the Fogg's stated obligation was to serve only Harvard students who want to become curators, and to make its collection available, not through exhibitions, but through catalogs (p. 7). This focus may be the result of successful efforts of the Museum of Fine Arts and other Boston museums to attract local audiences. Some museums also emphasize their uniqueness by developing a regional or local angle. For example, both the Detroit Institute of Art and the North Carolina Museum highlight the circulating exhibits they organize and send to all parts of their home states. Denver mounts shows of western art (cowboy art, frontier photographs, Indian artifacts). The Brooklyn Museum stresses its unique contribution to the borough of Brooklyn (in contrast to the Manhattan museums, which ignore Brooklynites). This localism has three angles: First, it strokes local elites who may donate works of art. Second, it makes the museum more worthy in the eyes of state and local government funders who care about the educational and outreach programs of the museum. And third, it builds audiences, by attracting local people to exhibitions of local significance.

Homogenization/Differentiation

The research shows several examples of increasing isomorphism among museums in the sample (annual reports, professionalization, orientation toward funders and management, orientation toward exhibits, etc.). This is a recognized result of the structuration of organizational fields.[15] However, the study also uncovered examples of differentiation and specialization among museums. This suggests that organizations in fields involving competition (in this case, for funds, especially in a national arena) will become distinct in substance (exhibitions, collections, focus) while becoming structurally similar.

Organizational fields are described by three features: network, culture, and historical aspects (Scott, 1983). This research suggests a fourth aspect: ecological features that appear when the societal sector operates as a community ecology.

I argue that community ecologies and organizational fields are different cuts of the same phenomenon, and both isomorphism and differentiation pressures manifest themselves in organizations drawn into these networks. As sectors become structured, environmental pressure leads to isomorphism (coercive isomorphism), and organizations also become similar as they come into contact (mimetic isomorphism), and as they come to share similar definitions of the situation (normative isomorphism). However, as sectors become structured, niches are articulated, which leads to diversity among museums. Organizations that once existed in their own local environment are drawn into national environments where they must compete for resources with other organizations. Interestingly, the same entities that help structure the sector (in this case, the NEA along with other institutional funders), and thus foster isomorphism among organizations, can also lead to increased competition in the sector and increased diversity among constituent organizations.

How can organizations become more alike and more distinct at the same time? While this sounds paradoxical, it has to do with the loosely coupled nature of organizations—all parts of the organization do not have to change in the same way. Further, networks of organizations exert several types of pressures on each of the organizations within them. Different pressures imply different outcomes. I believe that organizations become more alike structurally, but differentiate in substance.[16] The isomorphism comes from being drawn into a societal sector, and undergoing all the pressures described by DiMaggio and Powell. The differentiation comes from competing in a community ecology and striving to find a niche (Hawley, 1950). These two tendencies are not contradictory, and can come from the same source.

Discussion

In the past 30 years, museum decision makers have (1) implemented new museum missions (less curatorial, more educational), (2) redefined museum governance (less "impresarial," more managerial), (3) changed the relationship between the public and art (interactional rather than isolated, inclusive rather than exclusive), (4) re-thought what constitutes an aesthetic experience (from one perfect painting on a white wall to be seen over and over, to a lively series of exhibitions with wall labels and descriptive panels that help observers put art into a context), and (5) witnessed increased structure in the museum sector (more isomorphism, but also more specialization). As external support of museums moves from individual philanthropy to organizational funding, museums have broadened the format of exhibitions, attracting a more popular audience; museums have become less elitist, more popular institutions. These changes empower a business-oriented museum coalition, which conflicts with one comprised of art-related professionals. This sparks controversy as museum factions vie for the ascendancy of the institutional visions that favor their coalition.

Museums made an effort both to stimulate and to tap new institutional funders in the late 1960s. Changes in the environment (the emergence of institutional funders) coupled with museums' efforts to utilize and encourage these changes transformed museums and the museum environment. Changes in museums that were stimulated by institutional funders were later sustained by internal mechanisms. Museums adapted their internal organizational structure to funders (e.g., they established development offices) and recast their internal beliefs and symbols (e.g., they revised expectations about the number and mix of exhibitions, and enhanced the definition of how many visitors comprise an "excellent" attendance). These internal changes perpetuate the environmentally driven changes. Further, museum policies reshape the environment when, for example, they lead managers to cultivate new funders or to attract new members, and then to attend to the alternative tastes and expectations of these additional environmental actors. In other words, museums reconstructed their environment and their internal arrangements in response to new funding sources. But these changes committed them to new courses of action, and established a self-sustaining dynamic. In adapting to their environment, museums have become new types of organizations that are more exhibition and audience-oriented.

Viewed from the level of the organizational field, the increasingly formalized, bureaucratic, and professionalized nature of museums can be seen as an increasing isomorphism between museums and their more ordered, articulated and structured environment. In the past, museums were dependent on a few individuals for funding. Today, they are dependent on a highly organized environment made up of other organizations. No longer impresarios charming Lady Bountiful, museum directors acknowledge funding ties in an explicit and organized way and plan funding, engaging in calculations that can be made public. Organizational features such as funder-acknowledging annual reports and the existence of development offices are evidence of this. When museums organize exhibits, they maximize calculable outcomes, like attendance, rather than just arranging display rooms with philanthropists' paintings, sculpture, and objets d'art. In organizational terms, they express their multiple, changing missions in terms of changing organizational charts that mirror the complexity in the environment. They explicitly encode conflict into departmental structure. The past was not free of conflict, as curators' rendering of the halcyon days suggests. Today, however, the conflict is now more explicit, and it is rendered in organizational structure. As these changes unfold, museums bureaucratize, professionalize, and copy each other's good ideas. They also specialize and differentiate, allowing them to fit into niches defined by the more articulated environment.

It is important to recognize that the changes in museums are associated with new environments with which they must mesh. Keep in mind that the old funding system was related to the old museum model and had its own set of constrictions. The picture is *not* a past with no constrictions that gave way to a new system with a great many. New funders do provide problems for museum management. The old arrangement did as well. But individual philanthropy was institutionalized in museums a long time ago. Museum managers "got used to" the philanthropists by establishing mechanisms (like directors' circles) to control individual donors. Seen from a macro-perspective, the changes in museums are "merely" adjustments to an increasingly rationalized organizational environment. But from the perspective of museums, the changes reflect a business logic that challenges and threatens to replace the scholarly logic that has been dominant during this century. The debates over the changes are particularly intense because they challenge the curator's place in the museum, and they challenge the status culture that the curator represents. In some ways, the changes in museums challenge the institutionalization of high culture, tearing down boundaries between high and popular culture in ways particularly disturbing to champions of the distinction.

NOTES

1. On the concept of rationalization, see Meyer, Boli, and Thomas (1987). They write: "We use the generic term *rationalization* to refer to the purposive or instru-

mental rationalization: the stucturing of everyday life within standardized impersonal rules that constitute social organization as a means to a collective purpose. Denotatively, through rationalization, authority is structured as a formal legal order increasingly bureaucratized; exchange is governed by rules of rational calculation and bookkeeping, rules constituting a market, and includes such related processes as monetarization, commercialization, and bureaucratic planning; cultural accounts increasingly reduce society to the smallest rational units—the individual, but also beyond to genes and quarks" (pp. 24–25).

2. This is especially true for foundation giving. Foundations are subject to much more stringent financial reporting, when giving to charity, than are individuals and individual corporations. Corporate foundations have the same reporting mandates as other types of foundations. For individuals and direct corporate gifts, the IRS cares only whether or not the recipient of the donation is a nonprofit 501 (c) (3) corporation (in which case, the donated money is tax-deductible). In response to charges in the 1960s that many so-called charitable foundations were not so charitable, Congress changed tax laws in 1969 to require foundations to acount for how money given out was spent (Odendahl, 1987a, b; Simon, 1987). This means that recipients of foundation funds need to provide careful financial records to the foundation. This change in tax law marked an important increase in the demand on museums for accountability. Foundation personnel were at first annoyed by the new legislation, but they came to see it as an advantage as it allows them more control (Barry Karl, personal communication).

3. Professionalization refers to credentialing in schools for a particular subject (Larson, 1977; Collins, 1979). It is an issue which has become important for many types of nonprofit organizations. In arts management, professionalization may entail hiring accountants and business school graduates, as well as requiring art historians to hold Ph.D.s. A related issue concerns arts educators: Although there are schools offering degrees in museum education (Georgetown, The Bank Street School), some outsiders do not recognize it as an established field and believe that it should be professionalized under the general heading of education rather than under museums.

4. Some aspects of this process resemble a "garbage can model of organizational choice" (Cohen, March and Olsen, 1972; March and Olsen, 1976). The garbage can model emphasizes separate flows of events, and the post-hoc rationalization of their merging, which may actually be highly random.

5. Paul DiMaggio, personal communication.

6. The esteem consensually granted to individual philanthropists is likely a recent historical development. In the first half of this century, trustees and wealthy donors were often the enemy—seen as conservative, naive or philistine obstacles to curators' creative ideas (see DiMaggio, 1988a).

7. The director of this museum, attuned to organizational dynamics, told me that she finds organizational charts useless unless one can also learn about the "flows" between the departments.

8. Scott (1987, p. 505) calls this the "incorporation" of organizational structure.

9. John Meyer, personal communication.

10. The situation is a bit more complicated than this, however. Decision-makers from different factions within the museum do not always work to the best interest of the organization as a whole. Rather, they are interested in furthering their own agendas and increasing their own leverage in the museum.

11. It is difficult to define precisely the concept. Indeed, the various names of this phenomena reflect the lack of consensus: It is called, variably, "organizational field" (DiMaggio & Powell, 1983), "societal sector" (Scott & Meyer, 1983), "indus-

try system" (Hirsch, 1981), "interorganizational network" (Benson, 1975). Economists have studied financial flows in industries, and policy analysts are interested in "policy arenas" or "policy areas" (e.g. Wildavsky, 1975). All of these different names imply somewhat different definitions and different research foci, as Scott (1992) points out. For me, however, the similarities among the definitions—the fact that organizations are increasingly tied in complex, interdependent networks, which are culturally and institutionally articulated—is the important issue. I follow DiMaggio and Powell (1983) in using the term "organizational field". An organizational field incorporates "all organizations within a society supplying a given type of product or service together with their associated organization sets: suppliers, financiers, regulators and the like." (Scott & Meyer, 1983, p. 129); it is a level of analysis that takes as its focus the structured aspects of organizational environments.

12. Art museums have always been connected, even early in their histories, if only to exchange objects for shows. Larson mentions that although the art field was fragmented in the 1940s, it became increasingly organized through the 1950s until, in the 1960s, it established an "arts lobby" (1983, p. 5). It may be useful to evaluate this change in museum networks.

13. The "community ecology approach thus conceptualizes population forms in terms of their functional roles vis a vis other populations within technologically interdependent communities" (Astley, 1985, p. 225).

14. Most empirical studies by community ecologists are limited to a single geographic area (Carroll, 1984). Scott (1992) suggests a vocabulary to describe these differences: "areal field" for a level limited by geographic areas and "functional field" for societal sectors.

15. Although the idea that organizations become isomorphic is now central to institutional theory, early formulations of institutional theory by Meyer and Scott in 1983 (see Meyer and Scott, 1992) focused more on potential differences within sectors: centralization versus decentralization, fragmentation versus unification, federalization versus concentration. Further, they suggested that very different organizations may fulfill similar functions—for instance medical practices built around M.D.s versus those comprised of chiropractors or faith healers or holistic practitioners—and that all those organizations should be considered as part of a single sector. Whether organizations become more alike as sectors become more articulated is an empirical, rather than theoretical, question. Structuration and isomorphism are two distinct processes, so the two are not necessarily concomitant.

16. Population ecology of organizations suggests that each "population" of organizations is like a species that fills one niche. Organizational ecologists would argue that if "similar" organizations within organizational fields fill different niches, then organizations within fields are not from the same population. In part, this depends on how one defines the sector, which is an analytical construct. One could argue that sectors only include organizations that face exactly the same environment and thus can only become more isomorphic. I believe this formulation eliminates, *a priori*, the possibility of understanding what happens in real networks of organizations, by theoretically defining away variation that exists in practice. Even if one examines "mainstream" organizations in a sector (for instance, all hospitals, leaving out such things as acupuncture centers or fasting clinics), they may evidence a variety of isomorphic and divergent strategies and structures that emerge from the dynamics of the sector in which they are located.

V

CONCLUSION

MUSEUMS AND MAMMON?

This study suggests that between 1960 and 1986 museums and museum exhibitions changed a great deal. Museums became more attuned to audiences, exhibitions, and educational programs. Further, the content and especially the format of exhibitions have changed. Funding does affect exhibitions, but not in a simple way. Rather, external funding flows through museums, which are formal organizations. In order to understand museum exhibitions, and indeed to understand art, we must understand organizational behavior. I contend that the output of museums—exhibitions—is shaped by practical concerns and mundane matters, such as financing and budgeting, along with more "noble" (and legitimating) aesthetic criteria.

This project has implications for the sociology of culture and the sociology of organizations. It addresses questions about how culture organizations affect aesthetic choice and informs thinking about organization-environment interactions. On a practical level, this research has applications to the array of nonprofit enterprises that garner major support from outside donors, suggesting that funding may affect the outputs as well as the governance of nonprofits.

Research on the production of culture (Becker, 1982; Peterson, 1976) suggests that institutional arrangements affect cultural outputs. This occurs through various mechanisms: gatekeepers, who filter cultural objects flowing through an industry system (Hirsch, 1981), legal incentives, which favor some styles or genres of art over others (Griswold, 1981), industry competition, more of which provides an outlet for creativity (Peterson & Berger, 1975), and market systems, which, unlike patronage systems, popularize the output of arts organizations (DiMaggio & Stenberg, 1985). This study suggests a different mechanism: In a manner just about opposite to the strainer effect of gatekeepers, funders, by favoring certain types of exhibitions, which already exist in museums, encourage the proliferation of those exhibition types and thereby change the overall mix of exhibitions mounted by museums. Funders do not force museums to change exhibition policy. Rather, funders have an implicit portfolio of exhibitions they wish to fund, and museums have a portfolio of exhibitions they would like to mount. More exhibitions happen where these areas overlap. In other words, by funding exhibitions that appeal to their own goals—as well as those of museum personnel—funders can broaden the audiences for art exhibits, perhaps beyond what museum personnel initially envisioned. This project suggests, then, that researchers in the sociology of culture should attend to opportunity-providing arrangements in culture production systems, which induce niche seeking, along with the better studied opportunity-reducing gatekeeping arrangements.

The research suggests that the sample frame can be divided into three eras with regard to exhibition support: the philanthropy, transition, and funding periods. The transition period was a crucial time when directors came to implement and articulate new visions of museums. Museums moved from more internally focused organizations concentrating on collections, conservation and scholarship, to more externally oriented organizations geared towards funders, exhibitions, and audiences. As exhibitions reached broader audiences, museums became somewhat less elitist, more populist institutions.

The initial changes in museums during the transition period—a shift from a curatorial model towards a management (or perhaps, an education or an entertainment) model, and an increasing orientation to and sophistication about external funders—were spurred by the entry of institutional funders into the cultural arena and by museums' efforts to tap that funding. These changes, however, may have been kept in motion not by the continued influence of external funders but by organizational change. In other words, museums reconstructed their environment and their internal arrangements in response to new funding sources. The changes then led to a self-perpetuating organizational transformation, though conflict over the transformation still remains.

This study suggests that museums have played a role in laying out the path that they have followed in the era of increased institutional funding. Though museum exhibitions have grown more popular, in the aggregate, and considerable conflict exists in museums because of these changes, curators do not relinquish autonomy in the face of the institutional funders. Indeed, the existence of many funders allows museum personnel more leverage and freedom to do what they want than would the existence of a few funders. Curators creatively use funders, picking and choosing among them when they can easily find overlapping goals and innovating to find new types of artworks or exhibitions that meet both museum and funder goals when the goals do not immediately mesh. Further, funders can be used to influence one another, as can be seen in the success of matching grant programs and in research showing that the existence of other corporate arts funding encourages corporations to start or to continue to donate to museums (Galaskiewicz, 1991; Useem & Kutner, 1986). New funders provide the leverage, and the spur, curators need to bring certain forms of creative expression into museum shows.

This is one of the most important insights suggested by this research: Managers creatively manipulate their environment and autonomously reshape the demands of funders. They are actors, not reactors. The environment is not a pool of demands to be passively met. Rather, it is an arena from which organizations pull in certain factors, shaping these factors to meet their own ends. The multiplicity of external demands provides this leeway to managers. This study has shed some light on how museum managers try to innovate to preserve their autonomy, given pressure to conform to outside demands, and how multiple external funders allow innovation, often changing the internal balance of power, and how they can drive fundamental change in the exhibition pool, the nature of art museums and, ultimately, in art itself. My research suggests a rethinking of organizational-environment relationships in organizations by elaborating the innovation process.

This process appears in other organizations, notably nonprofit organizations reliant on donations. For instance, Stuart (1992) discusses funding and innovation in settlement houses. He demonstrates that in the earliest phase at the turn of the century, settlement houses were funded by individuals and relied heavily on volunteers. During this time, innovation (defined as the diversity of programs) was high. In a middle phase starting around 1920, settlement houses began to hire professional social workers and to rely on federated funding, such as the Community Chest. During this period, settlement houses were stable, with greater physical capital , but less innovation. During the first part of a third phase which started around World War II, settlement houses relied on a mixed funding pool, including government grants. During the early part of this phase, innovation was high, as the government funded demonstration projects. In the middle part of this phase, however, government switched to service contracting rather than demonstration projects. This shift led to a decrease in innovation, which was furthered by government cutbacks. As government funding was curtailed, settlement houses cut back in similar ways, becoming quite isomorphic. Innovation was high when the field was unstructured and when ample funding was available from several sources. Innovation decreased when funding came from just one source (Community Chest and, later, the United Way). Innovation was also low when funding was scarce after the field had professionalized and become structured.

The research demonstrates that there are profound conflicts within museums. The conflicts are intense for two reasons. First, the conflict pits actors holding different normative visions against one another. These visions are based on two profoundly different institutional logics, one from business and one from scholarship. These two logics defy reconciliation. Consequently, the conflicts cannot be solved by compromise, as either side will feel undermined and de-legitimized by giving up their views. Compromise represents a distortion of the "right and proper" functions of museums. Second, the conflicts surround a reduction in the influence and status of the traditional "winners" in museums, art-historically trained curators. It is hard to satisfy people who are losing power and who feel undermined by their own institutions.

Along these lines, the research shows the value of using organizational theory to understand museums. Further, the research suggests that concepts from three theories of organization—institutional, resource dependency, and strategic decision making theories—are necessary for a thorough understanding of art museum actions. Elsewhere I have argued that these three theories must be folded together, under the umbrella of institutional theory (Alexander, 1996b). Institutional theory, with its focus on cultural constructs, which undergird human action, provides the best starting point for the combined theory. But institutional theory must be understood as allowing for conscious choice and the ability of actors to adroitly use cultural tools for creating new innovations, along with the more common use of the theory to explain how actors are constrained by, and fail to think about, socially constructed rules, roles, and meanings. Power is important, and though institutions shape interests, interests also shape institutions. These ideas have been themes in recent institutional theory writing and in work from the sociology of culture (e.g., Clemens, 1993; DiMaggio, 1988b; DiMaggio & Powell, 1991; Friedland & Alford, 1991; C. Oliver, 1991; Powell, 1991; Scott, 1995; Sewell, 1992; and Swidler, 1986), but they have not yet been accepted by organizational theorists, many of whom prefer to view institutional theory in its caricatured form, as it makes a better straw person that way.

The research suggests that it is useful to study organizations themselves and also to study them in larger networks, organizational fields. As fields become structured, three processes—coercive, normative, and mimetic action—lead to structural isomorphism of organizations in the field (DiMaggio & Powell, 1983). This research suggests that another mechanism—competitive pressures—leads to substantive diversity among organizations in societal sectors. Isomorphism among museums increases as funders draw museums into a more-structured "organizational field." Paradoxically, differentiation also increases as museums compete for funds in a national "museum ecology."

Managing environmental pressures and internal conflict are general problems in all organizations. The problems found in this study, however, apply with special force to nonprofit organizations, which are especially dependent on external constituencies. The dynamics of nonprofit organizations depend on the unstandardizable aspect of their products. The kind of conflict that encompasses two institutional logics is particularly common in nonprofit organizations. In fact, nonprofit organizations are increasingly operating on what Backman (forthcoming) calls the "institutional cusp." In museums, the conflict stems from business logic in conflict with professional/scholarly logic. In other types of nonprofit organizations, the conflict may be more a business logic competing with charity, religion, or democracy models. Yet, the dynamics inside the organizations may be quite similar. In these organizations, participants may disagree sharply on the goals of the organization and at the same time try (not always successfully) to retain autonomy from external constituencies (Alexander forthcoming).

There are many questions this research brings up but leaves unanswered. Museums have moved from more elitist to more populist conceptions of their duties and have become increasingly exhibitions-oriented. Further, museums have been moving away from domination by scholars to domination by managers. So museums have changed their goals. But when is a changed goal a distorted goal? When does the broadening of audience mean a democratization of culture, and when does broadening lead to insipidity?

The Broadening of Art

The research demonstrates that museums are faced with pressures for increasing the popularity and accessibility of art exhibits. However, museums have not responded, in general, by mounting large numbers of poor-quality crowd pleasers. Instead, museums have mounted many more shows that are multivocal—that appeal to different audiences on different levels. Faced with such pressures, museum curators innovate to find art that is both accessible and that can be viewed with a critical eye. The "rediscovery" of all types of American art—folk art, primitive art, craft, nineteenth-century masters—in the 1970s is one very good example. Still, popular and accessible exhibitions are more common in museums now than they were before the advent of institutional funding.

Legitimation of Middle Class Culture

The distinction between high and popular art is becoming increasingly blurred or "problemetized" (DiMaggio, 1987b). Though it appeals still today, and in fact seems obvious and inescapable, it did not exist a mere century ago. This underlines the fact that artistic boundaries are not immutable. They are, in fact, quite changeable and their composition is often based more on politics or hegemony than on merit (Smith, 1983). This amorphous nature of artistic boundaries suggests that changes in art worlds can bring about changes in artistic canons.

Museums play a role in the formation of artistic canons. This research suggests a broadening of the basis of art in the period of increased institutional funding. "Massification" is too crude a word to describe the trend, but perhaps it is accurate enough to say that it is the creation and legitimation of middle-class culture, as opposed to an aristocratic culture, in art. Art and aesthetics, once revered and sacred (Levine, 1988), are returning to a more pedestrian role. Art is to be enjoyed and aesthetics to be understood by broad audiences. Institutional funders, with their interest in popular exhibitions and audiences have had a broadening effect on museums and exhibitions. Further, the research shows that conceptions of art and the audience to which high culture "should" appeal is socially defined.

DiMaggio (1987b) argues that artistic classification systems, existing at the societal level, vary along four dimensions: differentiation, hierarchy, universality, and the ritualization of boundaries. In the United States, high art is one "genre," in a classification system that is "becoming more differentiated and less hierarchical, [its] classifications weaker and less universal" (p. 452). DiMaggio suggests that classification systems are generated by social structure ("ritual classification"), but are mediated by characteristics of the production system:

> One of these, *commercial classification*, is driven by efforts of culture producers in market systems to sell art for a profit, and tends to yield broader, more weakly framed genres than does ritual classification. A second, *professional classification*, results from artists' attempts to develop reputations and, under conditions common to Western democracies, produces narrower, less universal distinctions among genres. A third, *administrative classification*, stems from governmental regulatory activities and is variable in its consequences. (p. 449–450)

This research suggests that the influence of institutional funding on museums is similar to the effects of commercial classification: it broadens the definition of art, reducing the distinction between high culture and folk or popular culture. The NEA is a body of administrative classification and has two distinct effects on the definition of art: a popularizing effect in its funding of large exhibitions, and a narrowing effect in its support of contemporary art and small, scholarly exhibitions. Curators are professionals who classify art, though they do not operate under the same circumstances as artists. Like artists, curators are interested in establishing their professional identities, and some curators innovate about art forms, broadening the canon of high art. But unlike artists, curatorial status often rests on upholding traditions and maintaining the sacrosanct nature of high art. Overall, however, the classification of high art, like the society-wide system, is becoming broader, less hierarchical, and more differentiated, making room for traditional craft and folk art and new art styles.

The Commodification of Culture

"Our culture is a commodity culture, and it is fruitless to argue against it on the basis that culture and profit are mutually exclusive terms," writes John Fiske (1989: 4). But people do lament the commodification of high culture and argue against it in various guises.

> Behind such arguments lie two romantic fantasies that originate at opposite ends of the cultural spectrum—at one end that of the penniless artists, dedicated only to the purity and aesthetic transcendence of his (for the vision is a patriarchal one) art, and at the other that of a folk art in which all members of the tribe participate equally in producing and circulating their culture, free of any commercial taint. (Fiske, 1989: 4–5)

Though Fiske is speaking about popular culture, which is often produced by profit-seeking cultural industries, rather than nonprofit arts organizations, his comment is particularly cogent in explaining some of the changes in the wider museum environment. As our society continues the rationalizing process described by Max Weber, and as more and more aspects of life are subject to the criteria of the bottom line, more and more institutions resting on logics of the family, democracy, charity, religion, and others will increasingly come into conflict with business logic. These changes might occur within the organization itself, as in museums. Or organizations subscribing to one particular logic might come into competition from organizations in the same field mainly espousing another. For instance, nursing homes and hospitals can be either nonprofit (secular or religious) or for-profit. One amazing development in the art world is exhibitions for profit. *Treasures of the Czars* is an exhibition organized by Jim Broughton, an organizer of "art expos," with no formal training in the arts (Rogers, 1995). His shows appear in convention halls, rather than museums, and are designed to appeal to a large audience to make a buck; earnings come from ticket sales and from merchandising. Though the museums in my study have become more managerially oriented because of changes in their environment—institutional funders that demanded more accountability—it is possible that, in the absence of these funders, museums would have come under similar pressure from other sources.

The Art World

Other factors that may influence the broadening of artistic canons and the popularization of museums are not examined in this research. Many of these factors are related to the organization of art into art worlds. These issues merit further attention:

- Changes in structure of elites from family- and city-based to geographically mobile and professional, a change symbolized by a move from aristocratic to democratic culture.
- Changes in the discipline of art history. There are many more art historians today than in the past, which suggests a sociology of knowledge question: in order to be successful, all scholars must innovate and make previously unthought of claims about the subject of their discipline. This pressure can lead art historians to study new or previously ignored art forms.
- Changes in art markets. European painting has become too expensive for most American museums and collectors. Consequently, individual and institutional collectors must look to other forms of art, such as indigenous folk art, for acquisition.
- Related changes in artists' studios and galleries affect what museums and individuals collect in contemporary art.
- Changes in the nature of audiences who, in general, have more leisure, are better educated, and are more widely traveled than audiences 30 years ago. These museum visitors may be more demanding and better-informed about art history and, having seen the best examples of the Italian Renaissance in Florence and Rome, may be disappointed with the few examples by "the studio of" second-rate painters that hang in their local museum.

Other topics that deserve further study:

- Careers of directors (how are directors rewarded; if they continue to be selected from the ranks of curators, will curators split into two factions, with different attitudes toward art versus promotion?)
- Composition of boards of directors (how has this changed over time, how much business expertise exists on boards, and has this increased the administration/curator split in museums, interlocking directorates?)
- Differences between museums with strong boards and those with strong directors (weak boards)
- Funders' objectives (what do they say their goals are, how do they act on their goals?)
- The role museums played in bringing about the initial interest of corporate funders and in the early development of government agencies for art.

Funding in a Fourth Era

This study covered three "eras" of museum support: the philanthropy period (1960–66), the transition period (1968–1972), and the funding period (1974–1986). Given the current state of arts funding, we may already be in a fourth era: the retrenchment period. This era seems to be characterized by a dearth of funds, through government cuts and recisions and through reductions of corporate contributions stemming from restructuring, downsizing, or a poor business economy. Or perhaps our current time could better be characterized as the politicized period. Current controversies over government funding of the arts, multiculturalism in museums, and the viewpoints expressed in interpretive exhibitions (*The West as America* at the National Museum of American Art, and the Enola Gay installation at the Smithsonian Institution, to name only two), make it clear that museums are increasingly pulled by political debates.

The Potential for Censorship

Has the change in museum funding affected the character of contemporary art? This is a difficult question and one impossible to answer with the data in this study. However, I would like to suggest that funding has played some role. In order for artists to impose aesthetic standards, their views must mesh with the system of rewards (money and fame) and with those who control the rewards (dealers, galleries, and museums). These artists will receive legitimating one-person shows only to the extent that museums can handle the messages they offer.

In this regard, a story about the artist Hans Haacke provides a good illustration:

> In 1970, Haacke asked visitors to a show that included his work at the Museum of Modern Art (MoMA) in New York City to answer the question: "Would the fact that Governor Rockefeller has not denounced President Nixon's Indochina policy be a reason for you not to vote for him in November?" At the end of the twelve-week exhibition, the ballot boxes had registered the following results: 25,566 (68.7 percent) yes; 11,563 (31.3 percent) no. This was an especially ironic outcome, for MoMA has been a Rockefeller fiefdom since its founding in 1929. Haacke has not been given another show at MoMA. (Schiller, 1989: 57)

The Guggenheim canceled a one-man exhibition of Haacke's work in 1971 (see Burnham, 1971; Fry, 1971; Siegel, 1971). The museum objected to photographs of New York tenements labeled with the names of the individual or corporate owners of the slum properties. The Guggenheim publicly stated that they feared libel suits (though the photos were objective and accurately reported only publicly available information on the owners). By canceling the show, the Guggenheim made Haacke a folk hero in the art world, building up his status. Haacke continues his assault on museum funders. For example, his work *Mobilization* is composed of silk-screen images of documents, enlarged reproductions of Mobil Oil's printed philanthropy policy. The series highlights Mobil's non-aesthetic, commercial grant standards, which invokes an image of crassness despite the straightforward and seemingly apolitical tone of the piece.

This situation is quite similar to the infamous Mapplethorpe exhibition—the small Robert Mapplethorpe retrospective that initially gained national attention and notoriety not when the show was exhibited, but when it was *not* exhibited. The Corcoran Gallery in Washington, DC, canceled the show because it feared public outcry over NEA funding of the exhibit. The art world was shocked at the Corcoran's actions, and protests by artists' groups brought considerable attention to the show, not all of it positive. Likewise, it is possible to imagine a case where an exhibition is never *planned* because of a feared negative reaction. In such cases, the artist's work would not be mounted, nor would the artist gain status by being acted against, since no public notice or record would speak for the actions (or really, nonactions) of museum personnel. There is no evidence in this study of funders' censoring museums. But do museums censor themselves, to avoid alienating funders? External funders—government as well as corporate—cause museums to think twice about controversial content:

> Even Philippe de Montebello, Director of the Metropolitan Museum, calls corporate funding "an inherent, insidious, hidden form of censorship," though he hastens to add, "but corporations aren't censoring us—we're censoring ourselves." (Glennon, 1988: 42)

Art needs a social support system, whether it is based on a popularity or an art-critical standard. Museums are an important part of the support system of contemporary artists. But if museums shy away from possible controversy, they may disproportionately promote the less-controversial and more easily understood components of the avant-garde.

Art and Money

I have not taken a clear stand on whether funding has been good or bad for museums. Instead, I have cast the question as one residing in a struggle within museums, a struggle highlighted and crystalized by changes in funding. There are costs and benefits of funding to museums. But one's view on what is a cost and what is a benefit depends on professional training and background. So does the answer to the question: How do you characterize broadened, more active, and more middle-class museums? As inclusive and democratic? Or as trivializing pabulum?

I have argued that the new funders, especially corporations, are often seen as self-interested Philistines who sully art with their mere presence. But this pejorative view can be traced to the associated threats to museum autonomy. Moreover, patronage has always constrained art in one way or another. As Martorella (1990, p. 20) writes:

> It is somewhat romantic to assume that patrons of the past or present treat artists with deepest respect, allowing them freedom in creating, and acquiring their works for purely aesthetic reasons or for art's sake.

She argues that earlier patrons, as well as today's corporate patrons, "use art for the symbolic display of their own wealth and power." Similarly, both today's institutional funders and yesterday's elite patrons fund museums for a complex mix of reasons, not all completely benign or for the pure love of art.

I would like to suggest that funding of museums, no matter by whom, is beneficial to museums. Though funding can create sticky difficulties in museums over what the organizations are trying to accomplish, the changes in museums that I have related to funding are also related to other broad changes in society. Thus, without funding, museums might have made similar changes to the ones they made in the face of funding. Except that, without funding, museums would probably have quite a bit less than they have today. Art works wouldn't have been conserved, scholarship wouldn't have been published, publics wouldn't have been thrilled, members wouldn't have joined, and children wouldn't have been educated.

It is certainly more hip to assert that smarmy, popular shows have hurt museums, not to mention western culture. I do have some sympathy for this view and for curators. The Impressionist blockbuster I attended in San Francisco several years ago was too crowded to enjoy properly. Yet, as a museum outsider, I also find the liveliness of today's museums stimulating. The question remains: In a time when highbrows can "learn from Las Vegas" (Venturi & Scott Brown, 1984), what happens to institutions like museums that enshrine high art?

Government Funding and Art

In general, this research shows that government arts policy has had two notable effects on art exhibitions. Government sponsorship has led to bigger, more popular exhibits. But government panels, along with museum curators, want to support art that is scholarly or that is at the cutting edge of current trends in art. Consequently, museums are able to organize more exhibitions in traditional art-historical formats. In addition, museums mount small exhibitions of contemporary artists. This type of exhibition is more difficult to fund, but government funders may have encouraged it.

I would especially like to argue against government cuts in arts spending. NEA/NEH funding of museums has been especially successful. It has supported popular exhibitions that have entertained and enlightened millions of Americans. In addition, government-sponsored shows also have scholarly merit; they are not just so many pretty pictures. Government has also sponsored shows of living artists. Though shows of living artists are comparatively infrequent, supporting them enlivens the art scene. More people can appreciate fine art because of government funding, and I hope that Congress will continue to find it sensible to tax each American 65 cents per year for the good work the National Endowments achieve.

Interestingly, the national debate over arts funding can be analyzed with the same theory of competing models that allows us to understand the debates within museums. Though it is clear that part of the attack on culture is cynical posturing—an attempt by conservatives to get in the face of the liberal arts establishment—some of the concerns are genuine. In our society, we do not have an established, consensual definition of what constitutes art or how art should relate to society. Should art be intellectual, complex, and challenging? Should it glorify the patron or society? Or should it be beautiful? And what is "beautiful" anyway? The common view in our society, a view that is seen as naive by the art world, is that art should be sublime. It should be a pleasure to gaze upon and should uplift the viewer. Art might focus on high moral or spiritual sentiments or, in a more ordinary vein, it might be pretty or cheerful; but in any case, it should be well-executed by someone who has "more skill than a five-year-old." This is not the definition of art that has taken hold in the contemporary art world. Cognicenti prefer art work that is thought-provoking and striking, visually, intellectually, or emotionally. Being "deeply moved" by a work can mean being shocked, revolted, or enraged, instead of being soothed or awed. These are very different models of what "art" means. Having taught a course on the sociology of art for many years, I can safely say that partisans from one camp are very rarely able to tolerate, let alone understand or sympathize with, the other camp's views. Pejorative terms like 'philistine,' 'naive,' 'schmaltz,' or 'snobby,' 'elitist,' and 'offensive' are common.

Though it is true that political art has a long history (think of Goya's *The Third of May, 1808*), it is also true that in the past, the function of art was to glorify the patron who commissioned it. Michelangelo did not try to challenge the authority of the Catholic Church or to shock the Pope with the Sistine Chapel ceiling. Today, most recipients of government grants do not glorify the USA (or even the NEA). Most also do not produce art or exhibits that insult the nation or "its" ideals. But some art does exactly this. This is what has conservative critics up in arms, as they firmly believe in the older, and more common, model of what art is and how it should relate to patrons.

The NEA's efforts to depoliticize its funding is the most sensible strategy it could follow. Though artists and organizations that sponsor contemporary art find the idea of government "censorship" reprehensible, I believe they will lose the battle for completely open funding of "challenging" contemporary work. And by fighting too hard against the NEA's rejection of the most challenging political art, the vanguard arts lobby could lose the war for the 99.9 percent of arts grants that go to non-controversial projects to the enemies of the NEA. The conservative formula—"budget crisis plus Mapplethorpe equals elimination of the NEA"—is wrong.[1] But the NEA is a public agency, and it must be mindful of general public sensibilities. As Schuster (1991, p. 38) argues: "It is very easy for a particular arts institution with an interest in its survival and maintaining the status quo to be unmindful of, or to actively avoid, specific public interests in arts funding." This tendency is heightened through the peer-review system: The art world's position on public funding of the arts —"that only people in the arts should decide and that they should be given as much latitude as possible—is neither a particularly compelling position on which to base a public policy nor a particularly compelling position on which to stake one's claim on public resources," (Schuster, 1991, p. 55). The most radical art will not disappear even if the NEA does not support it; but it will not be as easy to produce, exhibit, and sell as perhaps it has been in the past.

Today, we have institutionalized a romantic view of the artist, struggling in a garret producing true art. The best art, this view says, is art unbiased by any outside effects. This is fiction. All art is shaped by external factors, and the truth is that throughout most of human history, most great art has been produced in very constraining patronage systems. Though I disagree with conservative critics, I also believe that public funding should increase the public good. The broadening of the audience for art exhibits is a public good, though it does not come without costs. As composer and musician Quincy Jones argues, government arts funding should not be eliminated: "Every country in the world is smart enough to know that you have to feed the soul of the country through its arts. That *is* the soul." (NBC Evening News, Friday, March 24, 1995). Let us hope that the United States continues to be smart.

NOTE

1. The claim that the NEA sponsors immoral and obscene art, though it must be taken seriously, can be parried. There is very good evidence that the NEA does not make an effort to sponsor offensive art and that the few controversial cases, if viewed as "mistakes" (a label the avant-garde resists), gives the NEA a very low

"error rate," much lower than that of most organizations. It will be harder, however, to counter the "fiscal responsibility" argument about cutting arts funding. This argument says, "Art is good, arts funding is good, but it is less necessary than education and food programs, so it has to go." In an era of budget cutting, it may be difficult to resist this pressure, unless the art world can coalesce around—and publicize—a vision of art that hightlights its public benefits.

REFERENCES

Books and Articles

Aldrich, Howard E. (1979). *Organizations and Environments*. Englewood Cliffs, NJ: Prentice-Hall.

Aldrich, John H. & Forrest D. Nelson (1984). *Linear Probability, Logit, and Probit Models*. Beverly Hills: Sage.

Alexander, Victoria D. (1996a). "From Philanthropy to Funding: The Effects of Corporate and Public Support on American Art Museums." *Poetics: Journal of Empirical Research on Literature, the Media and Arts*, Vol. 24.

Alexander, Victoria D. (1996b). "Pictures at an Exhibition: Conflicting Pressures in Museums and the Display of Art." American Journal of Sociology, 101, 797–839.

Alexander, Victoria D. (forthcoming). "Environmental Constraints and Organizational Strategies: Complexity, Conflict, and Coping in the Nonprofit Sector." In Walter W. Powell and Elisabeth Clemens (Eds.), *Private Action and the Public Good*. Yale University Press, (1996).

Allen, Barbara Jacobsen (1974). *Organization and Administration in Formal Organization: The Art Museum*. Ph.D. Dissertation, New York University.

Allen, James Sloan (1983). *The Romance of Commerce and Culture: Capitalism, Modernism, and the Chicago-Aspen Crusade for Cultural Reform*. Chicago: University of Chicago Press.

American Association of Fund-Raising Counsel (1994). *Giving USA: The Annual Report on Philanthropy for the Year 1993* (39th annual issue). Ann E. Kaplan (Ed.), New York: AAFRC Trust for Philanthropy.

Astley, W. Graham (1985). "The Two Ecologies: Population and Community Perspectives on Organizational Evolution." *Administrative Science Quarterly*, 30, 224–241.

Backman, Elaine V. (forthcoming). *Good Works, Inc.: The Effects of Corporate Structure on the Provision of Private Social Services*. Ph.D. Dissertation, Stanford University.

Balfe, Judith Huggins (Ed.). (1993). *Paying the Piper: Causes and Consequences of Art Patronage*. Chicago: University of Illinois Press.

Balfe, Judith Huggins (1989). "The Baby-Boom Generation: Lost Patrons, Lost Audience?" In Margaret Wyszomirski and Pat Clubb (Eds.), *The Cost of Culture*. New York: ACA Books.

Balfe, Judith Huggins (1987). "Artworks as Symbols in International Politics." *International Journal of Politics, Culture and Society*, 1, 195–217.

Balfe, Judith Huggins & Thomas A. Cassilly (1993). "'Friends of . . .': Individual Patronage through Arts Institutions." In Judith Huggins Balfe (Ed.), *Paying the Piper: Causes and Consequences of Art Patronage* (119–133). Baltimore: University of Illinois Press.

Baxandall, Michael (1977). *The Limewood Sculptors of Renaissance Germany*. New Haven: Yale University Press.

Baxandall, Michael (1972). *Painting and Experience in Fifteenth Century Italy*. New York: Oxford University Press.

Becker, Howard S. (1982). *Art Worlds*. Berkeley: University of California Press.

Benedict, Stephen (Ed.) (1991). *Public Money and the Muse: Essays on Government Funding for the Arts*. New York: W.W. Norton & Co.

Benson, J. Kenneth (1975). "The Interorganizational Network as a Political Economy." *Administrative Science Quarterly*, 20, 229–249.

Blau, Judith R. (1989). *The Shape of Culture: A Study of Contemporary Cultural Patterns in the United States*. New York: Cambridge University Press.

Boris, Elizabeth T. (1987). "Creation and Growth: A Survey of Private Foundations." In Teresa Odendahl (Ed.), *America's Wealthy and the Future of Foundations* (pp.65–126). New York: The Foundation Center.

Bourdieu, Pierre (1984). *Distinction: A Social Critique of the Judgement of Taste.* Richard Nice (Translator). Cambridge: Harvard University Press.

Burnham, Jack (1971). "Hans Haacke's Cancelled Show at the Guggenheim." *Art Forum*, 9, 67–71.

Burt, Ronald S. (1983). *Corporate Profits and Cooptation: Networks of Market Constraints and Directorate Ties in the American Economy*. New York: Academic Press.

Carroll, Glen (1984). "Organizational Ecology." *Annual Review of Sociology*, 10, 71–93.

Chaffee, Ellen Earle (1985). "Three Models of Strategy." *Academy of Management Review*, 19, 89–98.

Chandler, Alfred D. Jr. (1962). *Strategy and Structure*. New York: Doubleday.

Child, John (1972). "Organizational Structure, Environment and Performance: The Role of Strategic Choice." *Sociology*, 6 (January), 1–22.

Clemens, Elisabeth S. (1993). "Organizational Repertoires and Institutional Change: Women's Groups and the Transformation of U.S. Politics, 1890–1920." *American Journal of Sociology*, 98, 755–98.

Cohen, Michael, James G. March & Johan P. Olsen (1972). "A Garbage-Can Model of Organizational Choice." *Administrative Science Quarterly*, 17, 1–25.

Coleman, Lawrence Vail (1939). *The Museum in America: A Critical Study*, in three volumes. Washington, DC: American Association of Museums.

Collins, Randall (1979). *The Credential Society*. New York: Academic Press.

Corn, Wanda M. (1983). *Grant Wood: The Regionalist Vision*. New Haven, CT: Published for the Minneapolis Institute of Arts by Yale University Press.

Crane, Diana (1992). *The Production of Culture: Media and the Urban Arts*. Newbury Park, CA: Sage.

Crane, Diana (1987). *The Transformation of the Avant-Garde: The New York Art World, 1940–1985*. Chicago: University of Chicago Press.

Crane, Diana (1985). "Avant-Garde Art and Social Change: The New York Art World and the Transformation of the Reward System, 1940–1980." Paper presented at the meeting on the Sociology of Art at the Société Française de Sociologie, Marseilles.

Cummings, Milton C. Jr. (1991). "Government and the Arts: An Overview." In Stephen Benedict (Ed.), *Public Money and the Muse: Essays on Government Funding for the Arts* (pp. 31–79). New York: W.W. Norton & Co.

Cyert, Richard & James March (1963). *A Behavioral Theory of the Firm*. Englewood Cliffs, NJ: Prentice Hall.

Dahrendorf, Ralf (1959). *Class and Class Conflict in Industrial Society*. Stanford: Stanford University Press.

Danto, Arthur C. (1987). *The State of the Art*. New York: Prentice Hall Press.

Dauber, Kenneth (1993). "The Indian Arts Fund and the Patronage of Native American Arts." In Judith Higgins Balfe (Ed.), *Paying the Piper: Causes and Consequences of Art Patronage*. Chicago: University of Illinois Press.

DiMaggio, Paul J. (1991a). "The Museum and The Public." In Martin Felstein (Ed.), *The Economics of Art Museums* (pp. 39–50). Chicago: University of Chicago Press.

DiMaggio, Paul J. (1991b). "Decentralization of Arts Funding from the Federal Government to the States." In Stephen Benedict (Ed.), *Public Money and the Muse: Essays on Government Funding for the Arts* (pp.216–256). New York: W.W. Norton & Co.

DiMaggio, Paul J. (1991c). "Constructing an Organizational Field as a Professional Project: U.S. Art Museums, 1920–1940." In Walter W. Powell & Paul J. DiMaggio (Eds.), *The New Institutionalism in Organizational Analysis* (pp.267–292). Chicago: University of Chicago Press.

DiMaggio, Paul J. (1988a). "Progressivism and the Arts." *Society*, July/August, 70–75.

DiMaggio, Paul J. (1988b). "Interest and Agency in Institutional Theory." In Lynne G. Zucker (Ed.), *Institutional Patterns and Organizations* (pp. 3–21). Cambridge, MA: Ballinger.

DiMaggio, Paul J. (1987a). "The Professionalized Environment as a Source of Institutional Change: American Art Museums, 1920–1940." Paper presented at the Convention on Institutional Change, Center For Advanced Study in the Behavioral Sciences, Palo Alto, CA.

DiMaggio, Paul J. (1987b). "Classification in Art." *American Sociological Review*, 52, 440–455.

DiMaggio, Paul J. (1986a). "Introduction." In Paul J. DiMaggio (Ed.), *Nonprofit Enterprise in the Arts: Studies in Mission and Constraint* (pp. 3–13). New York, Oxford University Press.

DiMaggio, Paul J. (1986b). "Can Culture Survive the Marketplace?" In Paul J. DiMaggio (Ed.), *Nonprofit Enterprise in the Arts: Studies in Mission and Constraint* (pp. 65–92). New York, Oxford University Press

DiMaggio, Paul J. (1986c). "Support for the Arts from Independent Foundations." In Paul J. DiMaggio (Ed.), *Nonprofit Enterprise in the Arts: Studies in Mission and Constraint* (pp. 113–139). New York, Oxford University Press

DiMaggio, Paul J. (1983). "State Expansion and Organizational Fields." In Richard H. Hall & Robert E. Quinn (Eds.), *Organizational Theory and Public Policy* (pp. 147–161). Beverly Hills: Sage.

DiMaggio, Paul J. (1982a). "Cultural Entrepreneurship in Nineteenth-Century Boston: The Creation of an Organizational Base for High Culture in America." *Media, Culture and Society*, 4, 33–50.

DiMaggio, Paul J. (1982b). "Cultural Entrepreneurship in Nineteenth-Century Boston, Part II: The Classification and Framing of American Art." *Media, Culture and Society*, 4, 303–22.

DiMaggio, Paul J. & Walter W. Powell (1991). "Introduction." In Walter W. Powell & Paul J. DiMaggio (Eds.), *The New Institutionalism in Organizational Analysis* (pp. 1–38). Chicago: University of Chicago Press.

DiMaggio, Paul J. & Walter W. Powell (1983). "The Iron Cage Revisited: Institutional Isomorphism and Collective Rationality in Organizational Fields." *American Sociological Review*, 48, 147–160.

DiMaggio, Paul J. & Kristin Stenberg (1985). "Why Do Some Theatres Innovate More Than Others?" *Poetics*, 14, 107–122.

DiMaggio, Paul J. & Michael Useem (1978). "Social Class and Arts Consumption: The Origin and Consequences of Class Differences in Exposure to the Arts in America." *Theory and Society*, 5, 141–161.

Domhoff, G. William (1967). *Who Rules America?* Englewood Cliffs, NJ: Prentice-Hall.

Dubin, Stephen C. (1992). *Arresting Images: Impolitic Art and Uncivil Actions*. New York: Routledge.

Duncan, Carol & Alan Wallach (1980). "The Universal Survey Museum." *Art History*, 3, 448–469.

Ermann, David (1979). "Corporate Contributions to Public Television." *Social Problems*, 25, 505–514.

Feld, Alan L., Michael O'Hare & J. Mark Davidson Schuster (1983). *Patrons Despite Themselves: Taxpayers and Arts Policy*. New York: New York University Press.

Fiske, John (1989). *Reading the Popular*. New York: Routledge.

Fligstein, Neil (1990). *The Transformation of Corporate Control*. Cambridge: Harvard University Press.

Fligstein, Neil (1987). "The Intraorganizational Power Struggle: The Rise of Finance Presidents in Large Firms, 1919–1979." *American Sociological Review*, 52, 44–58.

Frey, Bruno S. & Werner W. Pommerehne (1989). *Muses and Markets: Explorations in the Economics of the Arts*. Oxford: Basil Blackwell.

Friedland, Roger & Robert R. Alford (1991). "Bringing Society Back In: Symbols, Practices, and Institutional Contradictions." In Walter W. Powell & Paul J. DiMaggio (Eds.), *The New Institutionalism in Organizational Analysis* (pp. 232–263). Chicago: University of Chicago Press.

Fry, Edward (1971). "Hans Haacke, the Guggenheim: The Issues." *Arts Magazine*, 45, 17.

Fry, Louis W., Gerald Keim & Roger E. Meiners (1982). "Corporate Contributions: Altruistic or For Profit?" *Academy of Management Journal*, 25, 94–106.

Galaskiewicz, Joseph (1991). "Making Corporate Actors Accountable: Institution-Building in Minneapolis-St. Paul." In Walter W. Powell & Paul J. DiMaggio (Eds.), *The New Institutionalism in Organizational Analysis* (pp. 293–310). Chicago: University of Chicago Press.

Galaskiewicz, Joseph (1985). *Social Organization of an Urban Grants Economy: A Study of Corporate Contributions to Nonprofit Organizations*. New York: Academic.

Galaskiewicz, Joseph & Barbara Rauschenbach (1988). "The Corporate-Culture Connection: A Test of Interorganizational Theories." In Carl Milofsky (Ed.), *Community Organizations: Studies in Resource Mobilization and Exchange* (pp. 119–135). New York: Oxford University Press.

Galligan, Ann M. (1993). "The Politicization of Peer-Review Panels at the NEA." In Judith Huggins Balfe (Ed.), *Paying the Piper: Causes and Consequences of Art Patronage* (pp. 254–272). Baltimore: University of Illinois Press

Gans, Herbert J. (1974). *Popular Culture and High Culture: An Analysis and Evaluation of Taste*. New York: Basic Books.

Garfias, Robert (1991). "Cultural Diversity and the Arts in America." In Stephen Benedict (Ed.), *Public Money and the Muse: Essays on Government Funding for the Arts* (pp. 182–194). New York: W.W. Norton & Co.

Gingrich, Arnold (1969). *Business and the Arts: An Answer to Tomorrow*. New York: Paul S. Eriksson, Inc.

Glaser, Barney G. & Anselm L. Strauss (1967). *The Discovery of Grounded Theory: Strategies for Qualitative Research*. London: Wiedenfield and Nicholson.

Glennon, Lorraine (1988). "The Museum and the Corporation: New Realities." *Museum News*, 66 (3), 36–43.

Griswold, Wendy (1992). "The Writing on the Mud Wall: Nigerian Novels and the Imaginary Village." *American Sociological Review*, 57, 709–724.

Griswold, Wendy (1987). "A Methodological Framework for the Sociology of Culture." In Clifford C. Clogg (Ed.), *Sociological Methodology*, 17, 1–35.

Griswold, Wendy (1981). "American Character and the American Novel: An Expansion of Reflection Theory in the Sociology of Literature." *American Journal of Sociology*, 86, 740–765.

Hannan, Michael T. & John Freeman (1984). "Structural Inertia and Organizational Change." *Administrative Science Quarterly*, 49, 149–164.

Hannan, Michael T. & John Freeman (1977). "The Population Ecology of Organizations." *American Journal of Sociology*, 82, 929–64.

Haskell, Francis (1963). *Patrons and Painters: A Study in the Relations between Italian Art and Society in the Age of the Baroque*. New York: Alfred A Knopf.

Hauser, Arnold (1982). *The Sociology of Art*. Kenneth J. Northcott (Translator). London: Routledge & Kegan Paul.

Hauser, Arnold (1958). *The Social History of Art*. New York: Vintage Books.

Hawley, Amos (1950). *Human Ecology*. New York: Ronald Press.

Hickson, David J., D. S. Pugh & Diana C. Pheysey (1969). "Operations Technology and Organization Structure: An Empirical Reappraisal." *Administrative Science Quarterly*, 14, 378–97.

Hirsch, Paul M. (1981). "Processing Fads and Fashions: An Organization-Set Analysis of Cultural Industry Systems." In Oscar Grusky & George A. Miller (Eds.), *The Sociology of Organizations: Basic Studies* (2nd ed., pp. 455–476). New York: The Free Press.

Holsti, Ole R. (1969). *Content Analysis for the Social Sciences and Humanities*. Reading, MA: Addison-Wesley.

Honan, William H. (1990, January 14). "Say Goodbye to the Stuffed Elephants." *New York Times Magazine*, pp. 35+.

Janson, Anthony F. (1986). *History of Art* (3rd ed.). New York: Harry N. Abrams, Inc.

Larson, Gary O. (1983). *The Reluctant Patron: The United States Government and the Arts, 1943–1965*. Philadelphia: University of Pennsylvania Press.

Larson, Magali Sarfatti (1977). *The Rise of Professionalism*. Berkeley: University of California Press.

Levine, Lawrence W. (1988). *Highbrow/Lowbrow: The Emergence of Cultural Hierarchy in America*. Cambridge: Harvard University Press.

Levitt, Arthur Jr. (1991). "Introduction." In Stephen Benedict (Ed.), *Public Money and the Muse: Essays on Government Funding for the Arts* (pp. 19–30). New York: W.W. Norton & Co.

Levy, Ferdinand K. & Gloria M. Shatto (1978). "The Evaluation of Corporate Contributions." *Public Choice*, 33, 19–28.

Lieberson, Stanley (1985). *Making it Count: The Improvement of Social Research and Theory*. Berkeley: University of California Press.

Lilla, Mark & Isabelle Frank (1988). "The Medici and the Multinationals." *Museum News*, 66 (3), 33–35.

Lynes, Russell (1973). *Good Old Modern: An Intimate Portrait of the Museum of Modern Art*. New York: Atheneum.

Lynes, Russell (1954). *The Taste Makers*. New York: Harper & London: Hamish Hamilton.

March, James & Johan P. Olsen (1976). *Ambiguity and Choice in Organizations*. Bergen, Norway: Universitetsforlaget.

Martorella, Rosanne (1990). *Corporate Art*. New Brunswick: Rutgers University Press.

McGuigan, Cathleen, with Shawn Doherty, Janet Huck, & Maggie Malone (1985). "A Word From Our Sponsor: Increasing Ties Between Big Business and the Art World Raise Some Delicate Questions." *Newsweek*, (November 25), 96–98.

McKelvey, William (1982). *Organizational Systematics: Taxonomy, Evolution, Classification*. Berkeley: University of California Press.

Metcalf, Eugene W., Jr. (1986). "The Politics of the Past in American Folk Art History." In John Michael Vlach and Simon J. Bronner (Eds.), *Folk Art and Art Worlds* (pp. 27–50). Ann Arbor, MI: UMI Research Press.

Meyer, John W., John Boli & George M. Thomas (1987). "Ontology and Rationalization in the Western Cultural Account." In George M. Thomas, John W. Meyer, Francisco O. Ramirez & John Boli (Eds.), *Institutional Structure: Constituting State, Society, and the Individual*. Beverly Hills: Sage.

Meyer, John W. & Brian Rowan (1981). "Institutionalized Organizations: Formal Structure as Myth and Ceremony." In Oscar Grusky & George A. Miller (Eds.), *The Sociology of Organizations* (2nd. ed.) (pp 530–554). New York: Free Press.

Meyer, John W. & W. Richard Scott (Eds.) (1992). *Organizational Environments: Ritual and Rationality* (2nd. ed.). Beverly Hills: Sage Publications.

Meyer, Karl E. (1979). *The Art Museum: Power, Money, Ethics*. New York: William Morrow and Co., Inc.

Middleton, Melissa (1986). "Nonprofit Management: A Report on Current Research and Areas for Development." Program on Non-Profit Organizations. Working Paper No. 108.

Miles, Matthew B. & A. Michael Huberman (1984). *Qualitative Data Analysis*. Beverly Hills: Sage.

Miles, Raymond E., Charles C. Snow, Alan D. Meyer, & Henry J. Coleman, Jr. (1978). "Organization Strategy, Structure and Process." *Academy of Management Review*, 3, 546–562.

Miller, Danny (1992). "Environmental Fit versus Internal Fit." *Organization Science*, 3, 159–178.

Molotsky, Irvin (1993, August 19). "Tax Break to Aid Museums." *New York Times*, pp. C11+.

Moulin, Raymonde (1987). *The French Art Market: A Sociological View*. Arthur Goldhammer (Translator). New Brunswick: Rutgers University Press.

NBC Evening News (1995, March 24.) Interview of Quincy Jones by Tom Brokaw.

Namenwirth, J. Zvi & Robert Philip Weber (1987). *Dynamics of Culture*. Boston: Allen & Unwin.

National Endowment for the Arts (1990). *Annual Report for Fiscal Year 1990*. Washington, DC: U.S. Government Printing Office.

National Endowment for the Arts (1974). *Museums USA*. Washington, DC: U.S. Government Printing Office.

National Endowment for the Humanities (1986). *Twenty-First Annual Report*. Washington, DC: U.S. Government Printing Office.

National Endowment for the Humanities (1966) *First Annual Report*. Washington, DC: U.S. Government Printing Office.

Odendahl, Teresa A. (1990). *Charity Begins at Home: Generosity and Self-Interest among the Philanthropic Elite*. New York: Basic Books.

Odendahl, Teresa A. (1987a). "Independent Foundations and Wealthy Donors: An Overview." In Teresa Odendahl (Ed.), *America's Wealthy and the Future of Foundations* (pp. 1–26). New York: The Foundation Center.

Odendahl, Teresa A. (1987b). "Foundations and the Nonprofit Sector." In Teresa Odendahl (Ed.), *America's Wealthy and the Future of Foundations* (pp. 27–42). New York: The Foundation Center.

Oliver, Andrew (1991). "The Museum and the Government." In Martin Felstein (Ed.), *The Economics of Art Museums* (pp. 91–94). Chicago: University of Chicago Press.

Oliver, Christine (1991). "Strategic Responses to Institutional Processes." *Academy of Management Review*, 16, 145–179.

Palmer, Donald, A. P. Devereau Jennings & Xueguang Zhou (1993). "Late Adoption of the Multidivisional Form by Large U.S. Corporations: Institutional, Political, and Economic Accounts." *Administrative Science Quarterly*, 38, 100–131.

Peterson, Richard A. (1986). "From Impresario to Arts Administrator: Formal Accountability in Nonprofit Cultural Organizations." In Paul J. DiMaggio (Ed.), *Nonprofit Enterprise in the Arts: Studies in Mission and Constraint* (pp. 161–183). New York, Oxford University Press.

Peterson, Richard A. (1979). "Revitalizing the Culture Concept." *Annual Review of Sociology*, 5, 137–66.

Peterson, Richard A. (Ed.) (1976). *The Production of Culture*. London: Sage.

Peterson, Richard A. & David G. Berger (1975). "Cycles in Symbol Production: The Case of Popular Music." *American Sociological Review*, 40, 158–173.

Pfeffer, Jefferey & Gerald R. Salancik (1978). *The External Control of Organizations: A Resource Dependence Perspective*. New York: Harper and Row, Publishers.

Porter, Robert (Ed.) (1981). *A Guide to Corporate Giving in the Arts*. New York: American Council for the Arts.

Powell, Walter W. (1991). "Expanding the Scope of Institutional Analysis." In Walter W. Powell and Paul J. DiMaggio (Eds.), *The New Institutionalism in Organizational Analysis* (pp. 183–203). Chicago: University of Chicago Press.

Powell, Walter W. (1988) "Institutional Effects on Organizational Structure and Performance." In Lynne O. Zucker (Ed.), *Institutional Patterns and Organizations* (pp. 115–136) Cambridge, MA: Ballinger.

Powell, Walter W. & Paul J. DiMaggio (Eds.) (1991). *The New Institutionalism in Organizational Analysis*. Chicago: University of Chicago Press.

Prud'homme, Alex (1992, January 20). "The CEO of Culture Inc.: Controversial Guggenheim Director Thomas Krens Is Changing the Way the World's Art Museums Operate." *Time*, 36–37.

Robinson, Rick E. (1977). "Why *This* Piece? On the Choices of Collectors in the Fine Arts." Paper presented at the American Sociological Association's Annual Meeting. Chicago.

Rogers, Patrick (1995, February 13). "Circus of the Czars." *Newsweek*, 76–77.

Rose, Barbara (1975). *American Art Since 1900* (revised and expanded edition). San Francisco: Holt, Rinehart and Winston.

Rosenbaum, Lee (1977). "The Scramble for Museum Sponsors: Is Curatorial Independence for Sale?" *Art in America*, 65, 10–14.

Routledge, Anna Wells (1949). "Robert Gilmore, Jr., Baltimore Collector." *The Journal of the Walters Art Gallery*. 12, 18–39.

Schiller, Herbert I. (1989, July 10). "The Corporate Art Pitchers at an Exhibition." *The Nation*, 1+.

Schudson, Michael (1978). "A Critiques of the 'Production of Culture' Perspective in the Study of Mass Media." Paper presented at the American Sociological Association's Annual Meeting, San Francisco.

Schuster, J. Mark Davidson (1991). "The Formula Funding Controversy at the National Endowment for the Arts." *Nonprofit Management & Leadership*, 2, 37–57.

Schuster, J. Mark Davidson (1989). "Government Leverage of Private Support: Matching Grants and the Problems with 'New' Money." In Margaret J. Wyszomirski & Pat Clubb (Eds.), *The Cost of Culture*. New York: American Council for the Arts.

Scott, W. Richard (1995). *Institutions and Organizations*. Thousand Oaks, CA: Sage.

Scott, W. Richard (1992). *Organizations: Rational, Natural and Open Systems* (3rd ed.). Englewood Cliffs, NJ: Prentice-Hall, Inc.

Scott, W. Richard (1987). "The Adolescence of Institutionalization Theory." *Administrative Science Quarterly*, 32, 493–511.

Scott, W. Richard (1983). "The Organization of Environments: Network, Cultural, and Historical Elements." In Meyer & Scott (Eds.), *Organizational Environments: Ritual and Rationality* (pp. 155–175). Beverly Hills: Sage Publications.

Scott, W. Richard & John W. Meyer (1991). "The Organization of Societal Sectors: Propositions and Early Evidence." In Walter W. Powell & Paul J. DiMaggio (Eds.), *The New Institutionalism in Organizational Analysis* (pp. 108–140). Chicago: University of Chicago Press.

Scott, W. Richard & John W. Meyer (1983). "The Organization of Societal Sectors." In John W. Meyer & W. Richard Scott (Eds.), *Organizational Environments: Ritual and Rationality*. Beverly Hills: Sage.

Sewell, William H. (1992). "A Theory of Structure: Duality, Agency, and Transformation." *American Journal of Sociology*, 98, 1–29.

Siegel, Jeanne (1971). "An Interview with Hans Haacke," *Arts Magazine*, 45, 18–21.

Silverman, Debora (1986). *Selling Culture: Bloomingdale's, Diana Vreeland, and the New Aristocracy of Taste in Reagan's America*. New York: Pantheon.

Simon, John G. (1987). "The Tax Treatment of Nonprofit Organizations: A Review of Federal and State Policies." In Walter W. Powell (Ed.), *The Nonprofit Sector: A Research Handbook* (pp. 67–98). New Haven: Yale University Press.

Skloot, Edward (1987). "Enterprize and Commerce in Nonprofit Organizations." In Walter W. Powell (Ed.), *The Nonprofit Sector: A Research Handbook* (pp. 340–359). New Haven: Yale University Press.

Smith, Barbara Herrnstein (1983). "Contingencies of Value." *Critical Inquiry*, 10, 1–35.

Stout, Suzanne Kay (1992). *The Dynamics of Organizational Linkages: The Case of Higher Education and Philanthropy*. Ph.D. Dissertation, Stanford University.

Stuart, Paul H. (1992). *Philanthropy, Voluntarism, and Innovation: Settlement Houses in Twentieth-Century America*. Indianapolis: Indiana University Center on Philanthropy. Essays on Philanthropy, No. 5.

Swidler, Ann (1986). "Culture in Action: Symbols and Strategies." *American Sociological Review*, 51, 273–286.

Thompson, James D. (1967). *Organizations in Action*. New York: McGraw-Hill.

Tolbert, Pamela S. & Lynne G. Zucker (1983). "Institutional Sources of Change in the Formal Structure of Organizations: The Diffusion of Civil Service Reform, 1880–1935." *Administrative Science Quarterly*, 28, 22–39.

Tomkins, Calvin (1970). *Merchants and Masterpieces: The Story of the Metropolitan Museum of Art*. New York: E. P. Dutton and Co.

Useem, Michael (1991). "Corporate Funding of the Arts in a Turbulent Environment." *Nonprofit Management and Leadership*, 1, 329–343.

Useem, Michael (1987). "Corporate Philanthropy." In Walter W. Powell (Ed.), *The Handbook of Non-Profit Organizations* (pp. 340–359). New Haven: Yale University Press.

Useem, Michael (1984). *The Inner Circle: Large Corporations and the Rise of Business and Political Activity in the U.S. and the U.K.* New York: Oxford University Press.

Useem, Michael (1980). "Corporations and the Corporate Elite." *Annual Review of Sociology*, 6, 41–77.

Useem, Michael & Stephen I. Kutner (1986). "Corporate Contributions to Culture and the Arts: The Organization of Giving and the Influence of the Chief Executive Officer and of Other Firms on Company Contributions in Massachusetts." In Paul J. DiMaggio (Ed.), *Nonprofit Enterprise in the Arts: Studies in Mission and Constraint* (pp. 93–112). New York: Oxford University Press.

Veblin, Thorstein (1934). *The Theory of the Leisure Class*. New York: Random House.

Venturi, Robert & Denise Scott Brown (1984). *A View from the Campidoglio: Selected Essays*. New York: Harper and Row.

Wallach, Alan (1981). "Thomas Cole and the Aristocracy." *Arts Magazine*, 56, 84–106.

Webb, E. J., D. T. Campbell, R. D. Schwartz & L. Sechrest (1965). *Unobtrusive Measures*. Chicago: Rand McNally.

Weber, Max (1978). *Economy and Society*. Guenther Roth & Claus Wittich (eds). Berkeley: University of California Press.

Weber, Max (1946). "Class, Status and Party." In H. H. Gerth & C. Wright Mills (Eds.), *From Max Weber: Essays in Sociology* (pp. 180–195). New York: Oxford University Press.

Weick, Karl E. (1979). *The Social-Psychology of Organizing* (2nd ed.). Reading, MA: Addison-Wesley.

Weinberg, H. Barbara (1976). "Thomas B. Clarke: Foremost Patron of American Art from 1872 to 1899." *American Art Journal*, 8, 52–83.

White, Harrison C. & Cynthia A. White (1965). *Canvasses and Careers: Institutional Change in the French Painting World*. New York: John Wiley and Sons, Inc.

Wildavsky, Aaron B. (1979). *Speaking Truth to Power: The Art and Craft of Policy Analysis*. Boston: Little, Brown.

Williams, Raymond (1981). *The Sociology of Culture*. New York: Schocken Books.

Woodcome, Mary Elizabeth (1995). *Stories of the Self: Exhibiting Nubia and the Politics of Cultural Representation*. Undergraduate Honors Thesis, Harvard University.

Yoshitomi, Gerald D. (1991). "Cultural Democracy." In Stephen Benedict (Ed.), *Public Money and the Muse: Essays on Government Funding for the Arts* (pp. 195–215). New York: W.W. Norton & Co.

Yvlisaker, Paul N. (1987). "Foundations and Nonprofit Organizations." In Walter W. Powell (Ed.), *The Handbook of Non-Profit Organizations* (pp. 360–379). New Haven: Yale University Press.

Zelditch, Morris Jr. et al. (1983). "Decisions, Metadecisions and Non-Decisions," *Research in Social Movements, Conflicts and Change*, 5, 1–32.

Zolberg, Vera L. (1990). *Constructing a Sociology of the Arts*. New York: Cambridge University Press.

Zolberg, Vera L. (1986). "Tensions of Mission in American Art Museums." In Paul J. DiMaggio (Ed.), *Nonprofit Enterprise in the Arts: Studies in Mission and Constraint* (pp. 184–198). New York: Oxford University Press.

Zolberg, Vera L. (1983). "New Art—New Patrons: Coincidence of Causality in the Twentieth-Century Avant-Garde." *Contributions to the Sociology of the Arts* (Reports from the 10th World Congress of Sociology, Mexico 1982). Sofia, Bulgaria: Research Institute for the Arts.

Zolberg, Vera L. (1981). "Conflicting Visions in American Art Museums." *Theory and Society*, 10, 103–125.

Zolberg, Vera L. (1974). *The Art Institute of Chicago: The Sociology of a Cultural Organization*. Ph.D. Dissertation, University of Chicago.

Museum Annual Reports

Albright-Knox Museum (1978–79). *Annual Report, 1978–79.*

Albright-Knox Art Gallery (1966). "Annual Report, 1964–65." *Gallery Notes*, XXIX (March).

Albright-Knox Art Gallery (1963). "Annual Report, 1962–63." *Gallery Notes*, XXVII (December).

Art Institute of Chicago (1984–85). *Annual Report.*

Art Institute of Chicago (1980–81). *Annual Report.*

Art Institute of Chicago (1978–79). *Annual Report.*

Art Institute of Chicago (1974–75). *Annual Report.*

Art Institute of Chicago (1972–73). *Annual Report.*

Art Institute of Chicago (1970–71). *Annual Report.*

Art Institute of Chicago (1968–69). *Annual Report.*

Baltimore Museum of Art (1972). *Record*, December.

Brooklyn Museum (1982–86). *The Brooklyn Museum Report, 1982–86.*

Brooklyn Museum (1966–67). *Annual VIII, 1966–67.*

Brooklyn Museum (1962–63). *Annual VI, 1962–63.*

California Palace of the Legion of Honor (1965). *Bulletin*, Vol. 10, February.

Cleveland Museum (1965). "Annual Report, 1964." *Bulletin*, vol. LII, no. 6.

Detroit Institute of Art (1985). *Annual Report, 1985.*

Detroit Institute of Art (1983). "Annual Report, 1982–83." *Bulletin*, vol. 61, no. 3.

Fine Arts Museums of San Francisco (1983–85). *Report, 1983–85.*

Fine Arts Museums of San Francisco (1978–80). *Report, 1978–80.*

Fogg Museum (1974–75). *Annual Reports, 1974–76.*

Fogg Museum (1966–67). *Annual Report, 1966–67.*

Metropolitan Museum of Art (1982–83). *One Hundred Thirteenth Annual Report of the Trustees of the Metropolitan Museum of Art for the Fiscal Year July 1, 1982 through June 30, 1983.* Presented to the Corporation of the Metropolitan Museum of Art, October 15, 1983.

Metropolitan Museum of Art (1978–79). *One Hundred Ninth Annual Report of the Trustees of the Metropolitan Museum of Art for the Fiscal Year July 1, 1978 through June 30, 1979.* Presented to the Corporation of the Metropolitan Museum of Art, October 15, 1979.

Metropolitan Museum of Art (1970–71). *One Hundred First Annual Report of the Trustees of the Metropolitan Museum of Art for the Fiscal Year July 1, 1970 through June 30, 1971.* Presented to the Corporation of the Metropolitan Museum of Art, October 18, 1971.

Museum of Fine Arts, Boston (1972–73). *The Museum Year: 1972–73, The 97th Annual Report of the Museum of Fine Arts, Boston.*

Museum of Fine Arts, Boston (1970–71). *The Museum Year: 1970–71, The 95th Annual Report of the Museum of Fine Arts, Boston.*

Museum of Modern Art (1980–81). *Annual Report.*
Museum of Modern Art (1937). *Annual Report.*
Newberger Museum (1986) *Fall '86 Calendar.*
San Francisco Museum of Modern Art (1988). *Annual Report.*
Wadsworth Atheneum (1981). *Annual Report.*
Wadsworth Atheneum (1979). *Annual Report.*
Whitney Museum (1967–68). *Whitney Review.*

METHODOGICAL APPENDIX

The research presented in this book rests on two separate data collection efforts: (1) in-depth interviews with museum personnel and (2) an analysis of archival information (annual reports) produced by museums. I analyzed the annual reports qualitatively, as well as using them to build a quantitative data set of exhibition formats and contents.

The use of multiple methods, sometimes called triangulation, is highly recommended in empirical research (Miles & Huberman, 1984). The term, coined by Webb et al. (1965), refers to "validating a finding by subjecting it to 'the onslaught of a series of imperfect measures.'" (quoted in Miles & Huberman, 1984, p. 234) There are many advantages in using multiple methods, especially in the reconfirmation of a finding. In addition, as Glaser and Strauss (1967) point out, qualitative methods are especially useful in generating grounded theory, while quantitative methods are useful for confirmation of theory. Since generating theory is as important in this study as learning about the relationship of funding and exhibitions, a judicious mix of quantitative and qualitative analysis is in order.

In-Depth Interviews with Museum Personnel

I conducted in-depth, unstructured interviews to learn how museum personnel understand and react to their funding environment. I interviewed twelve people from eight northeastern museums. The shortest of the interviews was one-half hour, the longest, about three hours. Most were about an hour long. The sample was not random: I wrote people whom I knew through personal contacts. However, I did try to interview people from a range of occupations and types of museums (see Table A-1).

TABLE A-1
Type of Museum Personnel Interviewed by Museum Characteristics

Type of Museum	*Person Interviewed*
Small, Rural, Modern Art (1 museum)	Director/Curator
Large, Urban, General Collection (5 museums)	Director (3) Curator (2) Assoc. Curator (2) Educator
University (2 museums)	Director Educator (2)

I interviewed one director-curator from a small, rural, modern art museum; three directors, two curators, two associate curators, and one educator from five large, urban, general-collection museums; and one director and two educators from two university museums. The interviews were conducted in 1986.

The people with whom I spoke were curators, directors, and educators. *Curators*, who are generally art historians, organize exhibitions and work with the actual objects used in such shows. *Directors* manage and run the museum, and are often not involved with curatorial issues, although museums vary in this regard (with small museums more likely to require double duty from their directors). Although directors are predominantly art historians, many of their staff are trained in other fields such as public relations or law. *Educators*,[1] a mixed bag as far as training is concerned, run the museum's public programs. These programs introduce children and adults to various aspects of art history and link the museum's exhibits and its public. The education directors are the most aware of the audiences museums attract, or would like to attract. The museums themselves range from very small, new, specialized, museums in small towns to large, general, well-established museums in the nation's largest cities. Some are public museums, some nonprofit, and two are university museums.

Each of these factors—the museum's size, its location, whether it is a specialist or generalist—combine with the individual's staff position to shape each respondent's perspective on the art scene. Other important factors include the size of the museum's endowment, its membership (large, small, wealthy or not), and how many other museums (i.e., competitors) are located in the vicinity.

In keeping with the spirit of grounded theory, I did not develop a formal questionnaire. Instead, in the interviews I addressed several sets of questions concerning changes in art funding. These questions were open-ended to allow the respondents a great deal of freedom in answering. I focused on current issues (1986) and only occasionally relied on respondents' recall of the past. I asked museum personnel their opinions of corporate and government funders, how they thought the process for applying for corporate and government money worked, and what the different types of funders look for in exhibitions and demand from museums. I asked about the ramifications of changes from individual to institutional funders and how museum staffs manage in light of the changes. I asked about museum missions, specifically about broadening audiences and building education programs. Finally, I asked about a concern that is routinely expressed in art circles: Are corporations' instrumental interests hurting rather than helping the arts? The interviews were intended as a pilot study, but the results were important. Interview data supplement academic research on the goals of funders in Chapter 2, and they supplement the archival research in Chapters 3 and 4.

Analysis of Museum Annual Reports

The second research design for this study involves a longitudinal analysis of exhibitions mounted by large museums since 1960. I collected information on approximately 30 large museums, spanning almost three decades, to document changing patterns in exhibitions.

To collect information on museums and exhibitions, I consulted annual reports of museums at the Thomas J. Watson Library at the Metropolitan Museum of Art in New York City, and then at the Ryerson and Burnham Libraries at the Art Institute of Chicago. I employed a comprehensive sample of the largest American art museums, based on their 1978 operating expenditures (described below) and coded exhibitions mounted by a subset of these museums. I developed a coding scheme for exhibitions based on art historical research. In addition to coding exhibitions, I also collected financial, attendance, and other general information for each museum-year. Quantitative results are presented in Chapter 3. Further, the analysis of annual reports yielded interesting qualitative results concerning organizational-level effects of funding which are reported in Chapter 4.

There are many advantages to building a data set from original archival materials. Although the format of annual reports varies by museum and by year, these reports provide enough similar information, which I extracted and coded. As with all documentary source material, annual reports reflect the concerns of museums at the time they were written; thus, they are well-suited for longitudinal analysis. This is the main advantage of coding museum publications. I began the analysis with 1960—five years before the advent of federal funding and major corporate sponsorship of the arts—and collected data for even years from 1960 to 1986. That works out to be 14 time points for each museum. Significantly, the data set ends before the current crises in federal arts funding over what is funded and how much funding should be available.

I chose to examine large museums. Large museums form a conceptually distinct population, since they play a gatekeeping role in the visual arts sector that small museums do not (Crane 1987, Chapter 7). In other words, big museums disproportionately define what is art, and small museums follow the pace-setting large museums. Given the theoretical considerations detailed earlier, a thorough analysis of the large, "kingpin" museums is more appropriate for detailing the effect of funding on art itself than is a broader investigation of both large and small museums that lacks the focus necessary to fully examine this small but crucial subgroup.

I have also chosen to focus on museum exhibitions rather than other aspects of museums influenced by patronage, for example acquisitions and programs. There are several important advantages in focusing on exhibitions. Most of the public, and many critics and art scholars, experience art through exhibitions; consequently, exhibitions may be more important than acquisitions for defining art. Further, exhibitions are under more direct control by museum personnel than are acquisitions,[2] allowing for a broader understanding of curatorial intention and how it might be influenced externally. Finally, the mix of funding for exhibitions has changed much more than that for acquisitions. Consequently, studying exhibitions provides a greater opportunity for understanding the impact of the institutional funders on art.

This does not mean that acquisitions are unimportant to museums; on the contrary, museums cannot produce shows with art they do not have or cannot borrow. Since museums borrow from other museums and from private collections (the very collections from which donations are made), in the long run, acquisitions are extremely important. Wealthy individuals are still the primary source of acquisitions for museums, and perhaps they have become even more important in that area.[3] There are several reasons for this: First, corporations rarely give paintings to museums (although some corporations do have in-house art collections). Second, the purchase program of the NEA was discontinued in the late 1970s. Third, changes in the tax law of 1969 made it expensive for artists to donate their own work to museums.[4] Finally, with the exception of a few museums with substantial endowments (like the Getty), most museums cannot afford to buy paintings, (a) because paintings have become very expensive, and (b) because museums' endowments are often small relative to purchase prices—some endowments are small because of mismanagement, others because their blue-chip investments have not grown fast enough to produce a surplus. Given the importance of wealthy individuals in donating art works, ignoring acquisitions *understates the importance of elite patronage* in museum operations.

Corporations, government agencies, and elite donors may also fund very different aspects of a museum's operation. For example, elite patrons may wish to donate paintings, while government agencies prefer to fund educational programs. Corporations seem to favor a third strategy, choosing to sponsor large traveling exhibitions. Because I study only exhibition funding, the research does not capture these differences.

Sample Museums

I developed a "large museum universe" by taking the top 30 museums ranked by the institutions' annual expenses for museum-related items in 1978. Operating expenses were taken from the 1978 National Center for Education Statistics (NCES) Museum Universe Study. Five of these museums were excluded because they were not suited to the sample.[5] To this list of 25, I added six museums for which museum expense was "missing data," but which listed total expenditures for 1978 (including expenses for other activities, such as an art school or library), of $1 million or greater.[6] In addition, the J. Paul Getty Museum was listed in the NCES universe but had no information on either museum or total expenses. I added the Getty to the my sample because I knew it was a major museum. (Other museums with both variables missing tended to be small, obscure museums.)

The National Gallery,[7] the Los Angeles County Museum of Art, the Dallas Museum of Art, and the Kimbell Museum in Fort Worth, Texas, were not in the NCES universe at all, so I added them to my sample.[8] This made a total of 36 major museums in the universe (See Table A-2).

Building the Data Sets

I attempted to gather data on every museum in my large museum sample. Six museums[9] were dropped when information on them was not available in either of the archives I visited. I coded all annual reports collected: 6,337 exhibitions from 30 museums. The final data sets, however, are somewhat smaller. To increase the validity of the longitudinal analysis, I limited the data sets to museums for which there is data from at least 10 of the 14 time points. Consequently, the final data consist of more than 4,000 exhibits from 16 museums. There are two data sets used for the analysis. One uses the museum-year as the unit of analysis,[10] with information on a total of 198 museum-years, and a total of 4,370 exhibitions (16 museums aggregated by museum-year). (See Table A-3 for a summary of the coding for the museum level data.) The second is an exhibition-level data set, described in detail below, with information on a total of 4,026 individual exhibitions 15 museums).[11] The data sets contain only museums which have information on at least 10 of the 14 time points in the sample, and which have the most complete information. (These tended to be the larger of the large museums.)

Coding

I developed a coding scheme for exhibitions which tapped various measures of exhibition format and content. I coded each exhibition mounted by sample museums by its format, the source of the art work the museum used in the

TABLE A-2
Large Museum Universe
with Museum Expense, Rank, and Total Expense

Museum:	*Museum Expense*	*Rank**	*Total Expense*
The Metropolitan Museum of Art	$17,372,955	1	$37,762,523
Museum of Fine Arts, Boston	7,654,000	2	9,778,000
Philadelphia Museum of Art	5,809,000	3	5,809,000
The Brooklyn Museum	4,800,000	4	5,100,000
Cleveland Museum of Art	4,489,520	5	4,489,520
Whitney Museum of American Art	3,700,000	8	3,700,000
Fine Arts Museums of San Francisco	3,500,000	9	4,000,000
Detroit Institute of Arts	2,221,568	10	2,366,892
The Toledo Museum of Art	2,042,635	12	2,108,847
St. Louis Art Museum	1,876,020	13	2,039,385
The Minneapolis Institute of Arts	1,852,237	14	2,340,286
Art Institute of Chicago	1,780,422	15	139,176,200
Fogg Art Museum (Harvard)	1,769,742	16	.
Walker Art Center	1,725,000	17	2,327,300
The Baltimore Museum of Art	1,574,255	18	1,655,619
The Denver Art Museum	1,500,000	19	1,650,000
Wadsworth Atheneum	1,400,000	20	1,400,000
Walters Art Gallery	1,364,500	21	1,364,500
Worcester Art Museum	1,212,937	23	1,284,051
Nelson-Atkins Museum	1,200,000	24	.
Cincinnati Art Museum	1,076,014	26	1,143,605
New Orleans Museum of Art	1,063,000	27	1,063,000
Clark Art Institute	1,000,000	28	1,300,000
North Carolina Museum of Art	993,000	29	993,000
Joslyn Art Museum	925,000	30	.
Albright-Knox Art Gallery	.	.	1,335,732
Yale University Art Gallery	.	.	1,200,000
Indianapolis Museum of Art	.	.	2,500,000
Museum of Fine Arts of Houston	.	.	2,800,000
The Solomon R. Guggenheim Museum	.	.	2,547,126
The Museum of Modern Art	.	.	8,684,385
The J. Paul Getty Museum	.	.	.
National Gallery	x	x	x
Los Angeles County Museum of Art	x	x	x
Dallas Museum of Art	x	x	x
Kimbell Museum	x	x	x

Source: 1978 National Center for Education Statistics (NCES) Museum Universe Study.
Notes: . = missing.
x = not in NCES Museum Universe Study.
* Rank based on museum expenses.

exhibition, and the art historical style of the art in the exhibit. I was able to identify major funders and coded whether the exhibition was externally funded and by which types of funder (corporate, government, foundation, or individual). See Table A-4 for a summary of the aspects of exhibitions coded.

I developed the coding scheme using techniques recommended by content analysis researchers (e.g., Holsti, 1969; Namenwirth & Weber, 1987). I used a set coding scheme, which was designed to test hypotheses about the effect of funding on a range of exhibition characteristics. I pre-tested my coding scheme on a sample

TABLE A-3
Museum Code Summary

EXHIBITIONS:
1. *Separate list of exhibitions?*
   1 Yes
   0 No (exhibitions listed in text of annual report
   . missing (data not taken from an annual report)
2. *Exhibition sponsors listed separately?*
   1 Yes
   0 No
   . missing
3. *Description of exhibition with list?*
   1 Yes
   0 No
   . No list
4. *Description of exhibition elsewhere?*
   1 Yes
   0 No
   . missing, or with list

ATTENDANCE:
Record attendance if reported, missing, if not reported.

PARTIAL YEAR:
1. *Yes/No*
   1 Museum open only part of the year
   0 Museum open all year
2. *Percent*
   Record the percentage of the year the museum was open.

SPONSORS:
1. *List of general sponsors?*
   (Is there a list at the end of the report, by type of funder?) Code 1 for yes, 0 for no, or missing, for each type of sponsor:
   Corporate
   Foundation
   Government
   Individual
2. *Corporation/Government funders on general list?*
   1 Yes
   0 No
   . no general list
3. *Sponsors thanked in text?*
   Code 1 for yes, 0 for no, or missing, for each type of funder:
   Corporate
   Foundation
   Government
   Individual

FINANCIAL INFORMATION:
1. *Reported?*
   1 Yes
   0 No
2. *Amounts:*
   Record amount for each of the following categories (or missing, if not reported)
   Total expenses
   Total revenues
   Exhibition expenses
   Exhibition income

of exhibitions not included in the final analysis. In this pre-test, I looked for potential areas of ambiguity and for categories that might have been overlooked in the initial scheme. From this pre-test, I developed a set of "coding rules" that solidified coding categories. As I coded exhibitions, I kept a "coding journal" that allowed me to resolve ambiguities in the same direction each time.[12]

TABLE A-4
Exhibition Code Summary

Code	Category
Style:	
1	Postmodern
2	Modern
3	Contemporary
4	European, medieval to 19th century
5	American, not modern
6	American, ethnic
7	Classical
8	Primitive art, Asia, South America, Mexico, Africa, and Oceana
9	Asian art, not primitive
10	South American and Mexican art, not primitive
11	Craft, costume, European or American decorative arts, folk art
12	Commercial art, illustration, design
13	Architecture
14	Photography
15	Film
16	Local artists
17	Children/community
18	Other
19	Mixed
20	Unknown style (fine arts)
21	Unclear
Corporate Funding:	
1	Yes
0	No
Foundations Funding:	
1	Yes
0	No
Individual Funding:	
1	Yes
0	No
Government Funding:	
1	Yes
0	No
Format:	
1	Retrospective or One-Artist Show
2	Two or Three Artists
3	Style
4	Survey
5	Period
6	Location: country, continent or area
7	Theme
8	Mixed, fine art
9	Mixed, decorative or primitive art
10	Children/community
11	Media
12	Other
13	Unclear
Travelling:	
1	Travelling
0	Not travelling
Type:	
1	Blockbuster
2	Loan exhibition
3	Museum collection
4	Patron collection
5	Juried exhibition
6	Artist collection
7	Art School
8	Other
9	Unclear

I coded exhibitions on three different measures of format: layout, traveling status, and type. The category I called *layout* classified exhibitions into standard formats, such as a retrospective, a small group exhibition, or a survey of stylistic development. Other layouts include the accessible exhibition format called the theme show, shows that are oriented towards children, or those that are a jumble of styles with no art historical organization. I coded exhibitions as to their traveling status; *traveling* exhibitions appeared in and/or were arranged by other museums. Traveling shows reach a larger number of viewers than shows that appear in just one city. The variable I called *type* categorized the source of the art works in the exhibition. The majority of exhibitions were coded as "loan exhibitions." These are exhibitions where pieces come from a variety of sources, such as the collections of patrons and other museums as well as from the museum's own collection. A second type of show is the "blockbuster," a loan exhibition that meets several additional criteria. Blockbuster exhibitions are large-scale, mass-appeal exhibitions, designed to attract broad audiences. Blockbusters are defined in terms of reaching a large public, and are indicated *for the coding* by three factors (1) the use of advance ticketing, for instance, by Ticketron, (2) high attendance figures, or (3) mentions in the annual report of long lines of people waiting to get into the exhibit.[13] Other types of exhibitions include shows drawing from a museum's own collection, a patron's collection, or an artist's collection. Exhibitions were coded as coming from these collections when the collection was the sole (or vast majority) source of exhibited works. If a patron provides only a few works, with other sources providing additional works, the exhibition is a loan show. "Patron" usually means an individual patron, but occasionally, it indicates a corporate or foundation collection. Each exhibition is coded for each format variable; consequently, format measures in the analysis are not mutually exclusive. For instance, some, but not all, blockbusters travel.

I based coding of exhibition contents on canonical divisions standard in art history. I am personally knowledgeable about artistic styles through taking six courses in art history at Princeton and Stanford Universities, attending museums and studio art classes, and reading. The coding scheme divided exhibitions into twenty-one "style" categories, though some exhibitions are defined by the media of their contents (e.g., photography) without further reference to actual style. The final analysis rests on fourteen categories: (1) *Modern art*, including styles such as Post-Impressionism, Cubism, Dada, Surrealism, Futurism, Abstract Expressionism, Minimalism, and Conceptual art; (2) *European art, medieval through nineteenth century*, including these periods and styles: early middle ages (about 600 A.D.–1000 A.D.), early and late Byzantine, Romanesque, Gothic, Renaissance (Italian, northern), Mannerism, Baroque, Neoclassicism, Rococo, Romanticism, Realism, Impressionism; (3) *Classical art*, art and artifacts from these eras and areas, up to about 600 A.D.: stone age—central and northern Europe, Mycenae, Crete, Cyclades; Ancient Near East, Egypt, Assyria, Achaemenid, Greece, Roman Empire, Etruria; and early Christian; (4) *Postmodern and contemporary*, including such styles as contemporary figurative painting, Neo-Expressionism, Pattern Painting, Photorealism, and Pop Art (see below); also some video artists, and artists whose work is described as postmodern in an exhibition listing; (5) *American old masters*, early American portraiture, nineteenth century realists, such as painters from the Hudson River School, twentieth-century realists, such as Wyeth and Hopper, 1930s mural painters, naive painters, such as Grant Wood or Thomas Hart Benton, up to the Ash Can School; (6) *American ethnic*, a category reserved for shows that were explicitly billed in the annual report as containing works by minority artists;

shows that include minority artists where the museum did not make an issue of the artists' race or ethnicity are coded under their artistic style; (7) *Asian art*, art from all parts of Asia including India, Turkey, and Iran, except modern or postmodern styles or art that is made by so-called primitive cultures; (8) *Photography*, all styles of photography, including artists such as Daguerre, Edward Weston, Steiglitz (but not photojournalism, which is coded under commercial); (9) *Craft, costume, decorative and folk art*; examples include quilts, inaugural ball gowns, eighteenth-century English furniture, and Paul Revere silver; (10) *Commercial art*, such items as advertisements, posters, product development, and commercial design; (11) *Mixed styles*, art that spans more than one of the above categories; (12) *Local artists*, a category reserved for shows that are explicitly billed as including local or regional (professional) artists; a juried show is a common type of exhibition under this category (though not all juried shows are limited to local artists); (13) *Child- or community-oriented shows*, art that is specifically geared toward children or art made by children; art that takes into account specific community issues or art that is created by (nonprofessional) community members; (14) *Other Styles*, include art from several styles: primitive art (art made by aboriginal peoples, native to Asia, South America, Mexico, Africa and Oceana, regardless of date of origin), architecture (all styles and eras), film (films that are presented as art, but not films that accompany exhibits of other subjects, documentary films, or filmed lectures), South American, Mexican, and African art (art from these regions that is not otherwise primitive, modern, or postmodern—Diego Rivera, for example), exhibitions with unidentifiable contents (such as the show *Oom Pah Pah* at the Metropolitan, for which the title provided the only information) and, finally, exhibitions designated to a residual sub-category as "other" styles. Since this residual category is what is left over after coding for the traditional canon, for postmodern and contemporary art, and for non-western art (all of which are styles that are established in contemporary or traditional art history literature), it encompasses those "styles" which are not in any sense part of art history.

Exhibitions of living artists proved to be the most difficult to code. Here, I relied on lists of artists working in two modern and four postmodern styles (Crane, 1987: Appendix C, pp. 153–157), but the job was difficult because of the still-fluid definition of postmodern and modern styles, and because of the large number of contemporary artists exhibiting who were not on Crane's list and were unknown to me. The exhibition description sometimes made it clear that an artist was either "modern" or "postmodern" in style. I coded living artists as "modern" or "postmodern" if I was able to do so based on personal knowledge, Crane's list, or the exhibition description. Some living artists' styles were coded as "craft" or "American ethnic," if one of these was the primary way in which the museum presented the artists' work. I coded living artists whose styles I could not determine as "contemporary" styles. Similarly, I coded group exhibitions of living artists embodying both modern and postmodern styles as "contemporary." In the final analysis, I folded the categories "postmodern" and "contemporary" into one category indicating the newest thrust of art work produced mainly by artists who were still breathing and painting when the exhibit was mounted.

A great deal of work went into coding the exhibitions. In addition to the sheer number of exhibitions, there was a great deal of variety in the layout of annual reports. Further, ambiguity in exhibition titles and aims made coding difficult. As mentioned, I kept a coding diary of ambiguous cases and their resolution, in order to resolve similar ambiguities in the same manner and to keep the coding as uniform as possible and to keep coding reliability at a maximum.

Some of the exhibitions were difficult to code because they fulfilled multiple roles. For instance, many children's exhibitions were of interest to children, but had little art historical merit, such as *Drawings by Children of Chile*. Other children's exhibits, however, were didactic exhibitions of real artists—*Van Gogh in the Junior Gallery*—which could be coded as a children's show or with Impressionism as medieval to nineteenth century European art. In this case, I coded the exhibition as a children's exhibit, since it was explicitly billed as of interest to youngsters. Other multivocal exhibitions posed more difficult choices. For instance, exhibitions of local artists were coded separately as "local artists." However, if an artist born or living in the museum's community is well known, then the exhibition can have a dual purpose. I would code an exhibition, such as *Richard Diebenkorn, Famous San Franciscan* as "modern," just as I would a retrospective of his work mounted in other cities. Unfortunately, in such cases, the dual nature of the exhibit is not captured.

I also coded the funders of exhibitions. Externally funded exhibitions receive support from one or a combination of individual, corporate, government, or foundation donors. Exhibitions termed "internally funded," have been paid for by the museum's operating budget, earned income, an auxiliary entity, such as the "Ladies' Council," or small donations not directly acknowledged as exhibition support. It is important to note that museums do not report small donations which may help support an exhibit; consequently, my data concern major funding only. In other words, my data set is biased towards the effects of munificent and visible donors.

The data in the analysis speak directly to the environment-output link and sidestep the curator's role. Thus, they are strong indicators of the impact of environmental pressures on organizational outputs. I infer curator's role from output results, from anecdotal evidence in interviews I've conducted, and from qualitative information in annual reports.

Operationalization of Variables

The three main dependent variables are whether an exhibition is (a) popular, (b) accessible, or (c) scholarly. *Popular exhibitions* (those attracting broad audiences) are indicated by two variables: blockbuster shows and traveling exhibitions. Blockbuster shows attract a large audience in (at least) one venue, whereas traveling shows multiply their potential audience by the number of cities in which they appear. Both blockbuster and traveling status indicate the format of an exhibition. *Accessible exhibitions* are shows that are easy to understand without extensive training in art history, and are indicated by both format and content variables. An accessible format is the "theme show." Such exhibitions are organized around a theme, rather than around a traditional art historical category. These are shows such as *The Window in Art*, which included only paintings and drawings incorporating windows, or *A Day in the Country: Impressionism and the French Landscape*, which organized paintings by their subject matter instead of by the more traditional categories, such as the artist or chronology of the work. Several styles of exhibition indicate accessible contents. Though there are more accessible and less accessible artists within each style category, I assume that American old masters, craft and costume, commercial art, local artists and child/community exhibits are more accessible than other style categories.

Scholarly exhibitions are shows resting on solid art historical merit and research. A show can be designed in a way for scholars to learn more about the art in the show. A survey, which shows the development of a style or series of styles, and a retrospective, which shows the development of a single artist's oeuvre, are art historically based formats for exhibitions. In terms of content, scholarly shows are indicated by the traditional canon: "the" history of art (e.g., Janson 1986), which is now called the history of Western art. It is comprised of three style categories, classical art, European art (medieval through nineteenth century), and modern art. Postmodern art, a conglomeration of styles that draw upon, react against, or play with the conventions of modern art, also indicate art historical contents.

The data also address three additional concerns of funders. To test whether individuals tend to sponsor their own art works, I coded the source of art for exhibitions. The variable "patron collection" indicates that all or virtually all of the art in a given exhibition came from the collection of the individual or corporation who sponsored the exhibition. This variable indicates the format of exhibitions, since the content of a patron collection could be scholarly or accessible. Two content variables address government funding of living artists and art of interest to nontraditional audiences. Sponsorship of American ethnic art demonstrates an interest in nontraditional audiences. Contemporary artists and most of the postmodern artists were living at the time their art was shown, so for the purposes of this analysis, "living artists" are indicated by the combined style category for postmodern and contemporary art.

The four independent variables for the analysis are the funder variables. Four dummy variables, one for each funder type, indicate whether or not the exhibit was funded by an individual, corporation, government agency, or foundation. Exhibitions were often funded by more than one type of external funder. Exhibitions with no major external funding are indicated by a pattern of 0,0,0,0 on the four funding variables. Internally funded is the excluded funding variable.

All variables in the analysis are dummy variables. Dependent variables indicate either format (the five format variables are: blockbuster, traveling exhibition, theme show, art historical exhibition, and patron collection) or content (the 14 content 0,1 variables were created from the 14 categories of the style variable). The main statistical method used in this analysis is logistic regression, a regression method that is used for binary dependent variables (Aldrich & Nelson, 1984). A logistic regression equation was estimated, using the maximum likelihood technique, for each of the 19 dependent variables. Independent variables are the four funder dummy variables; thus the regressions test for associations between type of funder and each dependent variable. The four types of funders are not mutually exclusive (i.e., exhibitions can be sponsored by more than one funder). The omitted category is exhibitions that were not funded by any of the four external funders. In other words, the comparison group for the b coefficients is composed of exhibitions not funded by the given funder, including those exhibitions that are funded internally.

Logistic regression, like multiple (OLS) regression, is useful for analyzing the effect of several independent variables on one dependent variable. It calculates a coefficient for each variable while "holding the others constant." Thus, it is effective for testing the effect of one independent variable while controlling for the others. The logistic regressions control for the overlap in funding, but do not demonstrate the existence of coalitions among funder types. Using cross-tabulations, I check for significant overlap in funder types for each exhibition variable.

NOTES

1. The exact title of the educators was either "education director" (i.e., the head of the education department), or "education curator" (staff). Since these terms can easily be confused with director (of the museum) and curator (of art), I will call all personnel in the education departments "educators."

2. Museums are able to make fewer purchases of art than they have in the past, due mainly to the drastic increase in the price of art relative to museum budgets. Thus, acquisitions may have become more limited in terms of the desires of curators and directors as museum personnel are unable to compete for art work they would otherwise like to have housed in their institutions. Further, many acquisitions are gifts, and although museums actively seek these donations, they are, in some cases, a relatively passive recipient of proffered artworks.

3. Although purchase programs of the NEA have benefitted museums. Corporations, too, occasionally give money for purchase or donate works or collections.

4. The Tax Reform Act of 1969 discontinued artists' ability to deduct the market value of the paintings they donate to museums. Instead, artists can deduct only the costs of the materials used in creating the piece. Meyer (1979: 35) reports that during the two years before the change in the tax law, 97 artists donated 321 pieces to the Museum of Modern Art. During the following three years, 15 artists gave only 28 pieces, most of which were prints.

5. The five museums are the Carnegie Institute, Henry Francis Dupont Winterthur Museum, the International Museum of Photography, The Frick Museum and the Freer Gallery of Art (Smithsonian Institution). These museums are unsuitable mainly because they are not museums of modern art or general museums and, thus, do not have a range of exhibitions suited to my coding efforts. All of the Smithsonian Museums are problematic. They are under the Smithsonian Institution umbrella; consequently, it is difficult to know which is the proper level to study: the sub-unit museums or the overarching institution.

6. The one-million cut-off was chosen because most museums in the top 30 had total expenditures either exceeding or approximating that amount. In addition to the six museums added to the large museum universe, eight additional museums fit the criteria of total expenditures greater than or equal to $1,000,000. These organizations were excluded for several reasons; the most common reason was that the organization was an art academy (art school) with an associated museum (rather than vice-versa), so a great deal of the operating budget probably went to the school rather than to the museum.

7. Note that, the National Gallery is associated with, but not part of, the Smithsonian Institution. I had assumed that the National Gallery was not on the list because of a confusion with the Smithsonian's National Collection and Renwick Gallery. Indeed, the National Collection of Art (established in 1846) was called the National Gallery until 1937, when Andrew Mellon donated his own collection to the government of the United States. Mellon wanted his collection to be named the National Gallery. Thus, the old National Gallery became the National Collection, and the new collection from Mellon was duly named according to the benefactor's wishes. The National Collection is one of the Smithsonian Museums, while the National Gallery is merely associated with the Smithsonian, but has an independent, self-perpetuating board of directors.

8. These omissions cause some concern about how good a universe the NCES "universe" really is. Why were these major museums missing? It is possible that they could be miscoded as other types of museums? Indeed, there are examples of miscodings: "Public Utility Dist 1. Chelan City" in Wenatchee, WA is listed as an art museum.

9. Walker Art Center, New Orleans Museum of Art, Joslyn Art Museum, Indianapolis Museum of Art, the J. Paul Getty Museum, and the Kimbell Museum.

10. A museum-year is information on one museum for one time point in the analysis. Each museum-year is data for a given year, but note that data is collected only in even years.

11. I have more exhibitions in the museum-level data set because the exhibition data for the Albright-Knox museum was coded only at the aggregate level.

12. Coding data was a full-time effort for 3 1/2 months.

13. There is no established definition of a blockbuster. In the art world, some people consider blockbusters to have, by definition, corporate funding. This definition was not helpful, as it did not make sense to define away variation in one of the four independent variables, corporate sponsorship. Blockbusters can also be seen as shows that museums mount with the express purpose of attracting a large audience. My coding scheme was designed to find shows that museums planned to be large (advance ticketing) and that did reach large audiences (high attendance and lines). It is worth mentioning, however, that my definition leans towards discovering successful and/or unplanned blockbusters, as museums may not report the failure of shows they'd hoped would appeal to a large audience but which didn't draw crowds and museums may also gleefully point out the popularity of a show that wasn't designed as a blockbuster. Consequently, it is important to note that my coding scheme does not necessarily come up with a perfect correlation between shows I deem as blockbuster, based on the information in a museum's annual report, and shows that would be considered blockbusters by some other definitions.

INDEX

VICTORIA D. ALEXANDER is Associate Professor of Sociology at Harvard University.